UCD WOMEN'S CENTER

UCD WOMEN'S CENTER

EVERYDAY ACTS & SMALL SUBVERSIONS
WOMEN REINVENTING FAMILY, COMMUNITY, AND HOME

everyday acts
&
small subversions

Anndee Hochman

The Eighth Mountain Press
Portland ◆ Oregon ◆ 1994

"Extending the Picture: When Former Partners Stay Family" originally appeared in Ms. The challah story from "Marking Time: Charting a Feminist Calendar" originally appeared in Ms. in a different form and under the title "Slow Rise: Braiding a Tradition." "What We Call Each Other" originally appeared in Left Bank in a different form. "Finding Kinship with a Colleague" originally appeared in Just Out. The dining room table story from "Renegades and Exiles from the Wedding March" originally appeared in Just Out in a different form.

Cover art by Claudia Cave
Cover design by Marcia Barrentine
Book design by Ruth Gundle

Manufactured in the United States of America
This book is printed on acid-free paper.
First edition 1994
10 9 8 7 6 5 4 3 2 1

LIBRARY OF CONGRESS CATALOGING-IN-PUBLICATION DATA
Hochman, Anndee, 1962–
    Everyday acts & small subversions: women reinventing family, community, and home / Anndee Hochman. —1st ed.
        p.   cm.
    Includes bibliographical references.
    ISBN 0-933377-26-6 (alk. paper) : $24.95. — ISBN 0-933377-25-8 (alk. paper) : $12.95
    1. Women—United States—Social conditions. 2. Women—United States—Family. 3. Lesbians—United States. I. Title. II. Title: Everyday Acts and small subversions.
    HQ1421.H63   1994
    305.42'0973—dc20   93-43257

THE EIGHTH MOUNTAIN PRESS

624 Southeast Twenty-ninth Avenue
Portland, Oregon 97214
(503) 233-3936

To my parents, Gloria and Stan,
who showed me how to make a world with words

contents

acknowledgments

I THINK of this book as an ongoing conversation. It began on a winter afternoon in 1990, in a living room where I sat with two women friends to talk about family. By the time we finished, it was dark outside, our tea was cold, and my lap was full of scribbled notes that would form the first essays of *Everyday Acts and Small Subversions*.

In dozens of conversations over the next three and a half years, other women added their experiences, their triumphs, their frustrations in trying to build authentic and unconventional family lives. They challenged and provoked me, made me laugh and nudged me to tears as, together, we talked this book into existence.

I am grateful to the community of family, friends, and colleagues who enriched my own life as I worked. My loving thanks to Rachael Silverman and John Duke for endurance, musical interludes, and blackened-tofu sandwiches. And to Elissa Goldberg, who jumped up and down on Twenty-ninth Avenue, dared me to say yes to this project and continued to believe in it—and me—until the very last syllable.

My original family—my parents, grandparents, and a raft of aunts, uncles, and cousins—gave me the gifts of self-confidence, good humor, and love, a legacy that informs everything I do.

I was lucky to receive support for my writing from the Oregon Institute of Literary Arts and to spend a rare month of solitude at Cottages at Hedgebrook, a retreat where women writers are nurtured, respected, and freed from the distractions of daily life.

Many people read and offered crucial feedback on the essays; they include members of The 29th Street Writers, as well as Judith Barrington, Sally Brady, Susan Bryer, Elissa Goldberg, Kathleen Saadat and Thalia Zepatos. The astute eyes and good sense of Janet Howey, Julie Huffaker, Mary Catherine Lamb, Elizabeth Pollock and Mary Jo Schimelpfenig helped to weed inconsistencies and grammatical lapses from the final draft. My editor, Ruth Gundle, provided clarity, provocative questions, extraordinary intelligence, and faith that buoyed me through the most difficult days of work.

I want to give particular thanks to the women whose stories fill this book, who welcomed my questions and shared details of their lives with insight, wit, and candor. Nearly all of them chose to use their real names in the text; a few opted for first names only. Unfortunately, we still live in a world where women have reason to fear full disclosure.

Each conversation enlarged the book in some essential way. Together, they reminded me how much we need each other's words, each other's lives, to shape our own.

introduction: looking out of bounds

I OPENED the box of cards and and looked inside. It was a slow, sticky afternoon, and I was alone in the West Cambridge apartment two high school friends and I had sublet for the summer. Our two-bedroom flat filled the second floor of a sagging house on Cushing Street, a brisk thirty-minute walk from Harvard Square. The women who lived there, Wendy and Lynn, had sewn dark green cushions for the corner window seats. Their books covered one long wall of cinder block and pine shelving.

The night I arrived, several days in advance of my friends, Wendy and Lynn were still there, just back from a hiking trip. They ducked into the tiny bathroom for showers, then offered to double up in the larger bedroom so I could sleep on the futon in the smaller room.

The next morning they drove away, leaving their apartment in my care. For two years, I'd lived in college dormitories and had spent every summer with my parents. This was my first real venture into adult living; I was crazy to know how people did it.

So I prowled the kitchen cabinets. I examined Wendy and Lynn's collection of tapes, meticulously numbered and stacked. I perused the bookshelves. And then, although I knew I shouldn't, I snooped through the desk drawers in the second bedroom.

The note cards were printed and packaged with envelopes. "This is to inform you that Wendy Kavanaugh is secure and happy with her life and the people in it. She is not interested in meeting men for the purposes of courtship or marriage." I read the message again, and the puzzle of the tenants' lives suddenly snapped into focus. My face got hot. I quickly put the cards back where I'd found them.

My friends arrived several days later, and our life on Cushing Street eased into a laconic routine. We sampled the half-dozen brands of gourmet ice cream available within walking distance of Harvard Square. I wrote articles about seat-belt safety and salt marsh cleanups for *The Boston Globe*. Another intern there, a red-bearded MIT senior, sent me flirty messages via electronic mail, and I flirted back.

On muggy weekend afternoons, I gobbled my way through Wendy and Lynn's book collection: *Rubyfruit Jungle*. *The Tribe of Dina*. *Our Bodies, Ourselves*. And I returned to the desk drawer over and over, when my roommates had left for the evening and the apartment was mine. I pulled out the box of cards, slipped off the cover and read the message until I had it memorized.

SEVERAL years after that Cambridge summer, I moved to Oregon, propelled by a restlessness I couldn't quite name. "I want a more textured life," I told people at the time, leaving my friends and family alternately puzzled, worried, and envious.

In Portland, I began to meet women who lived differently from anyone I'd ever known. At the feminist bookstore where I volunteered, at Holly Near and Cris Williamson concerts and women's bars, my skin rippled with recognition and the sensation of "home," a vision of community that actually felt sexy in its openness and possibility. Yet this family, too, had rules, subtle but persistent codes of dress, attitude, politics. There were ways to distinguish "us" from "them," and a price for straying too far.

I bought a red spiral notebook and began to fill it with notes and thoughts on family, the things I watched on television, saw in the movies, observed in my friends' lives. When I wasn't writing, I read: an eclectic bibliography. Sociological tracts and contemporary essays, *Ms.* magazines from 1972 and 1989, *The Family, Sex and Marriage in England 1500-1800*.

When I house-sat for an older friend, I educated myself on her paperback collection of feminist classics—one whole weekend in an armchair with *The Dialectic of Sex*. In it, Shulamith Firestone claimed sexism was the basis for all the world's oppressions and condemned the nuclear family as its training camp. Further down the bookshelf, the writing of feminists such as Letty Cottin Pogrebin offered a different view: that women could re-frame family rather than refuse it. Perhaps, Pogrebin offered, a family could be a holdout against conformity, a place that nurtured free-thinking women and men.

I filled the red notebook, the pages restless with question marks, and bought an aqua one. Yellow. Blue. Hot pink. I pored over memoirs and fiction, feminist manifestoes and the Family Protection Act, Charlotte Perkins Gilman and Betty Friedan. I saw families everywhere I looked, a million variations on a theme.

At one Chanukah dinner, we lit candles, ate *pad thai* and talked about *Dances with Wolves*, its depiction of Native American tribal life. Gwenn said the movie made her ache for community—the visceral hold of people who share a history, a language, a piece of land. Rachael argued that a tribe could be as confining as any nuclear family.

I liked Pogrebin's notion—the family as subversive refuge. But Rachael was right; every clan had rules to ensure its own survival. Did inclusion always exact a price, I wondered. Could there be families in which it was possible both to belong and be seen?

I THOUGHT of all the families I'd tried out while growing up—brief, intense formations that bloomed with the startle of desert wildflowers. A group of sixteen-year-old poets from my summer at an arts camp. My college roommates, scattered now from New York to Raleigh to Chicago. The fourteen women who learned to frame walls with me at a week-long carpentry workshop in the Northern California woods.

In these temporary families, I had searched to fill my cravings—for siblings, physical challenge, sex, the company of women. In each, I stretched some aspect of myself, testing. Could I be an actress? A poet? A lesbian carpenter who lived on the land?

At thirty, I was beginning to hunt for permanence, to make decisions that would bend the rest of my life. There was much I wanted to know: how to sustain friendships that felt "like family" over time and distance. How to make choices about commitment and children. How to celebrate milestones, whom to gather at my table. How to balance tradition and invention, pull threads from my past and use them to weave a future. I craved the details of other women's stories: who earned the money, who baked the birthday cake, how each family coped with the muddle of making a life.

My friends and I grew up amid this century's second swell of feminism, raised with a concept that became the movement's signature: the personal is political. By the early 1990s, I could see the fruit of that philosophy. Contemporary feminists—lesbians and heterosexuals—in trying to fashion lives of integrity and joy, were changing not only their own relationships, the contours of their days. They were revising a centuries-old conversation about family; they made history daily, in their living rooms and kitchens.

My friends and I talked incessantly about our struggles to find community and partnership, to belong and be whole. We traded stories and asked questions. Still, we wanted more. Perhaps, I thought, women's lives were being carried out as quiet experiments, each discovery in a separate room, each setback and triumph unknown by the experimenters next door. With my journalist's training and my personal curiosity, I could track down these "living laboratories." Given a license to snoop, I might find acts of chutzpah and imagination, boxes of cards with other startling messages.

For three years I listened, asked questions, took notes. One voice led to another. I followed the trail. I knew I'd found something important when my whole body sizzled the way it had that afternoon in Boston. One woman's words could pry my world open, making it a larger and more promising place.

I focused my search on Portland, the mild-mannered, rain-soaked city that had become my home. Not because I believed it was "typical." Portland had special traits—a low cost of living that permitted nontraditional work arrangements, a medium size, a reputation for social tolerance. I wasn't looking for a microcosm so much as an area lush with invention.

Silence murders possibilities. But even a whisper can awaken them, breathe company into what seems an isolated existence. I left some women's living rooms giddy with ideas. Come and see what I've seen, I wanted to shout; come see the things women are doing and trying, all the ways life can be lived. Other conversations haunted me with the risks and sorrows that always measure change.

In seeking new kinds of kinship, in asking these questions, I joined a long line of women who were reinventing the most essential aspects of their lives.

I set out to find some more.

Anndee Hochman
October 1993

Growing Pains:
Beyond "One Big Happy Family"

I REMEMBER waking up to the smell of salt.

Each August when I was little, my parents loaded the car with Bermuda shorts and groceries, beach towels and Scrabble board, and drove to the New Jersey shore. My great-uncle Bernie Ochman had bought a $16,000 bay-front house there in the mid-1950s; he imagined it as a sort of freewheeling compound, where all the aunts, grandparents, and cousins of my mother's large extended family could gather each summer.

Bernie died before my parents were married, but my mother carried out his vision with her usual zest. She made sure the taxes on the house were paid quarterly, the water valve was turned on each May, and there were enough hamburgers for everyone on Memorial Day and the Fourth of July.

In August, my parents worked feverishly for two weeks, then packed up and headed to the shore for what my father used to call, with some sarcasm, "a little peace and quiet." We left at night to avoid traffic on the Atlantic City Expressway. I always fell asleep in the car and always woke up as we came over the bay bridge, where the smell of salt, moist and thick, would touch me like a mitten dipped in the ocean.

"Are we there yet?" I'd mumble from the back seat.

"Almost," my mom would say, and my dad would turn left, then left again, and park the car as close as he could to the big white house.

I LOVED the shore house because it was so different from home. The front steps tilted a little. Gray paint flaked off the window frames. Two daybeds in the living room were draped with pea green spreads, and the loveseats wore crunchy plastic slipcovers. The picket fence was red.

Even the architecture broke rules. The front room had been added as an afterthought, a low-budget job. The carpenters never removed what had once been the house's front window, now ridiculous in the wall between the front room and the kitchen. I used to sit on the stairs, tapping on the kitchen window and making faces until my mother or my grandmother or Aunt Sadie looked up from the dishes and waved at me. Then I would collapse in giggles.

Upstairs, there was no hall, no doors on the bedrooms. In fact, the bedrooms were not really separate rooms at all, just thin-walled divisions of the upper floor. The front stairs climbed right into the middle of Aunt Charlotte and Uncle Freddie's room; you could stand on the top step and almost tickle Uncle Freddie's feet.

Walk through that bedroom, and the next one, and the next, and you arrived at the bathroom, which had its own quirks—a white claw-foot tub, a hasty shower rigged up with red rubber tubing, and two doors. When I was older, I would check the sliding locks on both doors several times before I dared to unpeel my damp, sandy bathing suit.

Aunt Sadie and Uncle Izzy slept in the larger of the two rear bedrooms, in twin beds pushed together to make one. The very back room was long and narrow, like a single-lane swimming pool, with windows that let in wet salty air off the bay. My grandparents—Bubie and Poppop—slept here.

My mother loves to tell the story of my father's first visit to this family compound, during their courtship. He recoiled at the upstairs setup; a private motel room, with a door that locked, was more what he had in mind. My mother informed him firmly that she was a package deal; if he loved her, he would learn to love her family—the father who smoked terrible cigars, the sister who rolled her hair in Kotex sanitary pads, the mother who stewed bruised peaches in the hot, tiny kitchen. And he could start loving them here, in their peculiar summer habitat.

I thought the house was wonderful. The connecting rooms reminded me of a maze, the sort of place where surprises could hunch in old dressers, under beds. Later I realized how the physical space shaped our time there, dissolving the barriers that, in most houses, separate adults from children, private from communal space, eating from work. At the shore, my friends and I played jacks in the middle of the living room, hide and seek in the freestanding metal closets. When people got hungry, they helped themselves from one of the three refrigerators. If I wanted to be alone, I opened a book.

There was one last room upstairs, an odd sixth bedroom lodged in the center of the house. It was the only bedroom with a door, and it belonged to my parents. When I was younger, I assumed they took that room out of generosity. It was small and dark and hot, and you had to grope for the light switch behind a high wooden headboard. It was also the only room in the house in which two people could have a private talk, or take a nap, without somebody else clomping through on her way to the bathroom.

Much later, the summer I was twenty-two, I finally grasped the full significance of that room and made love with Jon Feldstein in it one June weekend when the family wasn't there. "Do you want to have sex?" he had asked, without expectation in his voice, as if it were a foregone conclusion. Later he said, "Well, you know, it gets better with practice."

I did not practice with Jon Feldstein again. In fact, I didn't practice with anyone until more than two years later. By then, I had fallen into a deep and surprising infatuation with one of my closest friends, driven my Datsun cross-country alone and settled in Portland.

EARLY in the summer of 1987, I flew back east to tell my parents I was in love with a woman and believed I was destined to be in love with women throughout the foreseeable future. It was Memorial Day weekend, the time we traditionally turned on the water valve and began to inhabit the house at the shore. My mother and I drove there in her blue Honda.

"I think that's how it's going to be for me. With women, I mean," I told her.

"Well, your father thought so," she said finally. "He thought so back in November. I told him that was ridiculous, that you'd always had boyfriends."

She said a lot of other things after that, about not having grandchildren and what a hard path I'd chosen and how she and my father weren't going to be around forever and had hoped to see me taken care of. I concentrated on driving and on the way blood was beating in my ankles, my thumbs, my neck, my ears. I wanted to go to sleep and not wake up until I smelled salt. When we came close to the bay, my mother asked me to pull into a parking lot so she could cry for a while. "I'm sorry," I said, but it didn't seem to help.

At the house, I walked around, touching things, while my mother told my father that he was right, I *was* having an affair with a woman. I wanted to eat something, anything, off the familiar mismatched dishes, play Scrabble until the stars came out, stand on the back porch and watch boats slip under the bridge, tap on the kitchen window until someone waved at me. Instead I went into the bathroom and locked both doors.

About midnight, while I lay sleepless in Aunt Sadie and Uncle Izzy's room, my mother came in and crawled into the other twin bed. "I feel so empty," she said. "I feel empty inside.... I don't feel any joy anymore. I feel like the family is breaking apart. I remember how the family was when Uncle Bernie was alive, how this house was...." And her voice, already thin, cracked like a bowl dropped on a tile floor—a splintering and then silence where something used to be.

2 A.M. 3 A.M. Everyone had trooped off to bed in pairs—cousins Joni and Gerry, cousins Debbie and Ralph. Except for my grandfather, who had always stayed up late to watch television and stayed up even later since my grandmother died three years before. Finally he switched off the set, and the house went dark and quiet.

"Don't you feel it's unnatural?" my mother asked. "Don't you feel it's just wrong, that it's weird?"

How can you ask me about being weird in this house, I wanted to shout. This house, with its bedrooms barging into each other and its mismatched dishes, its double-doored bathroom and its red picket fence. When I used to complain that our family wasn't like other families, you laughed and said, "Well, we may not be normal, but we have a lot of fun."

I didn't say these things. I only thought them. And it wasn't until much later, until very recently, that I began to understand why my mother could tolerate the quirks in that house. The madcap shell at the shore housed a solid, predictable center. Relatives came and went in pairs. Someday, presumably, I would join the procession; one of my children would tap on the kitchen window and giggle when I waved. The house might be a little cracked, but the family was predictable, enduring.

I understand why you are so upset, I could tell my mother now. The world has gone crazy and all the walls are too thin and your mother is dead and your sister divorced and your daughter loves women and everything is coming unglued and nothing turns out the way we plan.

4 A.M. 5 A.M. My mother stayed in my room all night, talking and weeping. Toward morning, as boats began to slosh in the bay, I fell into an exhausted, tear-stained sleep. When I woke up at noon, we ate tuna subs and drove back to Philadelphia.

THE New Jersey beach house was never just a summertime shelter. It housed my family's favorite image of itself at our expansive best—gathered around the huge dining room table, traipsing through the bedrooms, one big happy family. Just like all the television shows I watched and worshipped.

It is no accident that this particular image clung. The picture of such charmed and cheerful families took hold in the decade preceding my birth, a bit of postwar propaganda that paid homage to the supposedly idyllic families of Victorian times. Mass-marketed by television, the Cleaver clan and others were burned into our minds by millions of cathode-ray tubes.

The feminist movement challenged that postwar myth as women began to examine the contents inside the "happy family" cliché. Feminists of the late 1960s and 1970s urged their sisters to live authentic lives and to begin them at home. They insisted that personal choices had political import—that is, the daily, minute interactions of our lives *mattered*, not just for each of us alone but potentially for everyone, for the world. "When a woman tells the truth," Adrienne Rich wrote, "she is creating the possibility for more truth around her."

Women pointed out that families maintained the illusion of happiness only by denying important facts—about adoptions, abortions, illness and illegitimate births, divorces and deaths. Some families devoted their lives to maintaining the secret of a son's homosexuality, a grandmother's alcoholism, a father's violent rage. Melancholy and despair split family members not only from outsiders but from each other; certain topics, one understood, were simply not discussed.

In consciousness-raising groups, women discovered the exhilaration of telling each other unvarnished stories of their bodies, relationships, and families. Back at home, in their kitchens and living rooms, they began to apply these feminist ideals: that *how* people talked meant as much as the conclusions they reached; that the only way to solve problems was to actively engage them; that keeping secrets cost too much.

It was feminism, in part, that prompted me to tell my own family a difficult truth, one I was sure would cause misunderstanding and pain. I was frightened to disturb the jovial peace that was a source of such family pride; at the same time, I could not visit that unpretentious house and pretend I was someone else. I wanted to be known, and seen, in the ways I had come to know and see myself.

I did it because I chose truth over tranquility. Because I had come to believe that real families fight and resist, sob and explode, apologize and forgive. Beneath the fiction of happiness lies the raw, important tissue of human relationships.

And I did it because I had watched other women live without lying. For some, that meant no longer passing as heterosexual. For others, it meant acknowledging they did not want partners or children. Some urged their biological relatives and chosen kin to talk about subjects long considered taboo. Their example made my own convictions more fierce. Their bravery buoyed me.

"It's hard. We argue and struggle," Selma Miriam of the Bloodroot restaurant collective told me, with a glance around the room at her "cronies."

"You know each other's weaknesses," said Betsey Beaven, another Bloodroot member. "Love requires a lot of cultivation. It can be tenuous. You have to work on it all the time. It's very difficult at times, but so rewarding when you get through to the other side."

I remember my friend Susan's assessment, at the end of a long discussion about what separates family from friends. "Family," she said, "are the people I've struggled through things with."

Again, always, the personal becomes political. Women striving daily to make plain the good and the bad of their lives also contribute to a larger change, the breakdown of fictions that divide us from each other— white from black, lesbian from straight, old from young. Women who refuse to act out lies at home can turn the same honest scrutiny outside, demanding truth in their work, their education, their politics.

Maybe happiness, I have come to think, is a limiting proposition, a flat summary of human emotion in the same way a sitcom is a flat summary of real life. "Happy families" don't account for the ways people are knit by sorrow, the way bonds grow stronger through anger and grief.

This is it, I tell myself now; this mess is as real as it gets. I try to cherish flux—the mercurial moods, the feelings that flood and recede, the infinite chaos in which families become families.

Two days after I came out to my parents at the beach house, I returned to Portland, with my bicycle packed in a United Airlines baggage carrier and my grandmother's cameo ring on the pinky finger of my left hand. I'd found the ring in a jewelry box in my bedroom. It was delicate, a filigree setting with a small oblong cameo, the ivory-faced woman profiled on a peach background.

The thin silver band barely eased over the knuckle on my pinky—lesbians' traditional ring-bearing finger. Wearing it, I felt marked, as though I were bringing contraband across the border in broad daylight, all my conflicting allegiances exposed.

My head ached. Would my relatives still love me if I failed to do my part by marrying and enlarging the family with children? Could I ever bring a woman lover to the shore? Where would we sleep?

How would I reconcile my relatives with the various families I developed as a writer, a Jew, a lesbian, a social worker, an East Coast expatriate in the Northwest? How far could everyone stretch without snapping, refusing wholeness, flying apart like shrapnel?

I stumbled off the plane at midnight into a solid hug from Marian, a co-worker at the social service agency where I counseled street youth. At work that week, I walked numbly through my routine. On Friday, while cleaning up the drop-in center after the last round of kids, I looked at my left hand. Where the cameo of my grandmother's ring had been, a little rectangle of skin showed through the filigree window. In the agency's dim basement, I leaned against a paneled wall and sobbed.

All the rest of that summer my parents and I exchanged letters, envelopes full of anger and accusation, concern and caution, guilt and grief. I had been such a good child, cheerful, diligent, and brainy—good citizen awards in ninth grade, acceptance to Yale, an internship, then a job, at *The Washington Post*. It was bad enough that I had left the *Post* after two years, moved 3,000 miles away and begun to work with homeless teenagers. Now this! Where had I gotten such subversive ideas?

Perhaps in a certain south Jersey beach house, in a maze of doorless rooms.

From the West Coast, I glanced anxiously over my shoulder: Were my relatives still there, with their shopping and their sweaters, their softening faces and their stiff resistance to change? If I returned, would I be swallowed up? If I stayed, would I be left adrift? Is that the brittle choice that, ultimately, forms the boundary line of every family: Be like us, or be alone?

I took off the empty ring and put it in a drawer. I spent that summer prowling my past, looking for signposts to help navigate the present. I heard voices, comforting and cautionary, joyous and pained, voices that chased in endless loops through my head.

"You can do anything you set your mind to."

"Don't leave."

"The world is full of interesting people and places."

"This family is the only safe spot on earth."

"Follow your dreams."

"Stay put."

I listened, and remembered, and wrote things down.

Significant Others:
kinship without Categories

ONLY the intrepid visit the Oregon coast in January. Rachael Silverman and I trudged over sand the texture of concrete into skies the color of oatmeal, our jacket hoods up, rain needling our faces. I knew this was going to be a Serious Talk, the kind that required a long stroll with no particular destination. Rachael didn't waste much time with a preamble. "John and I have been talking about living together. And we want you to live with us. What do you think?"

Rachael was my best friend, as well as my housemate. Six months earlier, one woman left the house I shared with five other people, and Rachael showed up in response to our classified ad. With our coarse, dark hair and olive complexions, we easily passed for sisters. That first week after she moved in, I remember catching her glance and laughing riotously at something no one else in the house found funny.

That summer, we prowled the city together—morning runs through Laurelhurst Park, evenings at the Barley Mill pub, sipping Ruby Tuesday raspberry ale, grocery shopping on Wednesday nights at the twenty-four-hour Safeway, followed by frozen yogurt and reports on our love lives.

Soon she met John Duke. He was a bill collector by day, a musician by night, and the coordinator of volunteer escorts at the Feminist Women's Health Center, where Rachael worked. He was tall and rangy, with a dark ponytail, and he loved Raymond Carver stories as much as she did. Since they'd begun dating, I saw less of Rachael, and I missed her. But the prospect of living with both of them made me uneasy. Would I feel excluded? What if their relationship didn't last? Did I want to move in with a relative stranger, even if my best friend was in love with him?

Shortly after that walk at the coast, all three of us went to a John McCutcheon concert. We pooled money and bought five raffle tickets. At intermission, the first number was called—one of ours! John walked up to collect two tickets to a classical concert. Then my number won: a set of bells from Cameroon. As we were tapping the bells to make a hollow "klung" sound, another of our tickets was called. We'd won the grand prize, too—one night at a hot springs retreat in central Oregon.

A lucky omen? Perhaps. By then, I'd already made my decision. I loved Rachael and wanted to continue living with her. I'd spent much of my life in households of three, starting with my original family. I was willing to take my chances with John.

Within days, John and Rachael had scouted ads and put a renters' deposit on a blue clapboard house with a front porch facing west, just three blocks from our current address. One night, before we'd hauled a single piece of furniture, the three of us walked through the new house. I looked at the blank rectangle that would be my bedroom and writing studio, at the long cavern below the kitchen that John planned to insulate as a music room for himself and Rachael.

Compared to our current house, which was a drafty hodgepodge, this place looked like the set of Leave It to Beaver—linoleum kitchen floor, wall to wall carpet, sliding glass doors on the bathtub. "Wow, it's a real house," I kept saying.

We followed each other from basement to upstairs bathroom, smudging each doorway with a bundle of sage incense. John beat a drum in all the corners. Then, seated on the living room floor, we each contributed an object for a "special shelf"—Rachael's wooden truck, John's small drum, my vial of dried lavender. We talked about our hopes for the house, what we wanted from our lives there separately and together.

Rachael and John would be living together as lovers. I planned to quit my part-time job in the spring and write five days a week. For the first time, John would have his music studio and living quarters in the same place. "When I drum, I feel like something's breaking apart inside me," he said. Sitting there on the mustard yellow carpet, I felt that crackle, too. Life rearranged itself under my ribs.

Gradually we set up house. John, who had been living alone, brought a futon couch, armchairs, heavy enamel pots and about forty plants. I contributed my used piano and the two cartons of kitchen items I'd hauled in my trunk from Washington, D.C. Rachael, out of college for less than a year, owned books and a skillet. John's grandmother bought him a washing machine; Rachael and I each pitched in twenty-five dollars for a used dryer.

At first, John joined Rachael and me for our weekly grocery routine. We'd whoosh down the aisles at Safeway, playing bumper carts, then cluster at the register, each of us making a guess at the total. We never could decide how to reward the winner. Already, this was different from our former house, where each person kept his or her food, carefully initialed, in separate zones of the refrigerator. We added more hooks to the inside of the bathroom door, put all three names on the answering machine. On the wall outside the kitchen, we hung a framed portrait of each of us.

IF MY friendship with Rachael was instantaneous, fierce, and sometimes combative, my tie with John was the opposite—tentative, polite, and slow. Rachael was the spoke that linked us; the first time she left, for a week's visit to Ohio, I wondered what John and I would say to each other.

It helped that we were both home a lot. John was fired from his bill-collecting job in May and took a patchwork of part-time jobs. I was struggling to become a full-time writer. That first summer, we had too much time and too little work. In the morning, John drummed for several hours while I made phone calls in a vague attempt to feel busy. Then we'd have brunch, often lingering in the kitchen until two-thirty, do a bit more work and start dinner preparations at four.

While we sautéed eggplant or sliced potatoes, we began to divulge bits of our pasts. I talked about my parents, my job as a metropolitan reporter for *The Washington Post*, my first woman lover. John told me about his year teaching English in China, his drum teacher's enigmatic counsel, his first year in Oregon when he was so poor that both he and his dog ate lentils the last week of each month.

We began to show each other our creative work—my first, uncertain pieces of short fiction, his quirky, ironic stories written for performance with a drum accompaniment. We joked uneasily about Rachael, with her

$4.50-an-hour job, being our family's chief breadwinner.

By the end of the year, the three of us not only lived, but worked, together. John and I shared a job (he worked four days; I worked one) doing crisis counseling with homeless teenagers at a small social service agency. Rachael was hired to coordinate the agency's needle-exchange program for IV drug users. Our public and private worlds, work and home, overlapped. At dinner, "shop talk" about a fight in the drop-in center would segue into discussions of teen pregnancy, homelessness, racism, the Meaning of It All.

We gave each other rides to and from downtown, packed each other's lunches and folded notes into the bags: "This lunch was inspected by No. 36492." We spent our vacation together, bicycling in the Canadian Gulf Islands, joined a grocery co-op as a household and took turns working there on Tuesday mornings. Our birthday tradition began that year; we celebrated with fancy dinners followed by handmade gifts—a painted lunchbox for Rachael, a short story for John, a cactus terrarium for me.

There were other routines—summer dinners on the front porch in the lavender twilight, February nights huddled on the living room futon, weekend breakfasts of bagels and scrambled tofu, nightly hugs before bed. When one of us left or returned from a trip, we turned John's small stuffed tiger, a souvenir from China, to face out the window for good luck. A friend dubbed us the "RAJ Mahal," the acronym made of our three initials.

But not everyone understood. From some people, my domestic arrangement elicited blank stares or indulgent nods, as if Rachael, John and I were ten-year-olds attempting a sleep-out adventure in the back yard. As though we were playing at life, not living it.

Because our family fit no recognizable category, people failed to see an entity. They did not ask the questions people commonly ask about someone's partner: "How did you meet? How long have you been living together?" or even the simplest, "Say, how is so-and-so?" On the surface, we looked like a couple and a single woman, sharing a house. The truth was more complicated and harder to describe. I *appeared* single; in fact, I was deeply attached.

Sometimes I felt bereft, when I sat writing late at night in the living room armchair and heard the soft mingling of John's and Rachael's voices upstairs. Other times I relished the fluidity of my life—to have company or be alone, to go dancing as a threesome on Saturday night or stay home and eat granola for dinner. When we visited John's parents and sisters at Christmas, I enjoyed my undefined role, neither biological kin nor their future in-law.

Valentine's Day marked the anniversary of our household. One year, two, three. We still had no language for what we three meant to each other. On days when I felt fragile and craved definition, I chopped onions fiendishly at four o'clock, sizzled them in olive oil. The kitchen filled with smells of cumin and cornbread. I ladled up three bowls of soup at seven, reassured that we were, at least for that good moment, family.

I REMEMBER one summertime dinner. We lingered at the dining room table, eating tempeh Reuben sandwiches and discussing how women in films always seemed to be punished for sexual assertiveness. Rachael got up to answer a knock at the door.

"Is there a man in the house?" I heard a stranger's voice say, and then Rachael, sharply: "Yes, but is there some way I can help you?"

The man's truck had broken down, and he needed a jump-start. I hurried up from the table, pulled my Datsun into the middle of the street and jumped his car three times before it started with a wheeze. Rachael watched from the porch, smirking. John did the dishes.

I liked the way our household challenged expectations—other people's, my own. Every day I tripped on old beliefs, so carefully instilled: that only blood family endures, that one cannot depend on friends, that three is an unsteady number. I worked to silence those cautionary voices and listen instead to my own.

In that house, my writing flourished. I began to write opinion columns and personal essays, as well as short stories, stretching beyond the journalism I'd always done. After dinner, I sat at the computer in my room while the sounds of John's African drums and Rachael's singing floated up from the basement. I became a devoted fan of their duo, Clap Hands, attending so many gigs I eventually memorized their entire set. And they were boosters for my writing, buying flowers when I read in public and pointing out my newspaper articles to friends.

Two years, three, four. Time wound us together with simple repetition and unexpected crises. John's great-aunt died. A friend of Rachael's was raped. My father was in Candlestick Park during the 1989 San Francisco earthquake; Rachael and John wrapped me in blankets and fed me tea as I shivered for hours on the couch, watching the news and waiting for the phone to ring.

For a while, I thought our household might remain intact forever. Oh, Rachael and John would probably get married, maybe even have children. I fantasized about moving with them to a larger house, adopting a child of my own or helping to raise theirs as a sort of live-in aunt.

Later, when Rachael and John did decide to buy a house, all three of us sometimes trooped out on weekends to inspect the listings. We opened closets, wandered through bedrooms, tried to imagine our lives transplanted. Realtors looked puzzled. They always thought Rachael and I must be sisters; how else to explain our intention to live together?

"Good friends," we explained, explicating nothing.

The "special shelf" objects got scattered in our move to the house they finally bought, a blue gray Victorian just ten blocks away. Rachael's wooden truck sat in a downstairs cabinet. My vial of lavender ended up in a kitchen drawer. Bugs had taken up residence in John's drum, and he had to throw it out.

Our household rhythm changed, too. Somehow, without planning or discussion, we had all become busier. John joined another band. Rachael worked and enrolled full time as a graduate student. I spent evenings and weekends at the computer. We ate dinner at different times and went to bed at midnight. None of us had much time for videos.

By then I was dating Elissa and often felt pulled. Was I still part of a tight-knit, three-person family, or was I one half of an emerging couple? I was reluctant to let go of the sustaining patterns in my life; the first December Elissa and I were together, I debated for weeks about whether to accompany Rachael and John to visit his parents and sisters for the holidays, as I'd done before, or to go with Elissa and a few other women friends for a long weekend at the coast. We argued and wept; I defended my loyalty to the RAJ extended family.

At the last minute, I decided that what I really wanted was to stay at home, alone. I spent the holiday painting my room, eating Chinese takeout, and watching videos, my isolation confirming the uneasy limbo I felt, tethered to two families yet fully present in neither one of them.

In a photograph from the day we moved, Rachael, John, and I are sitting on the steps of the new house, grimy and disheveled. Our arms are looped around each other's shoulders. What I remember is that Elissa stood just out of the camera's range, and I watched her watching us, my focus half-in and half-out of the frame.

We are two couples now, in separate households, with new patterns and fresh dilemmas. I still rent office space in Rachael and John's house and spend my weekdays working there. We celebrate all four of our birthdays together and schedule two family dinners each month—one a leisurely Shabbes feast with challah and wine, the other a more casual Sunday night meal. My parents still send presents to Rachael and John; their grandparents ask about me.

Beyond this overlapping core, our circles have spun outward, grown more populous and complicated. Some occasions still leave me feeling pulled between competing loyalties. On Valentine's Day, while Elissa and I celebrate with a candlelight dinner, I feel a tug of sadness and longing for the day, five years ago, when Rachael, John, and I moved into our first house. My life is layered with these patterns, a fabric in flux.

I still imagine that Rachael and John, Elissa and I might someday share a large duplex or buy houses on the same block. I miss living with them sometimes, when being one in a couple feels too confining and tidy. At the same time, I know our triad could last only as long as I remained single; add a fourth point, and the figure must change shape.

When I spin out variations on my own future—how I will live, with whom—my memories of a half-decade in the RAJ Mahal make me confident that nearly any possibility is within reach. That household's legacy is my faith in the unnamed and the untried.

A Friendship Circle Sewn over Six Decades

At 11:30 A.M. each Tuesday, eighty-eight-year-old Rose Ettelson pushes her walker over the carpeted hallway of the Wyncote House and rings the doorbell at Ruth Myers's apartment. Or Dorothy Bennett's. Or Sajie Stein's. Or Sarah Blanckensee's. Unless it is the fifth week. Then, they all come to Rose's place.

Each woman pays one dollar, meticulously recorded by Sarah in a small ledger. She has been the treasurer since the group began sixty-four years ago. They were young women then with mending to do, newly married, eager for company. It was more fun to fix zippers and talk at the same time. They called themselves the Sewing Circle.

Then there were babies (announced coyly by the expectant woman, who placed notes under the other women's plates at lunch). There were baby blankets and socks and pajamas to make, and bandages to roll for soldiers, bulky sweaters to knit and mail overseas. Eventually the war ended, the children grew and wanted store-bought clothes. The members of the Sewing Circle put down their thimbles and switched to mah jong.

The Tuesday I visited, the women met in Sajie Stein's comfortable one-bedroom apartment in the Wyncote, a high-rise in the suburbs west of Philadelphia. The Sewing Circle had met, regular as the Sabbath, for more than twice as long as I'd been alive. If I looked closely at them, with a stride of imagination, perhaps I could see myself.

Would I be like Sajie, petite and bone-thin at eighty-nine, her light hair tarnished gray, the one who spoke least often and most bluntly of the five. Or more like eighty-seven-year-old Ruth, the youngest Sewing Circle member and the only one in slacks, with oversize glasses and a voice sandpapered by cigarettes?

Dorothy, whom everyone called Dot, was ninety and the most talkative. Sarah, the matriarch at ninety-one, wore neat pearl earrings, a peach skirt, and a striped blouse. Rose perched on a chair behind her walker, dressed in a high-collared ruffled blouse, knitting with ivory-colored wool while we talked. In the dining room, the table was set for lunch.

"WE NEVER missed a meeting. That was the important thing," Ruth answered, when I asked how they had remained together so long. "You wouldn't do anything else when it came to Sewing Circle day," Dot added. "That was a commitment. No other invitation was nearly as important."

"The amazing thing is, after all these years, that there's still the feeling, the closeness, the loving and care and the interest of each one for the other." That was Sarah, eager to give emotional shade to the facts. "It's just part of our life, that's all. The good and the bad."

After a while, their time together spilled from Tuesdays to other occasions. Birthdays, anniversaries, New Year's Eve. There were trips to Atlantic City, lectures and concerts and book discussions. Albums of photographs document Sewing Circle history. In one, the group was gathered around a table, the women in slim off-the-shoulder dresses, their husbands in dark dinner jackets. Later, the women sported beehive hairdos and almond-shaped glasses.

When I prodded for details of how they began and what kept them glued, the reminiscences tumbled out, each woman finishing another's thoughts, adding a snip of memory, until the picture became whole.

Ruth: "Don't give the impression that we only talked about our children. We also joined lecture groups, went to concerts, did book reviews."

Rose: "We don't do too much talking about our grandchildren or great-grandchildren, because everybody has them."

Sajie: "And we don't talk about our operations, 'cause everybody has them, too. We all went through a lot of those. And came back smiling. We're all so damn lucky."

The five women have their own biological families, children who they see with some frequency, but none as often as they see each other. They boast, as they should, of the Sewing Circle's long life. It was another way to keep count, to hold on in the fading ribbon of time.

I JOINED them for a brief, plain lunch—tuna fish salad on iceberg lettuce, sliced tomatoes, coffee, cake. Sajie, adhering to another Sewing Circle custom, refused to let anyone clear the dishes or help her clean up. Instead, they stayed at the table, each adding her piece to an ongoing conversation.

Sarah: "We're unusual in that we've stayed together so long."

Dot: "We never had a disagreement. We never had unpleasant words."

Sarah: "What one wanted to do—"

Dot: "We could discuss things—"

Sarah: "Whether it was a death, or a joy, or whatever."

Ruth: "One of the reasons none of us is in a retirement home is that we take care of each other. If we hear one of our friends is alone on a Saturday night, we will invite her in. We don't have to. But if we're free, we'll say, 'Do you want to go out to dinner with us?' We don't like to leave each other stranded."

Sarah: "That's the friendship behind the whole thing."

Dot: "Looking out for the other one's comfort and happiness."

The Sewing Circle withstood time partly because of luck and homogeneity; its members were all young, all Jewish, all married. No one challenged the group's unity by becoming a Buddhist or moving to Brazil or even getting divorced. Sajie and Sarah, Dot, Ruth, and Rose might have flinched under the label of "feminist." But many years ago, when they were young, these women made their friendships with each other a priority. By the time I met them, that commitment had outlasted three wars and four husbands. And they continued to choose it each Tuesday, as they moved slowly down the hallway, holding on.

We ate dessert—spice cake cut in rectangles—and then someone reached for the mah jong set, a fancy one in a red alligator-skin case.

"It's just become part of our life," said Sarah, looking around at her friends' faces. "Isn't it amazing we should end our days all here."

Finding Kinship with a Colleague

IT BEGAN over a beer. Renée La Chance and Jay Brown were both working at Portland's gay and lesbian newspaper. They spent frequent after-work gripe sessions at Wilde Oscar's, a bar a few blocks from the downtown waterfront, sharing frustrations about their jobs and the paper.

Soon the meetings became planning sessions—for a new gay and lesbian newspaper. Sometimes Jay and Renée would sit on the lawn near the Willamette River, with Renée's dog Punky in tow, and toss ideas back and forth. They scoured a thesaurus for suggestions on the name of their new publication, checking the listings for "out."

Leak out. Get out. Come out. Way out. Just out.

Just Out. That was it. They recruited a graphic designer to draw the masthead and began to publish a twenty-four-page paper twice a month on a skeletal budget, from an office so small they had room for only one desk. Jay sold his antique couch for $300 so they could pay the first month's rent and telephone bills.

Workplace groups can replicate the worst of family life—rigid hierarchies, power struggles, communication sticky as a clogged drainpipe. Even in the best situations, co-workers are often transient figures in our landscape. The project—the play we're producing, the fund-raiser, the campaign—defines the terms and depth of our attachment.

But sometimes there is more. Renée and Jay slipped noiselessly over that boundary between work and family into limitless terrain.

THEY made an incongruous pair. Jay was tall and gangly, with gray hair fringing both sides of a bald spot, gold wire-rims and a puckish face pitted with acne scars. Renée was short, stocky, and twenty-four years younger. At first, they fought. Renée wanted to place an ad on an eighth-page slotted for news. Jay insisted they needed the space to cover an important event. They made a stubborn, sometimes cranky match, yelling at each other in the tiny office or out on the ratty wooden platform they generously called their "loading dock."

But if Jay and Renée clashed over editorial matters, they agreed completely on the subject of family. Both were ostracized by their relatives, although Jay mailed a copy of the paper to his parents each month. For each of them, biological family churned up feelings of loss, anger, or the farce of having to pretend. They made a point of shunning traditional holidays. Instead, they celebrated their birthdays, Gay Pride, the anniversary of Just Out each November.

For a while, Jay worked as a janitor at the Rodeo bar, mopping the previous night's beer from the floors early in the morning. Renée had a series of jobs—as a carpenter, painter, driver of an ice cream truck. Still, there were months when one of them couldn't quite make the rent or had an empty wallet when the lunch tab came around. They loaned each other money, or one would agree to take home less pay that month so the other could have more. Slowly, their time together—and their expectations of each other—expanded beyond business hours.

Two years after they started Just Out Jay got sick. "He was diagnosed with ARC [AIDS-related complex]. I thought that was going to be it," Renée said. "It made me realize how much I cared about him. I tried to make sure he didn't get a lot of stress—like I had any control over it," she said.

In addition to publishing Just Out, Renée was then working full time at an insurance company and offered to marry Jay so he could gain health benefits as her spouse. She also told him that if he got so sick he couldn't live alone, he could come and stay with her and her partner. Instead, he recovered and remained fairly healthy for the next four years.

"When he got sick again, four years later, he tried to push me away by picking fights all the time," Renée recalled. "I think he was trying to keep me from knowing how sick he really was." But she noticed. Jay started to drive the four blocks to the post office instead of walking; it was a strain for him to climb the stairs. Once, he went home in the middle of paste-up instead of prowling around the flats, proofreading articles just one last time.

Perhaps Renée and Jay became so close because of the nature of their work—producing a paper that dealt with urgent, intimate aspects of both their lives, a job that could not be split neatly into political and personal components. Maybe it was just a lucky conjunction of timing, personality and need.

I'd written for *Just Out* myself and discovered the addictive freedom of the office. Men and women came to work there because they craved a respite from "straight" jobs that demanded suits and sanitized behavior. At *Just Out*, staff members could be sad, flamboyant, grouchy, enraged, ecstatic, whole-heartedly themselves—as long as they got the paper out on time.

Not that the work environment was a smoothly functioning paradise. Once, staff relations grew so ragged we enlisted the help of a therapist. The first thing she asked us was to describe our roles in terms of family relationships. I dubbed myself a "second cousin," connected but not intimately involved. Others said they were sister, uncle, best friend. Renée and Jay, without question, were "Mom" and "Dad."

"WHEN Jay got really sick, I felt a responsibility I hadn't felt before," Renée said. "I was there to decipher whatever the doctors were babbling at him. Other people would come over and help him pee in a little cup, give him a sponge bath. I didn't do any personal touching or caretaking that way; that didn't feel comfortable for either of us. I was more of a guardian, I think."

Renée visited Jay at Providence Medical Center every day, leaving only for quick stops to the office or to go home and sleep. Friends and colleagues visited him, called, and sent cards. But Renée was the primary support, the one who ran interference with hospital staff, who talked with Jay about the emotions and the logistics of death.

"Whenever Jay introduced me to doctors or nurses, he'd say, 'This is Renée. She's my family. You tell her anything she wants to know.'

"It was hard sometimes with the hospital staff because they're not used to dealing with alternative families. When someone's in intensive care, blood family is their criteria for visiting. We had to straighten that out with them first thing."

The night Jay died, with morphine dripping into his veins, he talked for several hours with Renée and a group of friends.

"He entertained us for four hours. He was talking about where he wanted his ashes. Point Lobos, near Big Sur, where the sea otters lived. He did sea otter imitations. He looked just like one. Then he said he was really tired and wanted to go to sleep. Everyone left but me. I told him, This is it, Jay. You're going to die now, and he said, 'I know.'

"Someone had given him a bunch of balloons, and as we left the hospital, we let them go."

WHEN Renée heads out to a gay rights rally or march, she inspects Jay's button collection to find one with an appropriate slogan. On the first anniversary of his death, Renée bought a stuffed animal, a small gray sea otter. She took it with her to the Gay Pride parade that June. "I miss the fights," she said. "I miss his input, his support, and his cynicism."

After Jay died, cards and bouquets of flowers arrived at *Just Out*, along with a small box wrapped in brown paper. The office was the logical place for the funeral home to send his ashes. And on a windowsill, boxed in glass like some family curio, Jay's gold wire-rimmed glasses stared unflinchingly at the whole business, watching the work go on.

"We had a little memorial gathering for Jay afterward, and everybody came up to me," Renée said. "They took my hand and gave me their condolences. They definitely recognized that he was more than just a business partner or friend—that we had a much deeper bond."

Inviting an Old Friend Home

L<small>IZ</small> Burke settled into an armchair in a living room that could double as the set for an early 1960s sitcom: big color console television, shag carpet the shade of avocado flesh, substantial armchairs. Her polo shirt was tucked into tailored pants. Her shoes were a flat and sensible navy blue. She was not, at first glance, the sort of person to ask a friend impulsively to move into her redwood ranch house, then punch a hole in the roof to make more room.

Liz told the story eagerly. She and Florence Fairhill had known each other almost forty years, ever since Florence was the director of Camp Arrah Wanna and Liz was a junior counselor. Florence, older by thirteen years, had worked as a Baptist missionary in New York's Bowery and told riveting campfire stories.

Camp ended. Florence returned to her job as statewide Christian education director for the Baptist Church. Liz went back to high school but continued to seek out the older woman as a mentor and confidante. "I'd go to her office and cry on her shoulder about the usual trials and tribulations of teenage girls. And she listened," Liz recalled.

For the next three decades, they kept in touch by mail—frequently, at first, then just once or twice a year. Florence moved to South Dakota, to the East Coast, to California. Liz stayed put; she married, had two daughters, got divorced, worked as a diabetes nurse and educator, raised her kids as a single parent.

Once, when Florence was visiting in the area, they met for lunch and talked as if no time had elapsed. When Liz sat down to write a Christmas letter to Florence in 1983, she decided to propose another meeting. "We've always said we should plan a visit," she wrote. "How about a vacation together this summer?" Florence wrote back: "Yes!"

"I told some of my friends," Liz remembered. "They were aghast—a week with someone you haven't seen for over thirty years? I had never thought that. I never thought there would be that much of a chasm between us."

The two women—then forty-eight and sixty-one—spent a few days in a cottage on the Oregon coast. They talked nonstop, wandered the long rocky beach, ate fresh strawberries. Florence described her work in a counseling center for Baptist ministers and their families, and Liz detected frustration and burnout in her voice.

Liz talked about her two daughters, who had recently moved out, her work, and her plans. She was interested in fashioning a future different from the patterns offered to women in this culture. "My parents always lived through their children, and my mother fell apart when her kids left home. I wasn't going to let that happen. I had a gob of other things I wanted to do."

The more time they spent together, the more comfortable Liz felt. The two shared values; they got along easily in the cottage, managing the cooking and chores with a kind of intuitive smoothness.

"One evening I said, Florence, how would you like to retire and come live with me? As soon as I said it, I thought, Wait, you can't do that. But suddenly we were really into Florence quitting her job and coming to live here."

That's when Liz decided to raise the roof. Her three-bedroom ranch house had been roomy enough for herself and her two daughters. But Florence, she knew, was accustomed to living in her own apartment, and Liz had come to expect more privacy since the girls left home.

Within a month after their visit, Liz called a contractor. Several months later, there was a second story on top of the house—a large suite with a bedroom, an office-library, a bathroom, and a deck. At the end of the year, Florence moved in.

Liz's family was startled at first. When she finally told her father she was remodeling the house to make room for Florence, she heard him half-cover the phone and shout to his wife, "Guess what my crazy daughter is doing now?"

The plan didn't seem crazy to Liz. Both she and Florence would gain companionship, at little cost to their privacy. They liked each other. And both could save money in the long run. Maybe it wasn't the most conventional arrangement, but Liz knew convention was not always the most satisfying guide. Sometimes friendship and faith proved more powerful ushers into brand new territory.

"We drew up a contract with an attorney. We agreed that since Florence had paid for the construction on the upper part of the house, she'd live here rent-free until I'd paid back my share. We'd share utilities." The attorney urged them to add a provision in case either woman wanted to end the arrangement. Liz and Florence felt sure that would never happen. But at their lawyer's insistence, they agreed that either one would give the other sixty days' notice if she wanted out.

At first they did everything in tandem—took weekend trips around the state, prepared the food for Liz's daughters' wedding receptions, traveled together to Washington, D.C., New Jersey, and Victoria. Neither one loved to cook, but they did try to eat together most nights.

The women made deliberate efforts to make a new family with room for their disparate ages, backgrounds, and idiosyncrasies. Liz had attended a Presbyterian Church, while Florence adhered to the Baptist traditions of her childhood. They shopped around for a church that both would like, and Florence finally decided to switch denominations so they could join a nearby Presbyterian congregation.

Their living arrangement sometimes raises eyebrows, and both women have fielded questions about whether they are lovers. Liz said she resents having to explain their choice to the curious; while their household may not be typical, she knows that heterosexual women through centuries have lived together in close platonic relationships. She describes her life with Florence as a "collaboration of practicality, friendship, and sensitivity to the other's needs."

After a while, their friends' and families' skepticism faded. Sisters in the Marylhurst Order, for whom Liz worked as a secretary, would ask, "How are you and Florence?" Liz's aunt and uncle began to call Florence "their other niece." Friends invited them out as a pair.

Occasionally they declined such offers, each believing the other should have time alone with friends and family. The set-up of the house and their various hobbies also guaranteed some separateness. Florence wrote dozens of letters; Liz spent her evenings with needlework. Florence handled most of the yard work; Liz did more of the cooking.

"The assumption has been that because Florence is thirteen years older, she would die or become ill first. We have discussed that. We each have our own wills. We've informally decided that I would take care of Florence as long as possible, with health care help in the home."

After forty years of friendship, after eight of living together, they still carry an unspoken understanding that transcends the age gap and the very different paths they took from Camp Arrah Wanna to the present. This friendship involves more than practical coexistence. Each woman provides a swatch of the other's history; they are living a life neither could manage alone. Words can't describe it; they refer to each other simply as "my roommate" or sometimes, on Liz's part, "my upstairs friend."

"We're not 100 percent in sync," Liz said. "There have been times when we don't understand the other's viewpoint. We get over it. We don't let that kind of thing build up. It's been an easy relationship—amazingly so.

"We plan to stay together forever."

Independence and Support in the House of Catharsis

THERE are times when being a family calls for some civil disobedience.

Twice a year, Laura Hershey and Robin Stephens join ADAPT—American Disabled for Attendant Programs Today—as 300 to 400 disabled people converge on a target city and hold a week of demonstrations, marches, and other actions. They make friends with people in wheelchairs from Nashville and Austin. They sport ADAPT's T-shirts, which proclaim, "Free Our People."

"We feel like we're part of a movement of people who are disabled and radical and militant. Those twice-annual protests are a reconnection with the national family of people with disabilities," Laura said.

In between those occasions, they live together in Denver, where their family includes friends, Laura's relatives, and a network of paid and volunteer attendants—all of whom share the couple's conviction that a life on their own terms is worth the struggle.

I ARRANGED to meet Laura and Robin at a local café. Robin was wiry and friendly, with a thin braid descending from her cropped hair, a wicked smile, and a habit of raising her left fist from the arm of her wheelchair in a thumbs-up salute. Her right arm went into frequent spasms, hooking back over her head.

Laura's hands sat still on the tray of her wheelchair. Plastic tubes delivered oxygen into both nostrils. Even though she did most of the talking, she seemed quieter than her partner, a calmer spirit. Both women wore buttons that read, "You Get Proud by Practicing."

"I have several families that are kind of overlapping and interconnected," Laura said. "Robin is one family. My parents and brother are another; they live near us. The network of attendants and friends that I rely on has become like a family to me, too."

Robin works as a national organizer for ADAPT, which aims to redirect Medicaid funding toward a national attendant program so more people like themselves can live at home rather than in institutions. Part of her job involves organizing the groups' demonstrations, which she describes as "chaotic but organized, like a big family reunion."

When our food arrived, she pulled the plate close and began to feed both herself and Laura. At first, I had a hard time understanding Robin over the hum of an air conditioner and piped music, so Laura repeated her answers for me. But as the interview went on, either Robin relaxed or I grew used to the rhythms of her speech.

All her life, Robin said, she was searching for a sense of family, of community. As a child, she read every book she could find about disabled children or adults. But except for a few summers at camp, she never met any disabled people face to face. As a lesbian, she sometimes felt doubly marginalized, sidelined by the homophobia of straight disabled people and the gay community's reluctance to include members with disabilities.

After college, Robin became involved with SOAR, an organization that sponsors outdoor adventure trips for disabled and nondisabled people. Soon Robin was lobbying the city bus system to get more, and better-functioning, wheelchair lifts.

"People with disabilities are bicultural," she explained. "Most of our parents are nondisabled. Our families don't reflect who we are."

Those words sounded familiar to me. I'd heard them in so many different contexts, from so many women. Lesbians raised by heterosexual parents, children of color in white homes. Robin and Laura's situation just made plain what is true, to some degree, in all families. Parents can offer only the stuff of their own lives and experience. Beyond that, a woman must find her own kin, her own kind.

On a typical day, Laura said, her first attendant will arrive between 6 and 8 a.m. to "drag me out of bed." Her morning routine—bathing, shampoo, toilet, and dressing—takes about three hours. Then she works at the computer on poetry or prose. Another attendant arrives to cook lunch; a third comes in the evening for dinner and bedtime routines.

"I do need a lot of help," Laura said. "But I consider myself as independent as you are. That doesn't mean I'm totally self-sufficient. That means I have control of the choices I make, what I do with my life.

"My feeling about that owes a lot to the way my parents raised me." Laura spent her first two years of school in a segregated "special education" classroom, which she remembered as being "horrible—very artificial, very unchallenging." Her parents insisted that the school system place Laura in regular classes.

"I was so happy to be mainstreamed," Laura recalled, "I didn't want to be around disabled people."

After college she received a grant to go to England and write about disability rights there. Far from her home and community, Laura discovered a new sense of belonging among disabled activists. When she returned to the United States she brought with her a sense of political urgency and a determination to express that in her work and in her writing. "I'm trying to be one voice for the disabled community," she said.

The same sense of empowerment that feeds Laura's political activity also shapes her daily life. "If I have an attendant who is screwing up, I can fire that person. I can control my situation. Some people don't work out. Some do and become very much part of our lives. The woman traveling with us has worked with me on and off for nearly ten years. She's traveling with us for two months. That really takes commitment."

When Laura needs to fill a shift with someone new, she advertises, conducts interviews, and looks for someone open-minded and willing to work for the admittedly small amount that Medicaid will pay. Often, she said, the attendants are people in transition, making difficult choices about their own lives. Emotions run high in their home, which they've dubbed "the House of Catharsis."

In the year and a half Robin and Laura have lived together, they've found ways to support each other and decrease the need for outside aides. Robin agrees to feed Laura so the two can go out to dinner unaccompanied. An attendant used to wake Laura and turn her once each night; now Robin does that.

"And I interpret for her in noisy environments. Or sometimes with phone calls," Laura said. "She can do a lot more physically. It's harder to see the kinds of things I can do for her."

At this, Robin made a face of mild impatience, an expression that said, "Partner, you do plenty."

I LEFT the café and felt conscious of my legs that moved me up the sidewalk, my arms that could swing and carry a notebook at the same time. I measure my freedom sometimes with such physical tasks, forgetting that there are many kinds of liberty. I have walked unaided along streets I did not choose, in places I would rather not have been.

Laura's and Robin's independence comes not from the number of things they can do without assistance but from their determination to live the life they want and to fight, if necessary, for the help to make that possible.

"There are millions of people in institutions who don't have the option of having a family of any kind," Laura said at the end of our talk. "We're not typical. That's why we're working so hard to change the system. Right?"

She glanced at her partner. Robin raised the thumbs-up and grinned her wicked grin.

Running a Restaurant, Sharing a Vision

EIGHTEEN years ago, Selma Miriam was running a weekly women's cooperative exchange called Bloodroot out of her living room. One woman brought and sold handmade jewelry; another did tarot readings. Selma was forty, about to be divorced, and trying to figure out what to do with her life.

Noel Furie, who sold her photographs each Wednesday at Selma's co-op, was thirty. She and Selma had met through a NOW-sponsored consciousness-raising group. She had two children, eight and nine, and a marriage that was rapidly unraveling. Noel wanted to cook vegetarian, she wanted to live by her own rules, and she wanted to work with women.

Betsey Beaven had moved to New Haven after graduating from college and soon found the only jobs available were baby-sitting for Yale professors' families. Graduate school held no appeal. At meetings of her lesbian rap group, to which Selma also belonged, Betsey talked about feeling adrift. She longed for something tangible to do with her mind and her hands.

Then Selma had a dream. Three dreams, actually, one after the other in a single night of busy sleep. In the first, a sociologist visited her consciousness-raising group and announced that a recent study showed parents were likely to end up supporting their divorced daughters. In the dream, that news brought Selma to tears.

Then she dreamed she'd won a commission to landscape a piece of property near the waterfront; she pored over books and manuals, learning what plants would thrive in that environment. Finally, she dreamed of coming downstairs in her house and finding her children serving brunch to room after room of people, using dozens of free-range chicken eggs she had received from a friend.

She wrote down all three dreams, because a friend had told her it was a good idea. And then she forgot about them.

Several months later, the memory of those dreams returned—a "hot flash," Selma said, that suddenly clarified what she would do next. "It was a Monday. In the middle of the day, I just got this physical rush: I know, I'm going to do Bloodroot full time, not just on Wednesday nights." She called Betsey and began hunting for a spot that would lend itself to a collectively owned, feminist, vegetarian restaurant and bookstore.

BLOODROOT sits on the Long Island Sound in residential Bridgeport, a depressed, steel-colored city. It is not easy to find. To get there, you trace a zigzag path over streets named Fairfield and Ellsworth and Thurston, then follow Ferris until it dead-ends at the water.

If I'd come across Bloodroot earlier, as a student in nearby New Haven in the early 1980s, it might have met some fragment of my own yearning, given me a glimpse of what women can do together. But I didn't know. I ate in Yale dining halls for four years and found the restaurant on purpose, much later, when I drove a rented Plymouth through New York and up Interstate 95 into Connecticut.

It was a Wednesday night, dinnertime. Women clustered around full plates in the low, honeyed cast of table lamps. I gave my order—grilled *ma-po* tofu—at a window where I could see the cooks moving swiftly, draining noodles, spooning out blueberry cobbler. Someone tapped out my bill on a tabletop adding machine. When I was finished, I bussed my own table. Later, after the kitchen was clean and the customers gone, Selma, Betsey, and Noel joined me at the table.

"You have to understand that we share a common vision. We're not simply a group that happens to like each other," said Selma. She talked fast, gesturing broadly, fistfuls of silver rings flashing. "We came together for a particular purpose—we wanted to live our feminism. This goal was more important to us than anything else."

In discussions that seamed their way through every hour the women spent together, they developed Bloodroot's principles—each woman would contribute an equal amount of start-up money, take home equal pay, and work the same number of hours. They would make decisions by consensus. Their commitment would be long term.

Bloodroot aimed to breach the separations between necessary work and inner passions, business and play, colleagues and family. But unlike the classic family farm or Mom-and-Pop grocery, where people were relatives first and business partners second, it was the work and shared philosophy of Bloodroot that made Its members kin.

"As we struggled to understand our relationship with each other and how we felt about each other," Selma said, "we kept falling back on this word, 'family.' And family, of course, is the possession of the man, patriarchal in its conception. So what do we call each other? Whatever our relationships were one on one, it's very different from the kind of thing we have together. We groped for a word to describe it."

Betsey took up where Selma stopped. "A woman came up to the counter one time, and she wanted to know if we were all related. I said, Well, we're all from the same tribe. It just fell right out of my mouth.

"We have been through so many experiences together. It's very hard to convey the power of that to other women when they first start working here. I think it's awesome. I think it's the beginning of civilization."

At first, starting a civilization required hours of garage-sale shopping, furniture refinishing, menu planning, gardening and poring through cookbooks and recipe files. When they found the site, a former machine shop, and Selma's dreams came flooding back, they negotiated for months with the owners. Selma had saved money from doing landscape work; eventually, her parents helped her buy the property. They had no furniture to fill the long rectangular room. Selma had never even balanced a checkbook. Noel was the only one with waitressing experience.

They worked sixty-hour weeks, standing in the kitchen until their heels throbbed. They skipped movies and concerts. Each week, Noel took her kids on the train to New York to see their father, then caught the return train back to Bridgeport and came to work.

"I wanted to live and work with women. I wanted to think about good and evil and ethics, and I had to be in a place where no one was stepping on my neck," she said. "I set my priorities so that Bloodroot was first. My kids learned how to do the laundry. They fed themselves. I felt I didn't have a choice. The only way I could survive was with Bloodroot."

The collective took its name from the bloodroot plant, *Sanguinaria canadensis*, which has an interdependent root system but grows separate, individual blossoms. The women say it's an apt metaphor for their work together. They abhor hierarchy and reject the notion, common to many families and workplaces, that some members are inherently more valuable than others. At Bloodroot, one woman schedules worker hours and plans the menu, one does local grocery shopping, one pays the bills. All three bake bread, wash dishes, and cook.

When she first joined, Betsey remembered, she thought a collective meant everyone would be the same. Instead, she found her strengths and her quirks thrown into relief by the group's close working relationship. In this emerging tribe that depended on each member's individuality, she could not disappear.

"One woman said you can't work at Bloodroot and not see yourself," she said. "It's like a mirror. Everything of who you are will appear in that mirror....

"You can't come here and not change."

"You work with a woman, and it's hard work, and there's a lot of customers, and everything's moving along, and you get mad and you celebrate together," Selma said. "You say, Wow, we fed ninety-five people tonight. You're sweaty and tired together, and meanwhile you argue politics and all the rest. And you fall in love with a woman like that.

"You don't fall in love with her because, you know, she's got pretty hair or you like the way she walks. You fall in love with her because you work with her and you care about the same things."

Over the years, various members of Bloodroot have fallen in love—and become lovers. When I visited, Betsey shared a house with Selma, and Noel lived with housemates. Their relationships overrode conventional notions of autonomy and private space; when Noel was shopping for a couch for her living room, she asked Betsey and Selma to check it out first. They take an annual vacation together. On days they don't see each other at work, they talk on the phone. Often, Betsey said, all three have similar flashes of insight at the same time, independent of each other, what she calls a "storming up of ideas."

Noel pushed her glasses up toward the bridge of her nose. "I know," she said, "that when I call them up, they will help. Whatever it is. I have total, total trust and faith in them. We've been through an awful lot, and through the very worst things we've been through, we have not left each other."

Some women have left, though, a painful consequence of such intense interaction. When work and family are one and the same, and someone grows restless, there's less room to maneuver, to change one aspect of life while holding another constant. At Bloodroot, it's all of a piece. You take it whole, or you leave everything—work, friends, family, ethics, food.

The regular customers, and women who come to chop carrots once a week but do not join the collective, form a large extended network of Bloodroot "cronies." Some members of their biological families—Noel's grown children, Betsey's mother, Selma's parents (now dead, but financial and spiritual supporters of the restaurant while they lived)—are also part of the clan.

"When my mother died, and my father was not doing well, we decided he should come here. He stayed until he died," Selma said. "We all took care of him. My parents were with me all the way." At various times, they offered financial support, practical advice, and bemused encouragement. "My mother would come in the kitchen and say, 'You know, the Russian Revolution didn't work. I don't know why you think this is going to work.'"

Bloodroot has worked now for more than eighteen years, outliving numerous women's bookstores, health collectives, and other like-minded ventures. The restaurant has earned rave reviews in *The New York Times*. Selma's hair is a wiry gray. Noel's kids have grown up. Betsey has learned homeopathy. They get tired more often, and more easily, than they used to.

Each year, they celebrate the restaurant's anniversary with a big party on the spring equinox. It is the point midway between the darkest day and the brightest, the edge of the growing season.

"We have each been able to make our own lives, carve them," Noel said. "I really want to do what I do every day. Sometimes I get a little tired of the dishes or something. But really, I am making my life. That's an amazing thing for somebody to have in the world."

One June evening, after all the customers had drifted out of the restaurant, Selma, Betsey, and Noel sat talking about nothing in particular. Even though they were exhausted, no one wanted to say good night and head home. When Noel finally climbed into her car and turned on the radio, an announcer said the summer solstice, the longest day of the year, had just ended.

She smiled. It made sense, then, that they had sat together in their restaurant, lingering and talking and reluctant to let go, through the last moment of available light.

First Person Singular:
Choosing an Unpartnered Life

WITH one hand, I balance my unbalanced meal—noodle kugel, potato salad, rye bread with Swiss cheese and sliced tomato. With the other, I reach out to greet the smiling, gray-haired woman who is headed in my direction. I'm at a party to celebrate my cousin's law school graduation; this woman coming through the kitchen doorway might be a distant relative, a neighbor, or a family friend.

She clasps my palm in hers, appraising me. I have just come from a grueling three-day job interview and stepped off a train on which I stood for forty-five minutes; I am rumpled, exhausted, and hungry. "How are you, dear?" says the woman, her glance taking special note of my wedding-ringless left hand. "I have four grandsons."

Several days later, it happens again: another party, another woman warmly patting my shoulder. "How would you like to be my granddaughter-in-law?" she asks. "I don't think so," I say. "How about just being your friend?" She pleats her brow, unsatisfied.

I should be used to this, by now, all these helpful, unsubtle hints. Part of the problem, I know, is the frequent, infuriating assumption that I am heterosexual. My close relatives, to whom I've been out for several years, no longer make such overtures. But to the rest, when I appear—young, unescorted, ringless—at a family gathering, I am simply a single woman, fair game for anyone with an eligible man in mind. Several years ago, when I *was* happily single, the comments irked me as much as they do now; the eager matchmakers presumed to know my wishes without ever inquiring about my life.

In the mid-1970s, the peak of my television viewing, single women held a brief, heady dominion over prime time. My favorite was Mary Tyler Moore's Mary Richards, the closest I had to a media heroine. She worked in a newsroom, had a passel of devoted and quirky friends and a terrific apartment with a view. And every week, without fail, she tossed her beret exuberantly into the air over a Minneapolis street as the credits scrolled. But the heyday of single female TV heroines soon ended, and I slowly began to grasp that such women were anomalies in a culture of pairs.

Of course there were a few exceptions, both fictional and real—the canny Miss Marple of my summertime reading; my mother's friend Marjorie, a busy news reporter and mother of two adopted daughters. But most plays, books, and popular music painted unmarried women as pathetic, unloved, hysterical, promiscuous, or crazy. Indeed, they were exceptions in my own biological family, in which women were either married, divorced, or widowed. In that world, no one *chose* to be single; it was a way you ended up after some unhappy circumstance intervened. And in most cases, it was a temporary state, a restless period marked with grief, longing, and the anxious search for a new spouse.

As early as elementary school, we were expected to pair up—for dances, record hops, parties, proms. It was all right for girls to attend those events in duos or clusters, but we knew each other's company was only a temporary refuge. We taught each other the hustle, practiced disco moves en masse, but we went home happy when we'd danced with boys.

When my parents invited their single female friends to dinner, it was usually a maneuver to introduce them to available men. "I wish I knew someone for her," my mother would say of an unmarried woman colleague. Always, they sought to match the unattached, to "fix them up," as if they were broken.

My mother often mentions the daughter of some neighbors, an ambitious lawyer in her forties whose parents fret over her single status. "Maybe she likes it that way," I suggest, and my mother shakes her head, refusing to believe that a woman might find fulfillment alone.

Even my paternal grandmother, Rose, who has lived alone since her husband died nearly forty years ago, did her best to steer me away from an unpartnered life. "I hope one of these days you'll have good news for me—if you know what I mean," she said on the phone. "It's no good to be alone."

"I'm not alone, Bubie, I have lots of friends."

"Ach—friends," she sputtered, and I could imagine her hand shooing me impatiently.

I SPENT most of my late teens and twenties single. In college, simple busyness made an acceptable excuse: with a full course load and work at the campus daily newspaper, who had time? After graduation, working sixty-hour weeks to prove myself as a reporter, everyone seemed to concur that I was just postponing relationships in order to establish my career. Many of my friends—male and female—were single then; the few weddings I attended in those years seemed weirdly premature.

It was not until my middle and late twenties, when I lived with Rachael and John, that I experienced firsthand the cultural tidal wave flushing women toward partnership. Friends and family looked skeptical when I said I was happy. Relatives questioned my decision to remain on the West Coast—after all, it wasn't as if I had a *spouse* who wanted to stay. When I talked about the importance of my friendships, my community, people's eyes wandered in disbelief.

After their initial dismay, my parents seemed to be more disturbed by my singlehood and my unconventional living arrangement than by my lesbianism. Over glasses of white wine at a neighborhood restaurant, my mother leaned toward me, her eyes glistening.

"I just don't want you to be alone," she said.

I look back at my daily calendars for those years, trying to recall how I spent my time, who peopled my days. With Pattie, I saw movies or spent hours in dense conversation on a Sunday as the sun crawled over the banks of the Sandy River. With Dolores, I tried backpacking, cross-country skiing, and canoeing for the first time. She was single then, too, and we were proud of our spontaneity, our ability to call each other at three o'clock and meet for a hot tub at six. Sometimes I stayed overnight with a friend, exchanging back rubs or foot massages, snuggling as we slept.

Once or twice a week, Rachael, John, and I slid a movie into the VCR and huddled under quilts on the living room futon.

Sometimes I had lovers. For several months, I conducted a long-distance romance through crackly telephone calls and long letters. An intense friendship swelled briefly into an affair, then ended by mutual agreement. A longer relationship finally broke with my realization that being a partner was not my priority then.

Throughout those five years, my life was busy, rich, and full of intimacy—it just didn't come from a single source. Still, both my gay and straight friends were eager to pair me up. They checked on my status—"Meet anyone interesting lately?"—as if finding a partner ought to be my main pursuit. What stung the most, though, was the way others regarded my life as a pleasant diversion, a rehearsal for the time when I would truly "settle down."

In fact, I did not know then if I wanted a partner; often, I imagined living into old age as a single woman, with John and Rachael as my immediate family and numerous friends as its extensions. But I hesitated even to voice those fantasies. They seemed so sharply at odds with what everyone expected me to do.

I struggled to weed those expectations from my own desires, to hear my voice clearly amid the coupled chorus. Was I merely "between relationships"? (Although, at that point, the "between" had lasted longer than any romance.) Was I precluding partnership with my workaholic habits, my refusal to compromise my independence? And if I was choosing to be single, either temporarily or for the visible future, why couldn't everyone accept that and leave me alone?

Why do we doubt single women so much? What do we fear? Think of the words—spinster, old maid—and the ways they were said (before feminists reclaimed them), with lips curled in pity, tongues clucking. Recall the centuries-old stereotypes, the very real hurdles that women faced if they chose to be alone. Most jobs were not open to women, and those that were rarely paid enough to make self-sufficiency possible. For working-class women, the choices were even fewer, and the pay more miserable. In some families, an unmarried daughter was both a social embarrassment and a financial burden; in others, single daughters became full-time, live-in caretakers, coerced by economic and social pressures into a life of servitude.

Outside the home, the paths of single women were literally curtailed; many hotels, restaurants, and clubs refused to admit them without escorts. At various periods in history, single women were automatically labeled as prostitutes, witches, or lesbians—shunned at the least, actively persecuted at worst.

Still today, to be a healthy, fulfilled, unpartnered woman is to wrestle with one of society's most cherished precepts. Women, we are taught, exist in relation to others, to *one* other, in particular. We are trained from girlhood to secure and nourish that lifelong bond. And if we choose otherwise, we throw into question the essence of our gendered role.

Women who want to be single expose the narrowness of common definitions. They alter patterns of intimacy, gathering companionship and support from multiple sources that may include lovers, friends, colleagues, housemates, children, and other relatives.

In their everyday acts, single women pose profound challenges—to men who may feel rejected by their choice; to women who might see in their sisters' lives a path considered but not pursued; to a culture that posits partnership as a woman's only route to adulthood.

SOMETIMES, on a damp Sunday when I have no other plans, I like to pretend that I am alone. I take my notebook to a café and practice the treachery of single-mindedness. Family, friends, and partner vanish for the afternoon. I think of nothing but the work. I let the words fill me utterly, until I am drunk with them.

Often I look back on my own history as a single woman for solace and information. I'm aware of the ways that even a healthy partnership sometimes confines me, of how guiltily glad I can feel when Elissa leaves for an evening or a weekend, when I move through the world solo, unchecked.

Other times, my experience as a single woman makes me think twice about the hidden assumptions on which my own relationship is based. Must we always live in the same house, or even the same city? Should we vacation together or alone? How can we continue to nurture our separate friendships? In what ways shall we resist the rules for behaving as a couple?

I watch single women closely, eagerly. By choosing lives that flout the culture of partnership, they become outlaws, claiming marginal territory. They call to me from that edge, brash and bright and encouraging, egging me on in my own disobedient dance.

Pledging Commitment to Friends

WHAT Beverly Stein now refers to, laughingly, as a "mini midlife crisis" took her by surprise. She is not the type to scour her soul for meaning, to languish in armchairs, questioning her purpose. In her private life and her political career, a strong drive to improve the world urges Beverly forward in a clear and unwavering path.

So it was disconcerting, about four years ago, when she suddenly felt worried about her place in the cosmos. "As a single person without children, what was the meaning of my life? What was I connected to?" she remembers thinking.

Beverly thought about her beliefs, her community, a group of friends that webbed across the country and the people she'd known since childhood. And she thought of two friends—a man and a woman—in particular. Both were people who felt like anchors in her life; she'd just never spoken her feelings toward them out loud.

"The man I'd known about ten years, the woman for fifteen. They're people I had a deep connection to, who I thought really loved me. I told them, I am committed to you for the rest of my life.

"I was nervous about it—that maybe they'd think it was silly. But they were flattered. It was a recognition that it's important to have some special people in your life whom you are bound to. Forever."

Beverly thinks of that pledge when she arrives home drained after a week of political battles and can hardly bear the thought of a phone call. She calls anyway. These friends keep tabs on each other's travel plans, work schedules, medical crises.

"It was like asking someone to marry you," she said, laughing. "I wondered, would they think that was weird? It's not a traditional way of relating. But it seemed to be what I needed. It was my way of resolving my midlife crisis."

IF POLITICS—most recently, a stint as a state legislator and now as the county executive of a large metropolitan area—created the warp of Beverly's life, then friends were the weft, the strands that made the fabric beautiful and gave it strength. Framed photographs of friends and family crowded her mantelpiece—except just before an election, when precinct maps and boxes of campaign literature defined her living room's aesthetic.

As her career gained momentum, she found both less time and more need for long-lasting friendships. "As I get to be more of a public person, there's a group I can retreat to and be my real self. The thing I've realized in the last three years is the importance of long-term friends to me. You can't substitute for time."

Beverly jots down birthdays and important dates in a book, sends cards regularly and keeps a "social list" of people to call, whether for a quick check-in or a Friday night movie. Once a month, she picks out a friend and sends her or him a bouquet of flowers.

When Beverly and her friend Susie, pals since age two, turned forty, they spent three days together in Chicago, seeing plays and celebrating their thirty-eight-year friendship. She schedules a phone date every three months with a friend in Detroit. She often spends Christmas Eve with a longtime friend, a gay man whose lover recently died of AIDS.

"I choose to live my life in the way I want to live it, which may preclude a lot of men from being interested in me," Beverly said. The last time she lived with a man, about twenty years ago, he introduced her to the burgeoning women's movement. She made instant friends; he ended up feeling bereft. "He was quite a feminist and couldn't find anyone to relate to. It was 1970. There weren't that many feminist men.

"I've had significant relationships since then but haven't lived with anyone. I would like a long-term partner, but I think in these times it's hard for heterosexual women like me to find one. There still aren't that many feminist men—men who are confident enough in themselves to want to be with a strong woman.

"I do have a certain amount of internalized oppression about being single—occasionally I think there must be something wrong with me. But usually I'm happy with my life. It has a wonderful richness and it's full of a whole variety of interactions with people. I like having a great deal of autonomy in how I spend my time. And I know that there's no way I could do what I do in my work if I had to be responsible to someone else."

ON THE campaign trail, people didn't always understand. Beverly might knock on a door, chat about the neighborhood, discuss her ideas for community safety or housing, offer to leave a campaign brochure. Occasionally the "family" question would come up.

"People who don't know me will say, 'Do you have a family?' I know they mean, do I have a husband and children. I used to say, No, I'm not married. But recently I got sort of annoyed with that and said, I do have a family. I have a mother, a father, a brother.

"Then I have—I don't call it a family—but I have a network of friends and acquaintances and a number of very close people. There's a whole group of them, my network here, my tribe or something, and then there are a number around the country, women primarily, whom I have known for many years."

One gauge of those longtime friendships, Beverly said, is their ability to withstand change. One friend was married for five years, then divorced. She and Beverly spent a lot of time together. When the woman began to date again, "I felt jealous for a while, left out. She was so enmeshed with this guy. I felt that I was not going to get what I needed.

"I finally decided to invite both of them over for dinner. Ultimately, their relationship settled in, and we went back to spending time together. You have to make adjustments.

"That might be why the long-term nature is necessary for me to feel like it's a real friendship, because you have to go through a certain amount of ups and downs to see if the person's going to hang in there. You can't find that out within a short time."

In State College, Pennsylvania, where Beverly was raised, the community of ten thousand felt small; a walk downtown usually yielded familiar faces. The same group of kids traipsed together from first grade to senior prom. In her family, marriage and children were unspoken expectations—but so was having a career. And example spoke louder than words; her mother returned to college after Beverly and her brother were born, got her doctorate and became a scientist.

At first, Beverly's parents were worried that being single meant a state of loss. "They were concerned that I wasn't happy. Now they've seen in the last few years that I'm very content with my life. My mother, more than a lot of parents, understands the trade-offs of married life."

ON A clear October Saturday, two weeks before election morning, most people in Beverly's neighborhood were raking leaves, putting in tulip bulbs. In her neat yellow house, Beverly drew red slashes on a calendar to mark off the days until the vote. The phone jangled every twenty minutes. Boxes of campaign literature were stacked by the fireplace. In an hour, she would start canvassing, walking around the blocks that defined her political home. "I'm very conscious of where those boundaries are, that these are my people.

"I don't have much wanderlust. The nature of my work is such that you can't move it around very well, because it's based on the relationships you have. That's the whole basis of my politics."

When Beverly lived in collective households, a single woman in groups that included couples and other single adults, people would sometimes imply that it was a temporary phase she was going through. "Now that I am in my forties, it's very clearly my life."

The midlife crisis has not revisited, although there are moments of loneliness. As a single woman, she has no obvious vacation partner. Her holiday celebrations—where and how and with whom—shift from year to year.

"One of the down sides is this—it's tiring to constantly create it. If you have a regular family, you don't have to think it out. I figure to have the kind of contact I need in my life, I have to make sure I write a certain number of letters, call people up and arrange to do something on a Saturday night. I just have to work harder. It has to be a conscious thing.

"I do feel like I'm inventing it. There is no model. I have to piece together the amount of intimacy I need from a lot of places." She'd learned to do that, Beverly said, partly from watching her friend Guadalupe, a nun with a large and passionate circle of friends. One woman's act makes space for another's. And the room in which we all move grows a bit larger.

"When I'm fifty," she said, "I want to bring together the women who have been there across my life, get them all together and go to the coast for a few days. That would be like bringing together my 'women family.' I must know half a dozen close women friends who are basically in the same situation I am. I don't feel like I'm on my own."

An Artist's Devotion to Living Solo

IN SANDY Diamond's hands, even a routine envelope becomes frame-worthy. Her first note to me came elaborately calligraphed, with tiny purple diamonds separating each digit of my zip code. A few months later, I visited her in Oakland, California. An uneven path wound from the street to the door of a house that made me think of Tolkien's hobbits. Sandy took me into her studio, a long room with bulletin boards, a drafting table on one wall and finished pieces stacked in every spare space. Quotations climbed across wide matted sheets, flowering into collages of paper, calligraphy, and paint. On the coffee table was a high school graduation photo of Gabriel, the son Sandy raised as a single parent.

It was not the life she was groomed to lead. Sandy recalled an "idyllic" childhood in Ohio, filled with stories of her parents' courtship. Later, though, she had a sense of "not being at home, at home." What she wanted lay outside her family's romantic mythology.

"When I was twenty-one and in art school, I was very enamored of painting," Sandy said. "I was also enamored of the painter who lived upstairs. I had a crush on him, right, and I was still a virgin. One day he and my roommate were making love upstairs, and I could hear the bedsprings."

Romantic passion upstairs; artistic passion below. If a woman could not have both, Sandy thought, she would choose the canvas, the colors, a life of creative work. Sandy had seen the flip side of such a trade-off. Her father, who yearned to be an architect, quit school during the Depression to raise his family. Her mother was an aspiring concert pianist who chose marriage and children instead. Maybe, as she often said, her hands were too small for her to have been successful. But Sandy always felt that, without the obligations of a traditional family life, her mother would have kept playing.

In a semiautobiographical short story Sandy wrote, someone tells the main character toward the end, "Maybe you'll be the artist who stays an artist."

SANDY sat in the rocking chair. She wore soft, loose clothes, sipped tea. In the hallway next to the kitchen were a dozen framed photographs—Sandy as a child with her mother, father, and sister, Sandy in a white dress with hair to her waist, Sandy cradling Gabriel in her arms. Artwork—her own and others'—covered the remaining walls.

Sandy broke her back when she was twenty-eight. "When my back was so bad I couldn't move out of the bed, I just saw that physically I couldn't engage in lovemaking anymore. Now I'm stronger than that, but I like it the way it is. I don't miss it. The work has filled up all those places. There really is no time, and I would not be willing to make time."

She cannot remember exactly when she last had a lover. "December of 1978," she said. "No, it might have been '77. In 1980 I started teaching calligraphy; it was all so heady. It was actually helping my back, too. Then I started doing my first book. That was totally engrossing. Maybe one day I looked up or somebody said, Don't you miss men?

"Who?" I said. "Oh, yeah. I guess not.

"A friend said to me a long time ago, 'You must be who you want to be. Be your own...' He meant that if I wanted a sweetheart, I must be that sweetheart to myself."

It was the art Sandy kept coming back to—the discipline of learning calligraphy, practicing alphabets day after day after day, completely absorbed in the lines and curves of a capital B. The quotes that inspired her collages. The short story collection she was writing, the first in a planned quartet of books.

"I started taking notes for what I was going to call *The Book of Celibacy*. There's a Filipina poet, Cyn Zarco; I do a quote from her. She starts out talking about a guy, I think, and then she says, 'I can't decide which I love best—you lying next to me like an open book, or an open book lying next to me.' When I've shown that, people just crack up. Especially women."

Sandy lives on social security disability payments and the money she earns from selling her work at art shows. She takes few commissions, has won the freedom to create what pleases her own eyes. Still, she feels out of sync sometimes. Friends call and want to talk about their latest dates.

Sandy wants to discuss her current collage.

"With the art, you can't convey to people how it feels to get the perfect phrase, the perfect quote, some sublime image. To my family, when I show my artwork and make a great deal of money on a weekend at a crafts fair, they say, 'Well, Sandy's turned out all right, after all.'"

The romantic dream clings like a mist. When Sandy's sister, seven years younger than she, was married at the age of forty-seven, their relatives seemed to rekindle hopes that Sandy might wed someday, too. She shook her head.

"Let me see if I can say this without crying...okay. I was thirty-four when my mother died. My sister was twenty-seven. And years later our father told us that on her deathbed she said, 'My only wish is that I could have lived to see the girls married.'

"I was really unhappy when I heard that. Maybe for my sister. . .but for me, I thought my mother would know that the art was everything. The art, and Gabriel."

I COULD see that there was no room for a partner in Sandy's house. It was already crowded with books and plants and her son and the strong voices of women. Emily Dickinson. Audre Lorde. Nina Simone. Georgia O'Keeffe striding over New Mexico sands, filling her pockets with bones.

"The picture I have of my old age," Sandy said, her face deadpan, her eyes mischievous, "is that I would get more silver hair. That I would not fall down and not break my bones. I just want to be writing and painting and doing collages until the end."

A year and a half later, Sandy left Oakland and moved to a hundred-year-old farmhouse in a small town near the Oregon coast. She walks among acres of thirty-foot noble fir trees; deer dart across her path. A rooster's crow wakes her each morning.

Art propelled her to this place, and art maps her days. For years in the Bay Area, she had traded with friends who owned a printing business—her work in exchange for the costs of printing posters. In Grand Ronde, she recently gave two pieces of artwork to the neighbor who mowed her waist-high grass. The house's second floor, with its sloping walls and dormers she installed, became her studio. "I don't have anything on the walls yet," she said. "It's the feeling of starting over, where you don't put out all your knickknacks at once.

"It wasn't hard to leave my friends," Sandy said. "The fact is that I was longing to be alone with the Muse. I'm very aware of being in my mid-fifties, not knowing how much time is left. I think my friends and I have loved each other enough for a lifetime, but there's so much more work to be done.

"I'm definitely not lonely. I relish solitude. Some days I don't even turn on the radio. Nothing but the sounds of the birds and the geese, the rooster in the morning, whatever noise ideas make."

Sandy is still working on her short story collection, and on a poetry manuscript. One recent project was a poster for the summer pow wow of the Grand Ronde Indians. Under an abstract painting of a ragged circle, resembling a chambered nautilus shell, she lettered a quote from Black Elk: "The power of the earth always works in circles, and everything tries to be round."

"For me," Sandy said, "there is zero separation between me, Sandy, and my work. If someone comes to visit me and doesn't look at the pictures on the wall, I think, Why are they here? They can't possibly want to know me.

"When you look at Georgia O'Keeffe, she and the person in her paintings are really one. Or Emily Dickinson—although she was portrayed so much as hanging her hopes on men who had no understanding of her genius—she really was content to be alone in her room doing her thing. Can you imagine her being a wife to some asshole? It's impossible.

"When I broke my back," Sandy said, "and was in the hospital, friends brought me my phonograph and my records of Nina Simone singing, 'My Baby Just Cares for Me.' That really spoke to me. Maybe it was like comfort. It seemed like 'my baby' wasn't a guy; my baby was myself. My own invention. My creation."

Two Women Creating a Home Base

THALIA Zepatos was feeling rootless. For several years she had been alternating periods of frenzied political work with spells of extended travel, including an eighteen-month trip around the world. As soon as the next election was over, she planned to leave town again—this time, for Mexico.

Elizabeth Kaufman divided her time between public school teaching and politics. The two met while Thalia was running the campaign of a state legislator; their personalities and politics "really clicked," Thalia remembers. Both were gregarious and busy single women, committed to political and social activism.

Thalia longed for a stable base but shied away from the commitment home ownership would entail. Liz wanted to own a house but felt daunted by the prospect of buying one alone. One day, shortly before Thalia left for Mexico, Liz suggested the two look for a house they could buy together.

While Thalia was gone, both women had plenty of time to think about the idea; they wrote long letters detailing their concerns and hopes. Thalia worried that homeowning would limit her wanderlust; would she have to spend money on furnace repairs instead of airline tickets? Liz was anxious about mechanical problems that might spring up; if pipes burst in a house of her own, she couldn't simply call the landlord. Both women, whose resumes included stints working for progressive politicians and groups such as NARAL, worried about financing a home and its maintenance. But other thoughts pushed them toward the idea of co-ownership.

"Neither of us had the money to buy a house alone," Thalia recalled. "We also wanted another person for support to go through the process of buying and owning a house. And, as single, straight women, we both felt strongly that we didn't want to wait to be in a relationship to do it. We thought, We can go ahead and have a home and make a life."

When Thalia returned from her trip, the two began hashing out details. They talked about what it would mean if one of them made significantly more money than the other; about the prospect that one, or both, might become seriously involved with a man. They discussed their work, social lives, and ambitions to travel—and the ways a house could be a stable springboard for all of those pursuits.

Thalia pictured her ideal home—a four-bedroom bungalow with a roomy front porch, plenty of light and an eat-in kitchen. Instead, they found a narrow Victorian with three dimly lit bedrooms and a skinny stoop. But the house made sense financially. She and Liz walked through the empty rooms and made an offer that same evening.

AT FIRST, Thalia and Liz set time aside regularly to discuss the logistics of living together. They opened a joint checking account for mortgage payments, taxes, groceries, and house repairs. They agreed to take turns shopping and to share food. Since Liz had more savings, she paid for workers to install skylights upstairs; Thalia, whose time was more flexible, spent hours painting the walls and wooden moldings.

"Both our families thought it was slightly odd to buy a house with a friend. They thought, You're supposed to be looking for a husband," Thalia said. Their relatives were also hurt, and a bit startled, when the women decided each would have the right of survivorship. She and Liz felt strongly that if one of them died, relatives should not have the right to sell the house and disrupt the other's life.

Quickly, they learned each other's quirks—and their strengths. Liz was tentative about her mechanical abilities while Thalia would enthusiastically grab a wrench and plunge ahead. With a thick book on do-it-yourself home repairs as their guide, they walked through the intricacies of plumbing, wiring, and wallpapering. On Liz's first birthday in the new house, Thalia gave her an electric drill.

After more than three years, many of their agreements have become intuitive. Thalia hates to vacuum, but Liz doesn't mind it. Liz abhors scrubbing the bathtub, so that is Thalia's task. They take turns shopping, entertain each other's friends, and love to throw big parties with music and dancing.

The house's aesthetic reflects a love of books and music, warm colors, and whimsical touches. They gave a friend carte blanche to paint the downstairs bathroom, whose walls are now decorated with cacti and bright geometric borders. In the living room sits a purple couch, a glass-topped wicker coffee table, and curtains that Liz sewed with bargain mill-end fabric.

"Having been married, I know it usually means you, as the woman, care more about the maintenance of the house," Thalia said. "I think we both feel equally responsible to one another." That shared accountability means both women go shopping for new couch pillows, or that when one is swamped with work, the other makes a pot of soup big enough to last for a week's worth of lunches.

By now, the bond between them is knit of practical and emotional strands. The women's close friends and relatives embrace both as members of their families. When Liz's parents call, they always ask about Thalia. When Thalia's parents visit from New York, they take both women out to dinner.

"Originally we decided we'd make a three-year commitment to living together," Thalia said. "Through that time, we've really grown in our relationship. We're always there for one another. We take care of each other if we're sick, rescue each other if we've lost our car keys.

"We weren't each other's closest friends at the time we bought the house," Thalia said. "I wanted to have a little separateness. But we've gotten to know and care for each other and protect each other. If one of us is working really hard, the other might say, Are you eating all right? Or, Here, I bought these vitamins. We've grown to share a lot of ourselves."

At the same time, they feel free from the gender-based expectations that often arise when women and men live together. "We're both very busy people," Thalia said. "When I worked on a ballot measure campaign, Liz was running the campaign for the state Democratic caucus. Neither one of us had someone at home grumbling at us for never being there or not doing our share of housework.

"We've talked about men, about what would happen if one of us got involved in a serious relationship. But I think the reality of having a very good living situation has upped the ante—it would have to be a really special person and a spectacular situation to make us leave one another.

"I think there's still an assumption on my parents' part that if I fell in love with a man, I'd immediately move out. That's a big question in my mind. I have a very happy home life."

Since Thalia and Liz bought the house, both of their lives have shifted. They have changed jobs, fallen in love, ended relationships. When Thalia was working on a book, she sublet her half of the house and spent quiet months at the coast and at a women writers' retreat. Liz traveled to Europe by herself. Sometimes, one of them talks about taking an extended trip or leaving town for a job in another city. When the topic comes up, they imagine ways the house can remain a steady refuge as both women pursue their ambitions and dreams.

"Liz has said, 'Let's never sell the house. Even if one of us gets into a long-term relationship with a man or gets married. Let's always keep it so we have this little haven.'"

Recently, the rhythm of their days changed again. A manic election season ended and both women began to spend more time at home. Thalia shifted her focus from politics to writing. "Since I've been writing full time, I've felt the house is too small. We each have a bedroom, and we have a shared study. I'm a late-night person, and Liz is a morning person. I feel inhibited, in the room next to her bedroom, clunking around on the computer late at night."

Very recently, the two began to talk about a possible solution—selling their home and buying another, larger one, together. "It's a testament to how great it's been," Thalia said. "We realize that our arrangement may be outgrowing this house."

Single and Single-Minded

EVELYN C. White is rarely more herself than when she is standing in the darkened main lodge at The Flight of the Mind writers' workshop on the McKenzie River in central Oregon. Her audience, seventy women seated in semicircles of chairs, fidget nervously and glance around the room. They are away from home, among strangers, wondering whether they belong.

Evelyn, who has taught at the workshop for seven years, stands by the cavernous stone fireplace, feet apart, her voice like a gulp of strong coffee. "There are straight women here; there are lesbians here; there are old women here; there are young women here; there are Jewish women here; there are African American women here; there are Latina and white and Asian women here." The workshop is an opportunity, she instructs— a chance to delve beneath fears and stereotypes about difference, to learn about the strangers around you, embrace the strangeness in yourself.

Not long ago, Evelyn gave herself the same provocative pep talk. She'd taken a year's leave from her job as a *San Francisco Chronicle* reporter to attend the Kennedy School of Government at Harvard University. When the year in Cambridge ended, she knew she wanted more of that life, its uncluttered pace, its autonomy. Her girlfriend, as well as her employer, were both waiting for her in San Francisco.

Evelyn realized she didn't want to answer to either of them.

A year later, back in San Francisco (the *Chronicle* extended her leave for another year) and on friendly terms with her former girlfriend, Evelyn described herself as "single and very, very single-minded."

For years, she tried conforming to society's two-by-two standard. By the time she was twenty, she'd turned down two proposals of marriage; by thirty, she'd left a string of disappointed ex-lovers. At the same time, her writing career flourished. In 1985 she published *Chain, Chain, Change*:

For Black Women Dealing with Physical and Emotional Abuse and in 1990, edited *The Black Women's Health Book: Speaking for Ourselves.*

"I'm not selfish, but I am very much self-referenced," she said. "It's what has helped me be successful as a writer. I have a hard time making the real sacrifices you have to make when you're in a partnership. If I'm working on an essay, and it's really happening, and my lover wants to go to the movies, I'm not going. No way.

"For a long time, I tried to conform. Then one day I woke up and said, Evelyn, you don't conform to anything else society wants you to do. I realized that just like pressing my hair isn't me and wearing dreadlocks *is,* being single is most me."

When Evelyn works—often spending days at the *Chronicle* and evenings or weekends at home on other projects—the writing claims her complete attention. During her relationship with another woman, they might agree on a Saturday schedule: Evelyn would write from 9 A.M. to 7 P.M., then at 7:30 the two would go out to dinner and to the movies.

"But at seven, I wouldn't be psychically removed from the work. It created this huge conflict. I would become mute," Evelyn said. "My priorities are such that I would rather spend two hours in my study fiddling with the structure of a sentence than two minutes with my girlfriend deciding where to have dinner."

Evelyn hates to plan. She hates to cook. Once a year, she and a friend take their dentist out to dinner—and that is the extent of her ritualized celebrating. She plans holidays as they come. Instead, her life is a series of spontaneous, sometimes intuitive, connections. When she misses a friend, she writes a letter. When she gets complimentary tickets to a play or concert, she invites the person she imagines will most relish the performance.

"This is what I think about: Who is the person who will really understand what I need to express about black women and body image? Who would like to go to the Napa Valley and have a mud bath? Who is the person who can teach me how to ski?

"I'm much more purposeful now and usually feel much better about my interactions with people. The people who are in my life are there because I have a great desire to see them. I'll think, Who do I need to connect with?

"This morning I was feeling a great need to talk to a friend in Cambridge. I started writing her a letter. Then I realized it wasn't to her, but a warm-up exercise for writing about the mental health of black women.

"I do pay a price. I am alone. I have to actively create support. Sometimes it's a drag. But it's a price I'm willing to pay. It's worth it to me."

Being single, for Evelyn, does not always mean being completely self-sufficient. In fact, it forces her to do the opposite—to examine her own limits and enlist caretaking from others.

While working on *Chain, Chain, Change*, she devoted hours to writing at the expense of her health. During long stretches at the word processor, she'd enter what felt like a trance, then snap back to awareness only from the gnawing, spacey feeling in her stomach and head.

"I knew that doing *The Black Women's Health Book* would be taxing for me emotionally. I went to my doctor and said, How can I prepare myself to have a really healthy relationship with this writing project?

"This black woman looked me dead in the eye and said, 'Evelyn, I know your body, as your physician. I have some idea of what you earn. Why don't you hire a cook?' I was stunned. The fact that a black woman would say that to another black woman was absolutely startling. It had never crossed my mind that I could do such a thing.

"So I was very careful where I mentioned it. I didn't want it to look like I was some privileged yuppie who was too lazy to cook my own meals. I knew it wasn't a question of privilege—it had to do with me not being very good at cooking."

One day at the *Chronicle* she saw a bulletin-board announcement from a colleague who was trying to help her housekeeper get more work. The reporter gave Evelyn the number for Gladys Griffin, a retired health worker in her mid-sixties. Soon the two developed a plan: Gladys would come on Mondays and make enough food to last Evelyn for the rest of the week.

"She had a key. I'd get home about 6:30. When I walked from the BART station to Alcatraz Street, I'd start searching for Gladys's navy blue truck. As I opened my door, I'd smell the aromas—macaroni and cheese, greens, these wonderful smells. There would be Gladys. She'd have on an apron; she'd have done all the dishes from her cooking. I'd walk into the kitchen and stare and smell.

"This black woman would stand at my side and look at me with pride and accomplishment and, I think, great love. I'd change my clothes, get a plate, take what I wanted, sit in the dining room and chat with Gladys. It was clear that part of the ritual was for her to be there when I first ate her food and see what my reaction was.

"It wasn't high cuisine, but it was very nutritious and soothing, very much what I needed. Baked or fried chicken, green salads, ham, tuna casserole, macaroni and cheese, rutabagas, red beans and rice, fish, cole slaw, carrot and raisin salad. She made an excellent carrot and raisin salad."

For almost a year, Gladys cooked and Evelyn wrote. They became a team, Evelyn says—each devoted to her portion of the task, aware that both kinds of labor were crucial to the outcome of this book.

"From the time Gladys started helping me, I never had to go to a store unless I wanted something special. It gave me this huge block of psychic and practical time. Also a great sense of comfort.

"I knew I had help. I knew someone else cared about this project. I didn't see my editors for three years, and some of the book's contributors I never even met. It was very helpful to have someone around who I could talk to on a regular basis."

The book was published. Evelyn stayed healthy. "Too often, creative women will just wish for things—you know how people say, I wish I had a wife. I realized I needed assistance and I got it. The experience with Gladys helped me learn that there *are* people who will help. We all have our different roles to play."

WHEN we talked, Evelyn was living with a married couple, an arrangement she described as "the optimum situation." Sometimes the three have meals together; other times, Evelyn eats alone. If her roommates go to the movies, they often ask her to come along. Usually she declines.

"There's no set expectation," she said. "I usually work on the weekends. Daniel rides his bike in the morning and comes back with a bag of bagels. He might knock on my door: 'Ev, do you want a bagel?' If I do, I'll have one with them.

"Last night, I went out to dinner with Daniel and a friend of his from Greece who spent the night here. I was going to work all evening, but about midafternoon, I realized what I needed was to go out. I do very little advance planning, and I try not to get anxious about it.

"I like companionship. The line got blurry for me with the extra expectations that come when you are intimate with someone. I think I will always be a person who has roommates. I am not a solitary, lonely person."

Evelyn's friends say they support her choice; she suspects that, deep down, some don't quite believe it. "They think, You have a fear of intimacy. What can I do about that? Nothing. I think being single threatens a lot of people, triggers desires they have within themselves.

"I get great joy out of saying I'm bringing *nobody* to a concert or party," she says. "Recently someone gave me a theater ticket and asked if I needed one or two. I said, It's just me, myself, Evelyn. I didn't feel pathetic or pitiful.

"We've gotten very directed in this culture to believe that only people can nurture us. I've worked hard to look at my needs. Sometimes I need to be with a river, with a dog, with the cereal aisle at Safeway. Oftentimes I need to be with music. Without a partner, I can see in a much broader way. My choices are infinitely expanded in terms of who I include in my life, who I extend myself to."

Who is your family, I asked, and Evelyn's voice rushed over the phone, an unhesitating current. "The universe," she said. "I believe the trees and the sky and the eggnog and the bookcase…I believe the earth is my family.

"Nature is filled with difference, and it all seems to work pretty well. We need to pay more attention to that as human beings. It doesn't mean I think there's no value or need for coupledom. But very little in our culture gives us the support to be different from that."

A world flourishing with difference: feminists, single or coupled, share that vision. They aim, like Evelyn, to rewrite the rigid scripts of female life and substitute a more fluid reality, to demonstrate that a single woman can be utterly complete and a partnered woman can retain her whole self.

I imagine Evelyn once again at the front of the lodge at The Flight of the Mind, giving the annual diversity message, meeting each woman in the audience with her singular gaze. Or sitting on the deck with a notebook on her lap, listening to the rush of the McKenzie River.

"I think my responsibility as a member of the earth's family," she told me, "is to be the most authentic Evelyn C. White I can be."

Renegades and Exiles
from the Wedding March

THIS is a story about commitment and ritual and dining room tables. Not necessarily in that order. In fact, it was the dining room table that got me thinking about commitment and ritual in the first place. It was the dining room table that made everything concrete.

A few years ago, on the eve of the summer solstice, Rachael and John decided to get married. As their housemate, I was granted the equivalent of front-row seats to the events that unfolded next. Here are some of the things that happened: Rachael's parents sent flowers. John's parents dusted off the diamond ring, a family heirloom. For a week or so, there were lots of phone calls to and from various relatives and a fair amount of shameless grinning all around.

In those first giddy days I found myself swept along on the tide of delight. I listened, and even shuddered with pleasure once or twice, as Rachael told the good news to her parents, her sister, both sets of grandparents, as John phoned his family. The whole thing seemed like such a desirable, such a necessary rite of passage, this ritual of separation and joining—children from their parents, members of the next generation to each other.

At times, I almost felt as though I were witness to a miracle—or at least, to a rich and ancient marvel. Two individuals' lives cross, quite arbitrarily, and they fall in love. From that unlikely collision, a community develops—of mutual friends and colleagues, grandparents and nephews and sisters-in-law. A ring handed down from the past. A promise cast like a net into the future. A whole happier than the sum of its parts.

The tradition unfolding in my house struck a chord of reverence in me. It just seemed so—well, so *right*.

Until the dining room table came along. A couple of weeks after Rachael and John got engaged, Rachael's mother came to visit from Ohio. The three of them spent several afternoons shopping for a table and finally, after much discussion, selected one. Before it arrived, they described it to me: beautiful and durable, made of oak, with a claw-footed pedestal and a leaf that turned it from a circle to an oval.

The idea of that table made me feel so ornery and sad, I wondered if I might just be jealous. Was I envious of the attention garnered by the soon-to-be-married? Did I wish my parents would buy *me* a solid piece of real furniture?

Perhaps. But there's more to this story than a sting of envy over someone else's durable goods. That table symbolized something—the willingness of one generation to honor the promises of another, the generous embrace that greets news of an engagement, a commitment. Two people decide they want to be together, for better, for worse, and everyone gets pretty excited about it. Excited enough to bank on that pledge, to want it to last, to buy furniture that will last with it.

The catch is, only some partnerships receive that kind of support.

Once, shortly after Elissa and I became lovers, we attended a holiday party for my freelance writers' group. A mutual friend, hearing for the first time that we were a couple, blurted "*Mazel tov!*" loudly enough to draw glances from the half-dozen people seated around us. Another time, as we walked arm-in-arm from a movie theater in downtown Portland, a young man wheeled toward us on a bicycle. As he swept past, he lifted one hand from the handlebars, grinned, and gave us a thumbs-up sign.

Those are rare moments. More often, it is like this: I attend the New Year's Eve party at Elissa's workplace as her "good friend" and spend the evening in diligent conversation with the nursing home residents, avoiding the glance of her supervisor, counting the minutes until we can leave.

Or this: we take a walk on a mild late-summer evening, holding hands. Half a block from the house, we walk by a teenaged couple, also hand-in-hand. Instead of exchanging nods of recognition, we get menacing glances. "Dyke," the man sneers once they've passed us. "That's right," Elissa calls over her shoulder, but we drop hands and dig them into our pockets.

You can say all the cynical things you want about marriage. You can talk about the sexist history and the staggering rate of divorce. You can say it's just a crazy promise on a sheet of paper. Truth is, there are couples who'd like to celebrate themselves, who want to make crazy promises to each other, in public, in front of their friends and tearful relatives. And they can't. What ought to be a ritual—affirming and enriching for everyone—is actually a privilege, accessible only to some.

Our story—the complete and multifarious human story—is really about love and separation, commitment and ritual, promises and trust. But it's also about who gets the dining room table and who gets snubbed by the grandparents, who wins custody of the children and who is left out of the family album. To leave anyone out impoverishes us all.

EXACTLY one year after they became engaged, Rachael and John were married. I stood under the white satin *chuppah* along with both sets of parents, John's sisters, Rachael's sister and brother.

You see, I go to weddings. I wear dresses and low-heeled pumps dyed to match. I carry small bouquets of tea roses and lilies. I sign my name as witness to the Hebrew contract between bride and groom. I raise my glass to toast their future happiness. I am genuinely happy for them. In complicated, alternating fevers, I am also angry, regretful, defiant, and envious.

And there are limits to my participation. I won't stand in a cluster of "single" women, arms outstretched to catch the bride's bouquet. I will not lie if asked when it will be my turn at the altar. Instead, I swing-dance with Elissa and introduce her as my partner. I want my presence to serve as a quiet reminder, like the glass broken at a Jewish wedding, that there is discord even in the midst of joy, exclusion on a day that celebrates connectedness.

In the end, I know, you can't legislate human attachment. You can't determine by law who will fall in love with whom, who will want to conceive and raise children, who will feel inclined to call each other family. But you can—and governments do, all the time—grant or deny public sanction to those human connections. You can build legal fences that mark some families as more worthy than others.

As feminists, whether heterosexual or lesbian, partnered or single, we live in the shadow of marriage as if in a land with an official religion. We are baptized into it the instant we are born female, and we learn its commandments as children, the first time we "play wedding" or serve as flower girls in a real ceremony, treading the aisle we are expected someday to walk.

A dozen times a week, I find myself eye to eye with the belief that marriage is the defining event in a woman's life. Every official form requires a check-off—single, married, divorced, widowed. Are these my only choices? Telephone solicitors call with a hopeful, "Mrs. Hochman?" The friends of engaged couples enlist my help with quilt projects and shower plans. My grandmother announces that she is waiting for some "good news" from me.

"Are you married?" someone inquires, and I consider the proper response:

"No. I'm a lesbian."

"Yes. I'm a lesbian, and I have a life partner."

"Well—not legally."

One year, Elissa and I spent my birthday evening in a hospital emergency room; she'd sliced her index finger on a chef's knife while cutting white chocolate for a mousse. "Next of kin?" the receptionist asked, typing as she talked. Elissa glanced at me, gave my name. "Relationship?" the woman inquired.

"Partner," Elissa said. It was a Catholic hospital, a quiet Thursday night. The receptionist left a blank space on the form.

Marriage patterns my emotional life, as well. When one longtime friend became engaged, my mother asked me how I felt. Suddenly, I forgot everything I knew about marriage—its roots as a property settlement, its questionable meaning at a time when the divorce rate is one out of two. I was nine years old again, left out of a game whose rules I didn't comprehend, unable to invent a new one.

"I'm sad," I said.

"Me, too," my mother agreed, her voice wistful and, I think, relieved, as if my admission had opened the gate to her own. "It's hard for me and Daddy. Very hard."

Later, off the phone, I was angry the way women in my family have always gotten angry—silently, with a slow burn. I was furious at the power of a wedding to define a woman's value, and at my own willingness to bear shame for not measuring up.

How had marriage become such a potent institution? I'd thought it was simple: a man and a woman agreed to "love, honor, and cherish," signed their names on a marriage license, and went on about their lives. But the more I read about the origins and legal history of marriage, the more outraged I became. Flowery customs smothered an important fact: religious bodies, then governments, had created marriage to advance and enforce a male-defined view of the world.

The blatant sexism at the root of marriage laws shocked me. Under the English Common Law that we inherited in the United States, a married couple effectively became one person—the man. "The very being or legal existence of the woman is suspended during the marriage," the law declared, "or at least is incorporated and consolidated into that of her husband." A married woman could not sign a contract, own property, inherit from her own biological family, or testify in court.

That sexism outraged nineteenth-century feminists, too. They worked, in public and private, to challenge marriage laws' enforcement of male dominance. Elizabeth Cady refused to let the preacher say "obey" when she married Henry Brewster Stanton in 1840. Lucy Stone kept her name and her convictions when she wed Henry B. Blackwell in 1855. The two wrote that their act "implies no sanction of...the present laws of marriage as refuse to recognize the wife as an independent, rational being." By the turn of the century, marriage reformers had achieved some important changes; for instance, married women could own their own wages and inherit.

This century's second wave of feminism picked up where earlier activists had left off. In "Marriage," a pamphlet widely circulated in the 1970s, Sheila Cronan argued that marriage duped women into a legal agreement whose terms were never made clear. A wife was obliged to give domestic and sexual services; her husband's greater economic and physical power typically ensured she would live up to the bargain. A husband, on the other hand, was supposed to provide for his wife, a requirement enforced only when a marriage ended. "Marriage is the model for all other forms of discrimination against women," Cronan wrote.

By the 1990s, a new wave of marriage law reform had swept out the grossest inequities, but many subtler aspects remain. In many states, a married man can insist that his children bear his, not his wife's, last name. In most states, under many circumstances, it is legal for a husband to rape his wife. Judges, priests and rabbis continue to declare newlywed couples "man and wife."

As an institution, marriage powerfully influences every facet of family life—who may legally parent a child, who may live in rent-controlled housing after the lessee dies, who may take bereavement leave. It determines who qualifies as "family" for health-club packages, zoo memberships, and train fares, how many unrelated adults can occupy a home, under what circumstances an assault is considered "domestic violence" and who can engage in oral sex behind closed bedroom doors. It regulates who can receive Social Security benefits, collect foster-care payments, claim a corpse.

Eventually, such laws can strike a woman in the teeth. I mean this literally. I have a mouth that looks like a dental student's final exam—impacted wisdom teeth, spongy gums, weak enamel, all aglitter with fillings, front teeth drifting toward entropy even after three years of adolescent braces. If Elissa and I were a married heterosexual couple, the dental insurance she receives at work would cover me, too. It would cost us money, of course, but far less than I pay, four or more times a year, for thorough cleanings, pokes in the gums with a steel probe, and solemn admonishments to floss.

Marriage is far more complex than I'd realized. It is a religious rite of passage, a set of social customs, a romantic trope. It is also a deliberately sexist legal framework that, like it or not, helps pattern every woman's private life.

SINGLE. Married. Divorced. Widowed. Other. I look around me for feminist strategies, ways to challenge and cope. Should we become rebels, refusing to marry or even to attend weddings? Or reformers, bent on rewriting marriage laws? Do we say the state has no business in our bedrooms, and hold nonlegal ceremonies to mark our intimate relationships? Or will we be *conversos*, pretending outwardly to keep the faith, asserting our discomfort with marriage only in private?

Journalist Lindsy Van Gelder explained her decision to stop going to weddings this way: "I've come, in these last six years with Pamela, to see heterosexual marriage as very much a restricted club," she wrote. "It seems apparent to me that few friends of Pamela's and mine would even join a club that excluded blacks, Jews or women, much less assume that they could expect their black, Jewish or female friends to toast their new status with champagne."

Some heterosexual women agree, eschewing marriage and choosing instead to remain unpartnered or create intimate relationships according to their own rules. They use living-together agreements, legal guardianship, powers of attorney and various other contracts to define their relationship to their partners, their property and their children.

Lesbian and gay couples, as well as some heterosexuals, have begun to celebrate their "lawless" relationships with eclectic and creative rituals. The names for these ceremonies—"webbing," "hand-fasting," "commitment ritual"—challenge even the vocabulary of marriage, its governance of our speech.

Others, continuing the work of earlier feminists, are trying to remake marriage laws. The most vocal proponents of reform today come from the gay and lesbian community, where some argue for the ultimate change: striking the heterosexual bias. After all, the institution of marriage rests on its ability to exclude; if anyone were allowed under the legal awning, surely it would yield to a roomier, more relevant shape.

Others push for domestic partnership provisions, which confer benefits such as health insurance on unmarried couples—both heterosexual and gay—who live in committed relationships and agree to register their relationships with local government agencies.

But not all lesbians and gay men agree on the crusade for same-sex marriage—or even on the notion of formalizing commitments with public rituals. Fiction writer Sarah Schulman raised a provocative argument in a published interview. "There's this push for domestic partnership laws, for gay marriage," Schulman said. "But if the gay community was divided up into privatized marriage family units, and wasn't a community, the response to AIDS would never have been what it has been."

I have a hard time imagining that civil marriage would dissolve our community's broader bonds. Still, Schulman's words haunted me. If gays and lesbians could marry, would an expansive sense of kinship to "my people" be replaced by a narrow focus on "my partner"? Would we alter the pattern, I wonder, or would the pattern shape us?

EVENTUALLY, John and Rachael's oak table arrived; it sat grandly in the middle of the dining room. We gathered around it for all of our birthdays, Valentine breakfasts, winter solstice feasts. I liked using it—cooking all day, gathering extra chairs, inviting some folks and serving up some celebration. I believed there was enough to go around.

At the same time, I watched Rachael and John work to maintain their new table—wipe with lemon oil every two weeks, sponge up any spills, worry about scratches, struggle it through the door when we moved. I felt relieved, sometimes, that this furniture's weighty responsibilities did not belong to me.

When Elissa and I take our turn hosting dinners, we often eat on the floor. A ring of candlelight, a swatch of bright tablecloth, a circle of familiar faces define our floating dining area. Perhaps it is Passover, or New Year's Eve, or the anniversary of our relationship. We pour wine, raise glasses, and toast to our improvised lives.

Celebrating a "Webbing" Ritual

JAN Corwin had no intention of getting married. Not even if they called it something else, like "commitment ceremony" or "ritual celebration."

It wasn't that she had doubts about her relationship with Linden Burk. The two had slipped easily into the routines of making a home together and raising Jan's son, Kerry, in a shared custody arrangement with Jan's former partner. Their house, on land that rises like a shelf over the Columbia Gorge, showed all the signs of nesting: pictures carefully placed, firewood stacked outside, coffeecake sliced on a plate.

I visited them on an October night so thin and clear the air felt astringent. Jan—dark haired, with an elfin face—knit while we talked. Linden—rangier, wearing green sweatpants, the one in the couple who more often craves privacy—sprawled at the other end of the couch, her bare feet in Jan's lap.

"When Linden first suggested a ceremony, I thought, I don't want to do that in front of all those people. Whose business is it, anyway? How I feel is so private," Jan recalled. "It was the fear of being invalidated, having what was so serious to me not be taken seriously."

Jan had always thought of herself as a "family person." She, her mother, and sister sound indistinguishable on the phone. She talks with her parents, who live in New York, once or twice a week.

The Burks, in contrast, were a study in separateness. Once, Linden's sister went to Eastern Europe for six weeks, and Linden's mother was the only family member who knew about the trip. By the time Linden came out to her mother, at nineteen, the reaction was more blasé than shocked. "Everyone in the family knows," her mother said. "Even Grandma. We've known since you were six." Creating a family with Jan and Kerry vied with Linden's natural hunger for separate time and space. And it was that daily, sweet tug-of-war she wanted to mark with a ceremony.

"I felt we needed to honor that it was a really wonderful thing we have. It felt important to stand up proudly and name it and not shrink from it."

It took Jan a few years to agree. "Not because of how I felt about Linden at all," she said. "Because, in a way, that commitment was made years ago. But to stand up in front of whomever—especially my parents—and say what was important to me was terrifying.

"Which is kind of why I did it. I felt I was standing over a precipice, and I knew I would never get to the other side unless I did it. I just couldn't keep being afraid."

ON AN evening in late August, a nervous, excited group gathered around a formally set dinner table in the home of one of Jan's and Linden's friends. Jan's parents and Linden's mother were there, along with both women's sisters and their partners, plus each woman's best friend, Jan's ex-lover, Kip, and Kerry, the son Jan and Kip were raising together.

Linden welcomed everyone. "Thank you for sharing, for being here, a courageous act for all of us," she said. "We spin forth from our first center, the family, in which all acts are first tried, to create new centers in ourselves and with others. This represents a separation and a coming-together.

"Jan and I want to acknowledge the strength and gratitude we feel at your presence here with us, to light a light for each of you as each of you has lit a light for us." Then they turned to each guest, reading a short statement and lighting a candle by his or her plate. By the time they were finished, nearly everyone was in tears.

It had been a difficult week. Linden's mother and one of her sisters weren't speaking to each other. Jan's father was tense and controlled; her mother couldn't bring herself to tell the hosts of their bed-and-breakfast why she was visiting Portland. By Saturday morning, Jan recalled, "We were wondering, Who the hell are these people? What do they want with our life?"

A small clothbound book holds the words they spoke that night, along with their vows, a written outline of their ceremony, and journal entries from each on the "webbing-moon" vacation they took afterwards. Reading them again makes Linden's voice crack, her eyes fill up.

"For me, part of the reason to do it was that it wasn't just about me and Jan," Linden said. "It was about our ability to swim in a sea. We live in a circle of people and we all affect each other. I wanted to be able to share what I was feeling and what I needed to do, so it wasn't something that I could make or break. It was something the community could sustain and understand and believe in."

THAT night, Linden and Jan slept restlessly in a bed they'd dragged outdoors. Every time Jan heard moisture drip from the leaves, she envisioned eighty drenched guests crammed into their tiny house. But by morning, the day was dry.

In a clearing in the woods above their property, Jan and Linden held a private ritual. For months, each had been collecting small stones, shells, and other objects. One by one, they talked about the meaning of the items and bound each to an alder branch with yarn.

Then their guests paraded up the hill. Children—including seven-year-old Kerry—led the way, blowing whistles and ringing chimes. Everyone walked through a curved-branch archway while Jan's sister and her lover waved a bundle of burning sage over each person as a purifying smudge. Then Jan looked out at the group, took a deep breath, and spoke.

"I talked about living in a patriarchal society and how hard it was for us to take ourselves seriously. It was very difficult to say this, especially in front of my father. It was very frightening. It was taking up so much space, saying, This is who I am, and it matters."

Linden talked about their vows, words they'd struggled for months to write. Each had scribbled in her own journal, then they compared notes. The statements they finally wrote were "not vows of ownership, demands and rights," Linden told the group, "but rather vows of determination to create together what we don't yet know."

They promised to "see change as our survival, knowing that nothing can stay the same." They vowed to seek help and support from their community. They pledged to honor each other's differences. They invited Kerry up, presented him with a "magic bag" of stones and treasures, and said they loved him.

One by one, guests came forward and offered wishes and blessings into a hammered pewter chalice full of water. Jan and Linden drank a sip each time, and spilled a drop or two on the ground. "Keep fighting," advised one friend. "Magic is everywhere," said another. Linden's mother told them how important it was to grasp love wherever it was found.

"My mother had written this thing welcoming Linden into the family. It was very wonderful," Jan recalled. "My dad came up and said, 'Well, I must say, this is most unusual.' He kissed us both and walked away."

They danced. They cut the cake, a three-layer concoction with spiderwebs painted on in liquid chocolate. Then Jan and Linden hopped into Linden's truck, the one with bumper stickers reading, "My Other Car Is A Broom" and "Live Simply So Others May Simply Live," and drove to an elegant downtown hotel.

At first the valet thought they were making a delivery. Then Jan opened the door, and her hand-painted silk dress wafted out onto the sidewalk. The valet parked the truck. Upstairs, they phoned room service and ate the first real meal they'd had all day.

BECOMING "webbed" was not easy to explain; often Jan didn't even try. When patients in her chiropractic practice mentioned a wedding they'd attended, she was tempted to talk about her own ceremony. But she didn't want to endure one more puzzled look or explain her intentions one more time.

"I couldn't just say to straight people, Oh, I'm getting married this summer. We had another name for it. It was this whole other experience," she remembered.

"We didn't call it anything for a long time," Linden said. "One day we just struck upon the name 'webbing.' The concept of the web was lines, each one very individual and very distinct, but they cross and connect and weave and create a greater whole. What happens when people begin to have common ritual? You do have a web that starts to be created."

Since the ceremony, both women said, their families have embraced the couple more warmly than before. Kerry seems more secure and has told Linden she is the only person who can drive him as crazy as his mother can. When Linden's younger sister visited them at Thanksgiving, she said, "Oh, how much fun to eat with a family I didn't even know I had."

In the album from their webbing day, there is a picture of Jan dancing with her father, a dapper man in gold-rimmed glasses and neat white hair. She remembered their conversation. "There sure is a lot of hate around here," her father had said.

"What are you talking about?" Jan asked.

"Against men. All that talk about the patriarchy."

In the videotape, Jan said, she could see her face becoming more and more tight. "But afterwards, when my father knew he'd never have to do it again, he said, 'Well, it was the most beautiful ceremony I ever was at. No, maybe not the most beautiful, but really the most meaningful.'" Linden's mother, who had started the day in tears, was snapping pictures and saying, "We straight people have a lot to learn from you girls."

"I think the ceremony was a real eye-opener for her, to see how seriously we take ourselves, and that she's allowed to do that, too," Linden said.

A few weeks after the ceremony, Jan and Linden packed the truck and headed east for a "webbing-moon" trip. They brought their commitment arrow, the alder branch bound with tiny objects. It was pouring at the Grand Canyon. Jan wanted to huddle in the tent, but Linden insisted they trek out to the edge and throw the arrow down. The first time they tried, it got caught in soaking-wet shrubbery. They scrambled down to retrieve it. Then, gripping the branch with all four hands, they drove it into the soil by the canyon's rim.

"JUST in trying to be who I am, I am always going against the grain," Jan said. "It makes me feel so shrill. If the world wasn't so different from who I was, I wouldn't always be taking that position.

"Also, as lesbians, I feel we erase ourselves a lot. Even before we give anybody else a chance to do it. We just quietly recede. Either we're out screaming or we're totally self-effacing and riddled with a lot of self-doubt.

"For me, the ceremony was a way of saying, I refuse to erase myself. At least, today. Today, at two o'clock, I am not invisible."

I stayed late at Jan and Linden's house, long after I'd turned off the tape recorder, and sat between them on the couch, paging slowly through the photo album from their webbing. There was the procession, led by children, streaming across the grass. Jan and Linden, wearing flower wreaths in their hair. A friend speaking a wish into the pewter chalice of water. Jan dancing with her father, both their expressions tense.

I got hopelessly lost on the way back home, somehow heading east instead of west on the unlit, winding roads, my gas tank needle quivering near empty. No map, no discernible street signs. I just kept driving, around curves, past huge trees, until, forty minutes later, I emerged in a clearing, where I could tell that the blackness beyond was the river, gushing and steady, showing me home.

Loving Living Apart

WE SANG it as a jump rope rhyme, our sneakers snapping the pavement. We sang it on the school bus in June, our legs slick against the dark green vinyl. *First comes love, then comes marriage, then comes Junior in a baby carriage.*

By the time Judith Arcana was in her twenties, in the middle of this half-century's tumult over war, marriage, and morals, the singsong refrain had taken on a different, rebellious tone.

I visited Judith in her office at the Union Institute Center for Women in Washington, D.C., because I wanted to hear about her relationship with her partner, Jonathan Arlook. They were not married. And for most of their twenty-year relationship, by choice, they had not even lived together. Sometimes they were just ten city blocks apart, sometimes on opposite sides of the country.

Judith told the story in a high-speed monologue. Her hands, moving quickly with her speech, took apart the air in front of her, patched it together again.

"When I hear the word 'family,' I generally think of traditional nuclear patriarchal family—parents who are married to each other, who are heterosexual, who have children the same race as themselves. That is the automatic image that word has had all my life, until these last many years when I have deliberately attempted to change that definition for myself and in the world."

Judith, born in 1943, grew up on postwar images of nuclear family, depicted in primary colors on the pages of grade school readers: Mother and Father, Dick and Jane, Spot and Puff. And then all the definitions, all the preset pictures, started breaking down. She married. She had a baby. But her daily life bore little resemblance to stock images of family. Several friends, all younger than Judith and her husband, moved into their large house and tried to fashion a communal life, sharing rent, chores, child care, and, occasionally, sex.

In women's groups, Judith and her friends talked about the limitations of blood family, the oppressions of marriage, the possibility of lesbian relationships. Nothing was sacred any more, and everything seemed within reach. Judith divorced, then pursued concurrent relationships with women and men—one of whom was Jonathan.

"The first time he and I tried living together, it was 1974. My kid was very little, two and a half or three. I know why I moved in with him. It was right after the group house broke up. I was frightened that, economically, I couldn't make it.

"We really liked each other a lot and had great sex, but that's not a good reason to live with someone. It was not a good basis to be together. So we separated after thirteen months, and I moved into an apartment with just the baby, and it was great. I was able to take care of myself. What a surprise. That was very wonderful—to come apart and find myself.

"I was disturbed, as was he; we thought, Uh-oh, this is the end. But we didn't say that. We said, We just can't live together. Maybe someday we can. We said, over and over, We'll see what happens. That's the line. It's become like a little joke in the family: We'll see what happens.

Jonathan moved less than a mile away, still in the same Chicago neighborhood, on the same bus line. "We had a good time; we liked it. We each loved having our own place. That space of ten or twelve blocks was really important and useful.

"I remember countless times that I would decide to stay at Jonathan's, we'd be in bed and would have a fight. And then I would have to decide, am I going to get up at two o'clock in the morning, put on my clothes, and go home on the bus? That's an interesting commentary on what it means to live together. I would stay there because it was too scary or hard *not* to stay there.

"When we began to live together as a couple a few years ago, we joked about that experience. Every now and then one of us will say, Get out of my house, and the other says, Too bad—I live here, too."

"I WAS very, very reticent, to put it mildly—I was phobic—about being in a couple," Judith remembered. "I was very frightened of what that would mean. Would I be able to escape the old patterns? Could I grow into a full person? I was very dubious, and I think I was right to be.

"We were so dumb," she continued. "We were such a happy couple that we started to live together again, five years later. We were in great shape; we screwed it up by moving in again. This time we went sixteen months and said, No good. Then we stayed apart for a long time. I believe that having separate lives and places made it possible for us to come back together."

Judith recalled one occasion during her marriage when she and her husband ran into a colleague of his at the theater. "This is my wife," said the man, and Judith's husband turned to her with the same possessive gesture.

"I thought, I'm not ever going to be in the position where someone turns to me and says, this is my..." she said. "I really feel marriage is not a good thing, especially for women. I don't like it. I even fear it. I fear the incursion of that structure, even after all these years. It's that powerful.

"I really needed to keep growing, to keep finding out who I was, not to have to concentrate on the dailiness of making live-in family. I was really careful about not losing myself in a couple. Also, I had a baby. I was completely committed to raising him, and Jonathan wasn't. Jonathan never wanted to be a father.

"We lived apart for eight years. We never considered living together during that time. We had figured out that it was stupid to try it again and make fools of ourselves. Then my son, at the end of his sophomore year in high school, called a little meeting on the sunporch of the apartment where we lived. He said, 'I want us all to live together again.'

"We talked endlessly about it for three days, about what it would mean. I was dubious. Jonathan was really dubious. He likes quiet. His house was like a Japanese garden; ours was like the alley. We said to Daniel, 'We're very happy living apart.' He said, 'I know. You're very weird.'

"The big line was, if we can find a place big enough for everyone to have her or his own room, and for me to be able to work at home, then we'll do it. And we did. Suddenly, there we were, Ozzie and Harriet. We had a house full of kids all the time. Daniel lived in the basement. It was a lot of fun. And it was not easy."

When Daniel left for college in New York, and Judith got a job in Cincinnati, there ensued another round of "high-level talks." Judith moved first and lived alone for about six months, then Jonathan joined her.

Later, when a better job came up in D.C., Jonathan followed Judith again, except for a nine-month stint when their relationship turned bicoastal. He worked in California and visited D.C. once a month for long weekends.

"We have a very fluid situation," Judith said. "It seems to me that I've been the pivot. Both of these guys have been together because of me. My job has made the family base move from Chicago to Cincinnati to Washington, and they are both relating to that home, which is bound up in the mother/woman. I sort of like it, because I'm into the older prepatriarchal forms. On the other hand, it's a lot of responsibility.

"We're like the contemporary late twentieth-century nomadic family. It's very American, I think."

Without a marriage, without the expectation that they will always share the physical boundaries of "home," Judith and Jonathan have spun out numerous variations on the theme of partnership. They fantasize about moving to the West Coast; Judith imagines another group house, full of women friends and Jonathan.

At forty-nine, she worries more about the future, about one of them getting sick. The legal boons of marriage enrage her even more than they used to; as she and Jonathan grow older, benefits such as health insurance and intensive-care visiting privileges become so much more pertinent.

"It's tough enough to be old, to be worrying about your health, but to have to worry that if something happened to me, he couldn't even get into the hospital. . .We're making steps with living wills and durable powers of attorney. A group house would complicate things even further, but I really think that's the way to go. Maybe even living with people we don't know yet."

Earlier I'd asked Judith where she drew the courage to break convention. Throughout her adulthood, she said, "I kept thinking, I can't live the way we did when I was growing up because I don't care for that way. That was really no good. We're going to do it differently now.

"It was the dream of that time. It was the sense that we could make it up. Don't get me wrong. There were terrible failures and painful eruptions and a lot of grief. It was very exciting to draw our own maps. At the same time, it was absolutely terrifying.

"There weren't any models. What I did have were other women who were trying to do it, too. We exchanged information, told each other about our lives. And I saw stuff working. I saw the courage of the women and thought, Well, if she can do it, I can do it."

We said good-bye at the corner of Nineteenth and Q Streets, just blocks from my old D.C. apartment, where three-story town houses nudge shoulder to shoulder and the everyday acts of women, provocative and impassioned, unfold within them. Judith headed home to the house she and Jonathan shared—at least, for the time being—her step rapid, her coat flapping behind her.

Refusing to Go to Weddings

LAURA Blue's feelings about marriage were clinched after she flew three thousand miles to attend her sister's wedding. The bride and groom had known each other for three months. Laura, as a member of the wedding party, wore a purple dress and strolled down the aisle with an usher to witness a perfunctory, ten-minute ceremony.

While Laura's sister was tying the knot, their mother was trying desperately to untie her own—and couldn't, because she lived in a state without no-fault divorce laws, and Laura's father didn't want the split. It was then that Laura decided marriage was not only oppressive to women, but hypocritical and irrelevant.

For Laura's partner, Tere Blue, weddings meant wearing dresses, and wearing dresses meant a fight with her parents, as far back as she could remember. By the time she was in her twenties, her Tennessee family had long since come to terms with her wardrobe, her cropped hair, even the tattoo that circled her left wrist. But memories of the two Methodist weddings she'd attended still made Tere uneasy. "Even as a kid, something didn't seem right about it," she recalled. "There was this whole farce of the maiden being given away."

On their way to the 1987 Washington, D.C., march for lesbian and gay rights, Tere and Laura debated about whether to join in the mass "wedding" planned for the day after the march. They weren't opposed to the idea of spoken commitments between couples; they'd made many such agreements themselves about money, shared belongings, and the prospect of raising children. But merely mimicking a heterosexual ritual that would not give them any real benefits held little appeal.

Laura and Tere marched in D.C. that fall, but they did not marry. In their community, where Laura worked for a feminist women's health clinic and Tere helped manage a food co-op, the issue rarely came up. Then two close friends—a man and a woman—nervously broke the news. They planned to be married, in a synagogue ceremony followed by a large dance party for friends and family. They had a request: Would Laura and Tere serve as emcees at the reception?

"We'd been with them as a couple, and they were great together," Tere said. "Obviously, we celebrated them. So their decision kind of caught me off guard, like an option I had forgotten about: Oh, people still get married?" She and Laura said they needed to think about their friends' invitation.

"We dreaded the decision," Tere said. "It wasn't something we could feel good about and support them in. We didn't know how to tell them without hurting their feelings. It wasn't anything personal. It wouldn't matter what couple it was. But I was faced with the possibility of losing them as friends. I had to examine what I really thought."

TERE and Laura talked together and hunted through feminist literature for theory to help them sort out their mixed feelings. What they found kept leading them back to the same painful conclusion.

"It was a very thoughtful process for me," Tere remembered. "They were asking us to emcee their reception, which was a way of honoring us as a couple. But for me, it's just this—the institution of marriage is a form of ownership. My basic feminist foundation is that the subjugation of women is the basis for every other form of oppression."

Besides, she said, her friends' choice to marry felt like an erasure of her own experience as a lesbian. They were using a privilege that would bring them emotional and financial support while Tere had to struggle even to find language that accurately described her bond to Laura.

The dilemma forced Laura to examine her own resistance to weddings. It was more than a natural aversion for rituals of any kind or her reluctance to masquerade as a bridesmaid in an itchy dress. She could even imagine how marriage might be the best of limited options for some women, but she couldn't forget what she knew about the institution as a means of keeping women in their place.

Both Laura and Tere had mixed feelings about the efforts of some lesbians and gay men to seek legalized marriage. Laura liked the outrage of their public protests, when a dozen lesbian couples would show up at City Hall and demand marriage licenses from flustered clerks. But a state-sanctioned relationship wasn't a model she thought gays and lesbians should emulate.

People need more options in their relationships, Laura argued, between the two extremes of lifetime commitment and no-strings-attached dating. "It's not just a straight/gay thing," she said. "Maybe you want to make a commitment to someone, have children, and then, when they're grown, reevaluate it. Marriage as it stands right now is not relevant to most people's lives. Why would lesbians and gays want it?"

Tere agreed. When lesbians and gay male couples sought recognition through legal marriage, she always thought about the myriad household arrangements that would still be excluded. What about adults who live in community, or those who choose to be single: didn't they deserve the privileges and support that came with sanction as a "legitimate" family?

ALL those factors made the answer clear; Laura and Tere called their friends and explained that they didn't want to be emcees at the reception. After that, Laura decided to make her feelings about marriage known in the hope of deflecting any future invitations. "I told all my straight friends, I hate weddings and I really don't want to go to any. Don't take it personally. It hasn't come up again—yet."

Meanwhile, in their own six-year relationship, Laura and Tere make agreements about various issues as they arise. They share money and belongings. When Laura got a new job two hours away, she commuted several days a week until the two could rent a house and move together.

For several years, they have talked in detail about their desire to raise children. Using a book designed for lesbians considering whether to become parents, they worked together through the questionnaires and discussions it suggested. The two have agreed, if they do have children, to remain in the same household, as a family, at least until the children are eighteen—whether or not they continue to be lovers.

Laura and Tere's discussions about even the most mundane matters, they said, are threaded with meaning, as they constantly redefine and affirm their relationship with each other. "We talk about our lives," said Laura. "We talk about what we want to do, how we're going to do it. We talk about what we can do legally to protect ourselves. Most of what we do is some sort of commitment ceremony."

Preferring to Be "Unmarried, with Partner"

ONCE, for about three days, Mary Scott thought she might marry Jay Harris. They had gone to help Mary's parents clean out her grandmother's five-acre farmhouse.

"We were going to spend the night," Mary recalled. "For some reason, my mother said she wasn't comfortable with us sleeping together." That puzzled her, because she and Jay had shared a bed on previous visits to her parents' house. But her mother was insistent, and the two left early, heading for the coast. On the way, they stopped at a Dairy Queen and talked.

"We realized that if it was that painful for my mother, if it mattered that much, maybe we should just get married. I don't remember who actually said it. It didn't feel like a proposal.

"There was a lot of pain that weekend," she recalled. "My grandmother had just died. My parents had basically been sorting through my mother's whole life. We wanted to do something that might relieve some of her sadness."

At the coast, they met Jay's sister and brother-in-law. When they announced their plans, Mary remembered, they were met with laughter and teasing. She recalled the long conversations she and her brother used to have on the way back from visits to their parents' home. He always said he wanted to spare their parents pain, and Mary, although she loved them, couldn't agree with that choice. "I'd always felt I couldn't live my life not to make waves."

As she lay on the beach, her body drenched with sun, she began to wonder about their decision to marry. When she and Jay talked again, something had turned over in their minds. "We questioned the validity of doing something like that for somebody else."

As unceremoniously as it had begun, their brief engagement ended, and their relationship resumed its unnameable path.

Mary had spent much of her young adulthood expecting not to marry. The daughter of a railroad worker and a homemaker, she remembered family as a tight-knit, traditional group. At one point, she fantasized about marrying a veterinarian or a forest ranger and having children. "Like a lot of women, I was going to marry what I really wanted to be."

But as she entered her teens, she began to question that prospect. It disturbed Mary that marriage, for her mother, had meant abandoning dreams of a career in radio. One day, when she was about fourteen, she announced to her mother that she was never going to get married. A few years later, she watched with ambivalence while several girlfriends swiftly tied the knot. "I still had these dreams of the forest ranger. But I know I didn't long to get married."

When I met them, Mary and Jay had lived together for ten years and had been lovers for thirteen. Their house, warm and cluttered, showed their myriad passions: Jay was a teacher, musician, mime, gardener, and inveterate garage-sale shopper; Mary a naturopathic doctor, a gardener, a kitchen wizard with food and herbal medicines. A copy of *Practical Homeowner* shared shelf space with the *Utne Reader*, half a dozen clay masks hung on one wall and a plastic skeleton wearing a cone-shaped hat stood in the corner.

Outside, a wooden porch held an assortment of rocks and shells and a confetti of signs: "Thank You For Not Smoking." "This Home Is Against Military Intervention In Other Lands." "Trees Are The Answer." Mary settled on a cushion facing into the sun, her back taut with a health worker's consciousness of posture. When she was trying to remember something, she closed her eyes for a long moment.

At the time she and Jay met, not marrying was a matter of principle. "One reason was in solidarity with gay and lesbian people who don't have a way to be legally married," Mary said. "But even if that barrier to gay and lesbian unions was lifted, I don't know that I necessarily would get married.

"We also had the feeling that our relationship shouldn't be defined in the eyes of the state. We had a wonderful relationship—sexually, politically. We really enjoyed each other. We didn't want to ruin it. We didn't want to define it, to have to call it anything. We wanted it to find its own natural evolution. I couldn't imagine a marriage ceremony that would really reflect how we felt about each other.

"I grew up with a very insular family. I wanted to show myself and them that that wasn't all family was."

Those traditional images of family cling tightly; it has taken years for Mary's and Jay's relatives to accept fully their choice to remain unmarried. Mary's father worried aloud about whether she would be taken care of; her mother was sometimes uneasy when she tried to explain her daughter's relationship to others.

After that summer weekend, though, neither parent has expressed concern about the two sleeping together. When Mary and Jay visit her parents now, they often make jokes about cold feet and stealing the blankets. "Maybe it's our way of not letting them deny it," she said.

Mary and Jay's lives seemed less governed by "shoulds" than those of the married friends I know. Their decision, Mary said, had helped to unlock them from the gender-based patterns in many married couples' lives. The family they are creating together remains a subject of constant question, challenge, and invention. They follow separate, sometimes widely divergent schedules—with Mary working days at a naturopathic clinic and Jay often playing music at night. While Mary was studying to become a naturopath and acupuncturist, Jay did all the laundry, all the food shopping. On holidays, they have no routine but decide on each occasion whether they will visit her family or his family, do things separately or stay at home.

And not being married, Mary said, makes it easier for the two to maintain an extremely simple lifestyle, in which possessions and money are of minimal importance. At thirty-eight, Mary dresses most of the time in bright, soft, secondhand clothes. For holiday gifts, she gives coupons to her friends offering them one-hour massages. After our interview, she was headed to a department store, where a friend was listed in the bridal registry, to pick out a wedding gift. She laughed about the errand, relieved to be a guest and not the recipient. "I don't want any part of that. Not being married has been a really easy way to sidestep all those expectations from other people."

During the few days she and Jay were engaged, "It made me feel very normal," Mary recalled. "I haven't experienced that feeling a lot in my life, because I haven't done a lot of traditional things."

Not being married means, sometimes, avoiding the issue with patients who might mistrust her medical skills if they knew she and Jay were not legally wed. And it means having to figure out, piece by piece, what the legal, financial, and emotional components of their relationship should be.

Mary and Jay own their house jointly. They keep separate accounts and split the bills in half. They don't tell each other what they do with spending money. Beyond the house papers, they have few legal documents to outline their obligations—no wills, no durable powers of attorney, no living-together agreement.

"Sometimes I get the feeling that people regard us, even though we've been together more than ten years, as if we haven't grown up," Mary said. "That we haven't been able to make that declaration to other people of our commitment to each other. But it hasn't seemed important. It's seemed important to say it to each other."

Her vow, made in a burst of adolescent defiance more than twenty-five years ago, has proven both prescient and durable. When those few days of engagement were over and they decided not to marry, after all, Mary recalled, it was like ending a game of "let's pretend," a swap of artifice for authenticity. "We felt more real to ourselves."

Standing Up as a Lesbian Couple

THE first time Susan Leo and Gloria Park publicly insisted they were family was at the membership desk at Costco, a giant discount warehouse where shoppers stock up on forty-roll packages of toilet paper and two-gallon jars of mayonnaise. Gloria, a nurse, had earned a free trial membership and wanted to sign Susan up as her partner. The two drove out to the nearest Costco, filled in their names and address on the form and handed it to the clerk.

"She said no, absolutely not," Gloria recalled. "We protested adamantly. We asked to talk to the manager, who said the law didn't see same-sex relationships as legal. 'It's the law.' That's what they always say."

Usually, Gloria and Susan talk back. They are assertive women, gregarious at parties and not shy of public confrontation. When they held a commitment ceremony several years ago, both women saw the event, in part, as a way to make their relationship more visible. And the effort did not stop there; it continues, daily, as they challenge heterosexist policies and presumptions everywhere from retail counters to insurance company headquarters.

When they were planning their commitment ceremony, they told the proprietor of a local coffee store about their plans. She gave them the free pound of coffee that the shop promises to all newlywed customers. Next, they took on their road-service company. Both women were members of AAA, and each paid the yearly premium. When Gloria's membership was up for renewal, she tried to switch them both to the same card. Another road service company had promised to enroll the couple as a family. But AAA said no. Both women canceled their memberships and wrote letters explaining why.

"I think the next step in our community is to confront people everywhere, to say: I want to talk to the manager. I think this is ridiculous,"

Gloria said. "We're totally out in our community. Our neighbors all know. The neighbor up the street, the really hard-core fundamentalist Christian, said he didn't approve, but it wasn't his place to try and save the sinner. I said, That's right."

"It's amazing," Susan continued. "The more we come out to people at businesses and other places, the more we challenge them to accept us on our own terms. And they do. Both Gloria and I are pretty outgoing. Also, we're pushy. And we don't have any doubts that we're wonderful people."

"I'm really shocked at the number of people who treat us well," Gloria said. "We say who we are, then we look at them as if to say, Isn't that great?"

THEIR latest struggles have taken place on the sensitive turf of the San Francisco Theological Seminary, where Susan is a student. At first, school administrators denied the couple, and their son, Kasey, family housing. For a year, the family lived off campus in a house much more expensive than any on-campus accommodations. They amassed $9,000 in credit card debt, and Susan felt isolated from the seminary community by the four-mile distance between their home and her classes.

In the meantime, they kept badgering administrators. "We're like these pit bulls that grab on and don't let go," Susan said. "They say it has to be blood family to qualify for on-campus housing. But married couples live in family housing. So do people with foster kids. So, of course, they make exceptions."

Finally they discovered a loophole in the housing policy. The next year, with Gloria enrolled in one class that provided her with "special student" status, the three, along with their two dogs, were granted permission to live in a two-bedroom seminary apartment just a block from campus.

That wasn't the end of their administrative struggles. "The school publishes a phone directory, and all the families have a picture taken at the beginning of the year," Gloria said. "We had our picture taken—Susan and me and Kasey. But only Susan's name was listed. My name was listed separately, with the P's. They'd taken it upon themselves to divide us as a family. We were hot. We marched over to the administration building, and they couldn't respond fast enough."

"They've since changed the policy," Susan added. "In the directory, people are allowed to describe whomever their family is for them."

"I'm interning this year at First Congregational Church in downtown San Francisco," Susan said. "I had a lot of compliments the first day I appeared in church and introduced Gloria as my soul mate and life partner and Kasey as our son. People were really touched that I did that."

The two have come out to teachers at Kasey's school, where Gloria volunteered to grade all the spelling books and accompany the class on field trips. Susan was umpire for Kasey's Little League team. "This is the way we run our lives," said Gloria. "We jump in and get involved. When we come out, other people have to stretch."

Susan began to laugh. "We're all set to give the seminary another of what Gloria calls 'opportunities to learn.' Next month, I'm going to try to get pregnant."

"It's going to be interesting," said Gloria. "We'll do what we always do. We'll walk around proudly, with our heads up, like we belong here."

Gradually, in daily, incremental ways, they change minds. Although they didn't win a Costco membership for Susan, they did introduce the clerk and the manager, perhaps for the first time, to a flesh and blood lesbian couple calling themselves family. Eventually the store may rewrite its policy. Societal shifts happen this way: one challenge, one small subversive act at a time.

"When I was making the case at school for us to be eligible for family housing, I said the families of the 1990s don't look like they used to— whether it's people living with aunts and uncles or foster kids or whatever," Susan said. "The benefits that society gives now to married heterosexual couples are going to have to be re-evaluated in light of all these changes.

"There's a theologian who has proposed that it's in the creative transformation of our lives that God is working. Lesbians and gay men and others are transforming the concept of family in ways that would have been totally unrecognizable twenty years ago."

Redefining Family in Public and Private

Ask the good people of San Francisco—all 723,000 of them—what constitutes a family, and you're likely to come up with 723,000 different answers. Roberta Achtenberg tried. As chair of the Mayor's Task Force on Family Policy in 1989, it was her job to coin a definition of family that fit the hugely varied lives of San Franciscans.

After interviewing dozens of people—gay and lesbian couples, older adults living alone, foster parents, multigenerational extended families, single mothers, divorced fathers—it was easier, Achtenberg said, to conclude what family didn't mean.

It didn't require, for instance, that all the members live together in the same house. It didn't necessarily have a sexual partnership between two adults as its core. It didn't mean children were always part of the configuration.

"It seems to involve a group, either related or not, who have a mutual bond of affection and have agreed to take care of one another, who have assumed responsibility for one another. My own view is that anybody who agrees to act in that way deserves the title of family."

She illustrated with a story of her own: "Many of us have taken care of somebody who has a terminal illness, have been there to share the responsibility for somebody in their dying days when their 'family' didn't do it or wouldn't do it.

"My friend Steven died two years ago. A group of his friends and I cared for him for a year and a half, willingly, without any expectation of return, because he was our friend. That's family. So I think it's the level of commitment—whether it's explicit or not. I never said out loud that I would take care of him, but I knew in my heart that I would."

Much of the testimony the task force heard from citizens struck home for Roberta; she knows firsthand the invisibility that visits people who do not fit the "family" norm. When Roberta's partner, Mary Morgan, attends judges' conferences, their son, Benjie, plays with the other kids, Mary sits in meetings, and Roberta lounges poolside with "the wives." When Mary was pregnant, people behaved as if she were the only one becoming a parent.

"They'd say, 'Oh, Mary, you must be so excited, you're going to have a baby.' I kept thinking, Well, what am I, chopped liver? We'd have to correct them and say, Well, yes, *we* are having this baby, and isn't it wonderful? You go through life and people try to invalidate your family."

Roberta had been trying for more than a decade to change that, for herself and for others. She did it first from the outside, as legal gadfly, the executive director of the National Center for Lesbian Rights. Then she became an insider, elected to the San Francisco Board of Supervisors, a body that has the power to make big changes in its small, but diverse, corner of the world. Recently she became Assistant Secretary for Housing in the Department of Housing and Urban Development—the first openly lesbian or gay person appointed by a president and confirmed by the U.S. Senate.

When we talked, a few months after her election to the San Francisco Board of Supervisors, her new office in City Hall still had a makeshift look about it, the desk and boxes of files dwarfed in the high-ceilinged room. Roberta was at once crisp and down to earth, dressed in a Katharine Hepburn-style suit of slacks and jacket, brown hair blunt-cut. Her manner was utterly professional, even a little brusque; yet when I asked what she wanted her five-year-old son to know about family, she paused for a long moment, and her eyes reddened before she spoke.

"Just. . .the idea that you take care of each other. That's what's been modeled for him. I hope he'll be able to bond with somebody and have a loving family for himself in the way we've been able to do for ourselves."

THE report of the Mayor's Task Force on Family Policy, issued in June 1990, gave voice to Roberta's personal conviction—that public policy needs to expand in recognition of the multiple ways families live.

The task force recommended that bereavement leave be made explicitly applicable to the death of domestic partners and that unpaid family care leave be available in cases of serious illness of a worker's spouse, domestic partner, parent, or a child "for whom the employee assumes parenting responsibilities."

The report also called for more pliable work rules such as flexitime, part-time employment and job sharing, more on-site day care and a family registry system to record extended and alternative families as well as committed, but unmarried, couples.

"Family life as it's lived doesn't always bear much resemblance to the strict legal notion of family," Roberta said. "Our assumption was, It's good public policy to promote constructive family life. The benefits are there to help protect these fragile relationships, to encourage them, to help preserve them."

One especially delicate issue is the definition of "parent." Legal parents include only those who bear, conceive or adopt a child. Custody and visitation statutes rest on these definitions.

"Suppose a guy moves in with his girlfriend," Roberta explained. "He's not the father, but he is the parenting figure and lives with the mother and child for many years. Then the mother and boyfriend break up. Should the mother have the absolute right to say, You can never see this child again?"

Policies based on narrow definitions of family grind away at the self-image of people in nontraditional groupings. "It turns out that our zoo has for many years had a very broad definition of family," Roberta said. "However, they have issued very few family memberships. Why? Because they don't advertise their policy. Most people don't ask for it. They assume that 'family' can't mean them.

"Now *we* have a lot of chutzpah, so we've had a family membership in the zoo for years. We said, Family? Oh, that must mean us. We're lawyers, used to shoving people around until we get what we want. But that's not most people's experience. Nor should it have to be.

"I'm in a relatively powerful position, so the kinds of things people can do to us because we're an unorthodox family are pretty small. One of the ways to protect yourself and your family is by acquiring as much power over the world as you possibly can—without achieving some misdirected notion that you ever control the world, because you don't.

"There's actually some protection in visibility. It also makes you a target. I don't mean to minimize that. I've had my share of death threats; I worry about someone trying to harm my child because of what we supposedly represent.

"But I know that if I call the police department because somebody's prowling around my house, the squad car comes immediately. I don't say that happily, but it's one of the ways in which I salve myself. By making a point of who we are, I also feel a corresponding obligation to protect my family from what the world has to say about us."

When the mayor's task force held hearings, witnesses came by the dozens. Many were grateful for the chance to talk publicly about their lives. Others were outraged that such a subject was even being discussed.

"Our hearings were commandeered by the fundamentalist religious right wing," Roberta said. "I heard this hour after hour: 'You're describing a definition of family that God didn't intend.... You're performing social engineering.'

"Gays and lesbians are one of the more organized communities around. It's not surprising to me that we would be out in front on an issue that intimately affects us. My feeling has been all along that if we do it only for ourselves, that misses the larger point somehow. So I constantly stress that this applies to us and to others as well.

"The truth is that the family has been changing itself. We're describing a phenomenon that exists. It's not any surprise that lesbians and gays are among those who are trying to force upon the larger society a recognition—hey, this is here. This is how people are living their lives."

On my way out, we stopped by the board of supervisors' chambers, a grand room with balconies and balustrades and, in the center, the giant table and swivel chairs where city government sits.

Roberta walked confidently into the middle of the chamber, swept an arm toward the dais as if showing off her own living room, and recalled the day of her inauguration. Her voice bounded back from the walls of the empty room.

"All the press, all the TV cameras were there," she said. "And in the middle were the families. Of course my partner and my boy were there, and my sister and her husband, and my other sister, and my good friend Bob. I had a whole slew of friends out in the gallery.

"Also seated there were Dianne Feinstein, former mayor of San Francisco, some of the senatorial candidates, Nancy Pelosi, our congresswoman, the lieutenant governor, our mayor—every muckety-muck you can imagine was sitting in that chamber. Of course the place was packed to the rafters. No gay people had ever won election to our county board of supervisors outright without having been appointed first.

"I introduced my family, and I left Benjie till the end. He was five. He had his little suit on. He stood up. Everybody cheered him and applauded.

"Then I said that Benjie was born in San Francisco and raised here, that he's never known any home other than this. Because of that, he's had such a rich experience. He's met and known all different kinds of people. Like a true San Franciscan, he has played with so many different kinds of kids from so many backgrounds that he already understands that having two moms is not the only legitimate form of family.

"The house came down. That's the only thing I said that was quoted later in the newspapers. It was taken differently by different people, depending on how charitable they felt or how odd a statement they thought it was. But I do think it was a little way of opening some eyes. Benjie's mind is open. He doesn't think the place he comes from is the only way to live.

"I don't mean to overstate the case. I don't think my contribution is any larger or more significant than the contribution any one of us makes when we introduce our nontraditional families to our families of origin or our friends or our neighbors.

"It's exactly that process that begins opening people's minds and gets them to understand that we're talking about the breadth and diversity of human experience and nothing more sinister or likely to produce anarchy than that."

Marking Time:
Charting a Feminist Calendar

It took me twenty-eight years to realize that challah wouldn't rise by it-self.

I was waiting, the way women are taught to wait, for the perfect conditions. Waiting for a family that fit some recognizable template, for a partner to share my home, for a synagogue to reach out and enfold me in its Friday night Shabbes ritual, for someone to assign me the task, for challah to spring spontaneously from the rightness of things.

I was behaving, the way women are taught to behave, patient and passive, hoping for someone to say yes, to endorse my idea, to invite me inside, to solicit my help, to say she was hungry and only challah would do.

Finally I took the ritual into my own hands. I followed Elissa's great-grandmother Lucoff's recipe: six cups of flour, a palm-sized toss of salt, make a well in the center, three eggs, half a cup of oil. When I'm finished, there are two braided loaves, brushed with egg and freckled with poppy seeds, steaming when I pull off the first piece.

Before, I thought making challah from scratch was a cultural mystery owned by another generation; I was not quite deserving of induction into its secrets. My cousins and I, after all, grew up in typically assimilated late-twentieth-century Jewish homes. I didn't go to Hebrew School. I did not have a bat mitzvah. I know more French and Spanish than I do Yiddish. Was I Jewish enough to make challah? Was I doing it with the right intentions, the appropriate reverence?

The first time I made it by myself, the process was pure magic—the yeast burping alive in a bowl of warm water, the eggs and oil and flour suddenly smoothing together in a pale yellow mass, the slow rise under a dish towel. Even the second time, the twelfth time, shreds of magic remain. I push and prod the dough and think of my great-grandfather, Samuel, in his Philadelphia bakery, tossing a few extra loaves into customers' bags.

But sometimes, I have to confess, it's just bread. It's raw eggs that I crack in a separate bowl to check for blood spots and flour that sticks to my clothes and, afterwards, a bowl to be scraped and washed and dried. A chore like any other chore. I mix the dough fast with my left hand, thinking about the deadline for my next article. I tear the dough roughly and wind it into quick, tight braids.

I do it anyway, because I am interested here in the big picture, the persistence of a private ritual I've begun. I want that even more than I want to indulge my desire, on any particular afternoon, to make phone calls instead, or to take a walk and buy challah at the bakery. Sometime in the course of measuring flour and pinching three strands of dough together, I feel my unruly thoughts slow down, my body settle into the routine like a carrying tide.

I look forward to interrupting my work on Friday afternoons, making the day different from any other. I like Shabbes, observing the spasms of activity and quiet that make the world. The challah reminds me that while I am a writer of articles, I am also a Jew, the great-granddaughter of a baker and a human being who needs to rest once in a while.

I'd like to say I am making challah as my mother did before me, as my grandmother did before her. But my mother's one botched attempt at making challah, in the basement of Samuel's bakery, is the stuff of family legend. She and her cousin kept adding powdered sugar, instead of white flour, while the dough slimed and oozed over a wooden board. I don't remember Bubie ever baking bread—in fact, it was her lack of inspiration in the kitchen, one time when Mom was sick, that launched my father on his path to gourmet cooking. I'm not so much continuing a tradition as searching the cultural tapestry for a bright, textured thread and tugging it into my own life.

In that life, I sometimes eat challah alone. Sometimes I share it with my partner, my housemates, or friends. I give one loaf to the neighbors across the street; I bring one to a dinner party. Sometimes we're busy and grab hunks of the hot bread on our way out the door.

The challah I make is different each week, depending on the season in which the eggs were hatched, the coarseness of the flour, the temperature in the house, the heat of my hands, the tightness of the braid, what I am thinking as I shape it. Each Friday night will be different from the last, no matter how much I try to make it familiar. Continuity does not mean sameness.

When it is time to tear the bread and recite a blessing, I hesitate. "*Baruch atah adonai, eloheinu melekh ha-olam....*" Blessed art thou, Lord our God, king of the universe. The Hebrew words comfort me, their sounds ancient lullabies. But they clash with my sense of the universe, where power and reverence are diffused, a bit to each of us, a bit to the flounder and Japanese maples, too. There is no king—nor queen, for that matter—in my prayers.

What I'd like to offer, whether anyone hears or not, is a blessing of my own invention. I'd like to feel glad for a moment that there still are places on this earth for wheat to grow. I'd like to acknowledge the alchemy of tradition and imagination that makes it possible for me to serve challah to my lover and friends three generations and a continent away from the site of Samuel's bakery.

I STUMBLED my way toward the making of challah, a ritual that now brings wholeness to my weeks. But so many other traditional markers of time leave me torn and uncertain. I examine the calendar: New Year's Eve, Valentine's Day, Easter, Passover, Memorial Day, the Fourth of July, Columbus Day, Thanksgiving, Chanukah, Christmas. As a feminist, these occasions—laden with customs and values of a male-dominated culture—prompt painful dilemmas.

I watch my Christian friends struggle each December, yearning for ways to celebrate the season but alienated by the symbols of American Christmas—a male god, a virgin birth, a heap of extravagant gifts. They cringe at front-lawn creches, loath to trace their spiritual ancestry to a white male infant. They cannot forget that Christianity's onset greatly accelerated the suppression of female ways of worship.

American Christmas celebrations tend to focus on the external—flashing lights, new clothes, parties, shopping—at a time when the darkness outside seems to beg for quieter pursuits and introspection. Working-class women, poor women, retired women, young women, and single mothers may find themselves priced out of the holiday; others simply reject its materialistic bent. Remove the external trappings, and the liturgical core is even more troublesome. The language of Jewish and Christian worship—God, King, Ruler, Lord, Dominion—speaks to a male-centered, hierarchical worldview.

Wintertime holidays—and, to a lesser extent, other holidays—also promote a particular image of family. Christmas glorifies the nuclear clan, with generations gathered around dining room tables, old grievances mended or forgotten. If your family doesn't fit this picture, you can spend the season in a state of painful dissonance, at odds with your culture at the very time you are supposed to be feeling most connected. And the emphasis on biological kinship offers scant comfort to those who remember family get-togethers marred by alcohol, anger or violence.

Christmas isn't the only troublesome time. Our patriotic holidays romanticize the country's wars. Thanksgiving may mark one moment of truce between white settlers and Native Americans, but it also reminds us of the brutal ways that Europeans claimed this country. Valentine's Day celebrates heterosexual love alone. And New Year's Eve, that arbitrary beginning, comes with social pressures to drink alcohol, spend money, and have an evening that rarely meets such heightened expectations.

I found some women who just say no, who will not participate in Thanksgiving, Easter, Passover. Or who actively rebel, sometimes with cleverness and humor. A particularly creative pair dressed in black last Christmas and paid stealthy nighttime visits to neighborhood lawn creches. By each infant's cradle, they propped a sign proclaiming, "It's a girl!" Still, rejecting traditional holiday rituals can leave women feeling isolated, cut off from the consensus that seems to mark such occasions. Resistance is hard, lonely work.

Perhaps because I come from a culture that has struggled to preserve its traditions from extinction, I'm reluctant to boycott my own history. I *am* a Jew, a citizen of the United States, as well as a woman, a writer, a lesbian, a feminist.

Besides, a stance of pure refusal, while intellectually refreshing, may not be emotionally honest. Many women still hold fond attachments, almost beyond reason, to holidays they find disturbing. Your head may say Christmas is a commercial fraud, but your heart feels the living room is empty without a Douglas fir brushing the ceiling. When we abandon tradition wholesale, we lose important links to our own childhood and to the customs of our families, communities, and cultures.

For so many women, holidays carry equal doses of expectation and loss, nostalgia and alienation. We swivel through the year, trying to make sense of such mixed feelings. Some women trace rituals to their genesis. Passover and Easter were grafted onto springtime festivals; Christmas and Chanukah are rooted in pre-Christian solstice rites. Kwanza, a relatively new holiday, harks back to African harvest festivals.

For Halloween one year, Chicago poet Maureen Seaton and a group of friends created a performance piece that juxtaposed stories of women persecuted during the Inquisition and targeted in witch trials with contemporary vignettes of violence against women.

The group's emblem is a silhouette of a woman about to be burned at the stake; in the performance, the women used art to challenge misogynist commercial images of witches and instead recall their strength, feminism, and refusal to conform.

"Halloween, or All Hallows' Eve," Maureen said, "is the time in pagan religions when dead souls come back or the living visit the graves of the dead. We wanted to bring these women back to say what really happened to them and what is happening now."

Through such events it's possible to skip back over centuries and connect with ancient traditions, times when people celebrated together the end of the dry season, the spring's first exhalation of rain, the winter solstice with its expansive, mysterious night.

I remember one winter solstice ritual, held in Dolores Kueffler's apartment, that invited participants to wrap ourselves up in the dark. First we passed a bowl of warm water and a towel to wash our hands. "Think about a time when you were afraid of the dark," Dolores said, and we each told a story—of nightmares, being lost in the woods, frightened and alone. "Now tell about a time when you loved the dark, felt at home with it." Women talked about camping trips and nights clotted with stars. I remembered sleeping on the floor of a half-built cabin in northern California, looking up through open rafters at satin-black wedges of sky.

Finally we passed a cup of pomegranate juice and each raised a toast to darkness. "I drink to the wildness of the dark," one woman said. "I toast the introspection of the night," another offered. "I toast its creativity, all the things that take root and grow in the dark."

Here, in the old calendar of solstices and equinoxes, lie occasions that can speak to feminists—cycles of season and weather, moon and tide. I know women who mark the moon cycle that we literally embody, celebrating menses with a special dinner or a massage and a sense of cleansing, strength, and renewal.

LaVerne Lewis lives by a lunar calendar, pacing her business and personal schedule according to the swell and ebb of the moon. Instead of working maniacally through dark winter days, she welcomes them as a chance to rest. She rearranges the furniture in her house each season.

"I start a kind of hibernation right after the new year, Hallowmas. I move the bed, shift to downstairs in my house, where it's darker and there's a fireplace. I tend to become more creative. In the summer, I camp a lot. It's like charging your solar battery so you can get through the winter. At home, I bring in flowers. I eat lighter and less. The lunar calendar is a natural rhythm, especially for women. I feel different—it's better than just wandering through life aimlessly."

Other women create private, daily pauses as a way to anchor themselves in time. Grace Silvia used to say the Shema, the central prayer in Judaism, each night before bed. It begins: "Hear, O Israel, the Lord is our God, the Lord is one."

"I felt superstitious about breaking the tradition once I'd begun," Grace explained. "I'd said it for many years but I didn't like the words. I realized that what the prayer did for me was to close the day, to say goodbye. Was there another way I could do that?

"I decided that I would try saying, Blessed be—and then say one thing that was important to me physically or that I noticed in the world. Blessed be the crisp air. Or blessed be the smell of the rose from this morning. There were some days I couldn't think of anything, not one physical thing. It helped me realize I'd better start paying attention."

Others strive for balance, something old and something new, something magical, something relevant. At Christmas, some counteract the shopping mania by giving gifts of hand-knit scarves or jam canned at home, volunteering at shelters or soup kitchens. They try to preserve the essence of the holiday—important relationships, mementos handed from friend to friend, the awareness of passing time.

That was my approach at Chanukah last year. Uneasy with a holiday that cheered a military victory, I focused on another theme: the rebellion of the Maccabees as a cultural minority, their refusal to assimilate. Elissa and I decided to celebrate the last of Chanukah's eight nights with a rebellious act of our own. In the magazine section of a downtown Safeway, we tagged two particularly offensive articles with large red stickers that said, "This promotes women-hating."

Other women take the framework of religious and cultural holidays and rewrite their texts, adding feminist prayers, contemporary songs and poetry, ways for their friends and families to participate more fully and bring immediacy to ancient rituals.

Teresa Jordan, a Nevada writer, transformed the notion of New Year's Eve resolutions into a ritual she has repeated with friends and family for several years. Each person writes down habits and traits she wishes to leave behind—such as constant complaining or disparaging her body—on special disappearing paper Teresa buys at a magic shop. Then they float the slips of paper in a bowl of hot water and watch them dissolve. Later, each person names things she wants to embrace in the coming year, lighting a small candle for each item until the circle blazes with light.

Holidays invite the creation of new ceremonies. Such rituals can be exquisite opportunities to reflect on the meaning of an event and infuse it with personal relevance. Yet they also feel odd, sometimes. Conventional holiday symbols create a kind of shorthand communication; when you alter the icons or add new ones, change texts or invent new celebrations, you must do a lot of explaining. No one knows, automatically, how to behave.

Gretchen Klotz, who holds an annual Valentine's Day potluck for women featuring "erotic" foods such as mussels, chocolate fondue and soft cheeses, said her guests are sometimes hesitant at first, uncertain what is expected at a Valentine's party designed to celebrate the love of self and friends. She urges them to wear their most comfortable clothes, bring exotic or unusual foods that they wouldn't ordinarily prepare and enjoy the occasion as an alternative to the holiday's emphasis on conventional romance.

I imagine tradition sometimes as a fine silver samovar, passed down through centuries, which I must polish and protect. Perhaps I should think of it instead as a quilt, expanding and changing with each generation, each new piece shifting the overall pattern, each pair of hands leaving their mark for future generations to read and revise.

In Marcia Falk's "Notes Toward Composing New Blessings," she writes about examining Jewish sources for language that points to a different image of God, not the fixed, singular, masculine deity referred to in most prayers. "Let us bless," Falk's new prayers begin, thanking the "source of life" that brings bread, ripens fruit, enables people to celebrate together. She notes that this effort to examine what has come before, sift it and change it, is not sacrilege, but custom, the very stuff of which culture is grown.

"We need to remind our critics, and ourselves, that tradition is not just what we inherit from the past; it is also what we create and pass on to the future," she writes.

So I press yellow dough into braids, on as many Friday afternoons as I can manage the task. Sometimes I recite the prayers I learned from Falk's essay: *N'varekh et eyn ha-hayyim, ha-motziah lehem min ha-aretz.* Let us bless the source of life that brings forth bread from the earth.

The new words sound foreign on my tongue at first, but I practice until the syllables roll easily. A changed ritual, a new ritual, brings with it a temporary sense of vertigo. Then the dizziness calms and the dissonance quiets. An internal leveling, true as a compass, places me firmly back in this time, my time.

Mothers and Others:
New Links to the Next Generation

A MIDWIFE kneels on the tattered carpet of the drop-in center where I work, holding a cardboard baby, head down, over her pelvis. "Birth and motherhood are the hardest and the most important work you'll ever do," she tells the group of homeless teenagers.

Rose and Cryz, who came in just yesterday with plastic spiders glued to their faces, have already offered detailed stories of their own labors. They talk authoritatively about contractions, dilation, episiotomy, bodily terrain I can barely envision. "Do you have children, Anndee?" the midwife asks, and I shake my head. I'm writing a book, I want to say, and the voice in my mind is defensive.

I am approaching the age when my biological clock is supposed to stir into action. Most of my married friends talk of children as a "when," not an "if." At my ten-year high school reunion, I had the same conversation forty times, yelling over the music: "What do you do now...are you married...any kids?" Classmates I wouldn't have trusted to baby-sit my gerbils were unfolding snapshots of their offspring.

Nearly every day, it seems, I read about a woman, single or married, shunning a fast-track career, rejecting a promotion, putting her unfinished novel away, getting pregnant at age forty-two, discovering that What She Really Wanted All Along was strained peas on her shoulder. I hear about fertility specialists offering high-priced counseling and treatment for those who can't conceive. Adoption agencies are welcoming single women and lesbians. Couples can inseminate with a vial from the sperm bank and a syringe.

Advertisements tell me I've "come a long way, baby" from my grandmother's day, when pregnancy was called "confinement" and middle-class women didn't leave the house from the fifth month until their delivery day. Now, it's seemly to be pregnant; actress Demi Moore, gloriously round and nude, poses on the cover of *Vanity Fair*.

The beliefs underlying all these visions hibernate in my unconscious, blanketed with centuries of history and myth, rhetoric and advertisement. Scratch the assumptions, and they roar awake.

Children will make you legitimate. Sometimes, at the social service agency where I worked, fifteen-year-old girls living on the street confessed that they knew all about condoms and how to use them, but frankly, they were *trying* to get pregnant. They wanted to be grown-ups. I understand such thoughts. When I'm around John's sisters—women my age who have, between them, four sons and a daughter—I feel young and inexperienced. I do not feel this way among childless friends who are twenty years older than I am. Motherhood seems a kind of adults-only club, and I feel jealous sometimes of its private, coded secrets.

Children will provide for you when you are old. A friend breaks up with her lover at age forty-two and begins talking about adopting a baby. I think her urge is partly to fill the sudden quiet in her house. Also, she wants insurance, a relationship that cannot be undone. I am relieved when she stops talking about children and instead rescues a mongrel puppy from the animal shelter.

Her fears of desertion in old age are terrors I share, though. When Elissa talks to me about a resident at the Jewish nursing home where she works, my first question is often: "Does she have any children?" I feel saddest for the ones who do not, who have no grown daughters or sons to visit, no photographs of grandchildren on their dresser tops.

I know this is not rational; many grown children neglect their parents. But I, too, jump to the conclusion that "childless" equals "alone." The message resounds in my own head, an ominous refrain: *We need children to take care of us because we cannot take care of each other.* It's an especially poisonous myth in the lesbian and gay community, where homophobia plants doubt about our ability to love each other long and well.

Children are a gift women owe to their families and cultures. I'm an only child. My father has one brother, who also had an only daughter. That cousin married, changed her name and gave the new one, Schenker, to her precocious, happy kids. If I do not have children, then, I will not give the name "Hochman" to anyone. The line stops here.

And I live in a society that values such links, the mysterious ropes of DNA, the resemblances and surnames that pattern our crowd. Within that larger world, I am a Jew, a female Jew, with a historical onus to reproduce: *Be fruitful and multiply.* It is an anti-assimilationist command; without children to take up the culture, the culture will die.

"I sometimes feel ready to dissolve in a great wash of tears because I have no child to contribute to this brave pool of survivors," writes Melanie Kaye/Kantrowitz, a Jewish lesbian essayist and poet. "As if I owe these parents aunts uncles cousins a birth—for those who died?"

I imagine, sometimes, that children would link me to my family. For all my parents' skepticism about lesbian parenting, I think they would welcome a baby of mine. A grandchild would resume a continuity they feared was ruptured. With a child in tow, I could honorably come home.

I THROW a surprise brunch for my mother on her recent visit. Ten friends gather around a picnic table, eating coffeecake and soufflé, drinking orange juice splashed with champagne.

My mother asks getting-to-know-you questions. Cynthia, a "recovering lawyer," is earning a degree in social work. Peg and Kate are renovating a house they bought as an investment. Anne just returned from leading a 150-mile walk for gay and lesbian civil rights. Mary is a naturopathic doctor. Janet works at an AIDS hospice. Amy is an accomplished poet.

As they talk, surges of pride crest in me. I admire these women, my busy and creative friends. Their lives are complicated and interesting. After the party, my mother wants to know more. Are these women single or with partners? How old are they? Do they have children? No, I say, they don't. In the car, a whole conversation passes between us, silently—her judgment and concern, my passionate defense.

In the current backlash against women's rights, childless women are depicted as the movement's casualties, independence gone awry. My friends' lives, and my own, defy these stock images. Still, I sometimes find myself believing rhetoric I detest, voices that urge me to have a child for all the wrong reasons—because it is "instinctive," because it would prove my selflessness, because it would make my life legitimate and whole.

In the meantime, I flirt shamelessly with the babies of friends and smile at toddlers in the bank line. I crawl on the floor and babble with my nephew, Ethan. But I feel relieved, after twenty minutes or half a day, to return these children to their parents. I listen for the urgings of my own biological metronome. Children or no children? If yes, then how? If not, what next? When my inner clock shudders into action, what will be the rhythm I hear—reveille or taps?

I THINK about the phrase "pro-choice," that familiar abortion-rights short-hand, and the day-to-day realities it conceals. I think of the numerous ways women are deciding to include children in their lives—and the many reasons others choose not to.

Some women are exercising for the first time a privilege to choose children. It's only in the last twenty years, for instance, that alternative-in-semination clinics have become accessible to nontraditional families, in-cluding women over forty, lesbians, and unmarried heterosexual women.

Of course, there have always been lesbians who raised children from prior marriages. But as greater numbers of lesbians started becoming pregnant, enrolling in childbirth classes and showing up at hospital de-livery rooms with their partners in tow, they rattled a favorite homopho-bic myth: that lesbians are "unnatural" women, sexual but not maternal, a biological conundrum. They also challenged this culture's fixation with origins and the misleading distinctions drawn between "natural" and "nonbiological" parents.

The latest generation of lesbian mothers has begun to alter legal concepts of parenthood, arguing successfully in some states that stat-utes on stepparent adoptions should apply to them as well. Kay, who adopted the biological daughter of her partner in the first such case na-tionally, said the judge's order supplied official protection for a relation-ship that already existed in fact. "The adoption lifted an incredible anxi-ety. It's been very convenient in terms of registering for school, getting medical care. We cross out where it says 'father' on forms and fill in 'mother' and 'mother.'"

No one knows how many babies have been born to or adopted by lesbians, but anecdotal evidence points to a parenting surge. Sha'ar Zahav, a gay and lesbian synagogue in San Francisco, organized a Hebrew school for the children of its members. Alyson Press has published several children's books depicting gay parents. Even the cautious *New York Times* noted the trend with a small article in 1989 about the "lesbian baby boom."

That boom coincided with the Reagan years, a time of "pro-family" rhetoric and celebration of domestic life. In congressional debate on subjects ranging from AIDS funding to school curricula, gay men and lesbians were cast as enemies of family, hazardous to children, and threatening to the American Way. In that context, lesbian parenting held contradictory themes. It was a way to gain legitimacy by joining the ranks of family-makers. At the same time, it was an exuberant "yes," an act of defiance, visibility, and hope.

"A pregnant lesbian shakes people up; it's a radical image in the world," Elissa tells me. It is a Fourth of July weekend, and we are driving back from the coast because we could not find a camping spot. The lot at the state park was crammed with cars and RVs. Now we're rattling in my Datsun past acres of "managed" forests, the timber-industry euphemism for stumps, wildflowers, and knee-high trees.

I imagine Elissa pregnant, her strong legs supporting a round belly. I see myself wiping sweat from her forehead and talking her through contractions. I try to guess the feel of an infant, wrinkled and wet, at her breast, in my arms. How would we do it, I wonder? Ask a male friend to donate sperm and then remain part of the child's life as a sort of uncle figure? Choose an anonymous donor from a clinic catalogue?

These questions remind me that my decisions about children are political choices; they exist in a context, and they affect other people. A heterosexual couple's decision to conceive, in a world of threatened resources, is political, too. It's just easier to pretend that theirs is a purely private act.

My mind jolts back to the road. Multiplying, I think, might have been a good way to populate the desert, strengthen the tribe and get some work done, but it seems much of the world's tasks now involve cleaning up the mess we've begotten these thousands of years. Perhaps, I tell Elissa, our time in history demands a different choice. It may be, in this overcrowded world, that *not* multiplying is the most fruitful thing to do.

Besides, there are other ways to become a parent. Some women, choosing not to add another human being to the planet, adopt instead. Agencies that for years favored young, white, heterosexual couples are slowly opening their doors to a variety of family types. Today's adoptions look different in other ways, often crossing ethnic and national lines. More and more women are raising children in families that are purposely multicultural; rather than try to hide the fact of adoption, they celebrate it, embracing their sons' and daughters' complex histories.

Yet such adoptions also raise questions about power, economics, race. I know that babies are sometimes bought from desperate parents in hungry countries to feed another kind of desperation—that of childless people in more comfortable places. I have read of the world's unwanted children, casualties of political terror, starvation, and war. When a child crosses national borders or racial lines to be adopted, she gets a family, but she loses the dimension of identity that is community, country, life among people who look alike and share a history. How do we tally these losses and gains?

So CASUALLY, thoughtlessly, we speak of women "having" children—"have," with its connotations of property and possession. Feminist mothers are questioning the language—and through it, the most basic assumptions—of child rearing. More and more, I see women viewing parenting as a collective endeavor, enlisting friends, relatives, whole communities in the task.

Successfully blended families make room for multiple kinds of mothering—that of birth parents, stepparents and co-parents. Other women are opting not to raise "their own" children, but to become involved in the lives of nieces and nephews, the children of friends, colleagues or neighbors.

Dolores Kueffler and Pat Hunter became *"comadres"*—literally, "co-mothers," to a young couple they know, offering support to the parents and guidance to their older daughter as her *"madrinas,"* or godmothers. A few months before the child was born, Dolores and Pat drove to their friends' home for a prebirth ceremony; the four adults sat on the bed and offered wishes and prayers to the baby. Since then, as one of the "special adults" in the child's life, Dolores makes a point of staying in regular contact, celebrating her birthdays and other important junctures.

Another couple, Kao Rhiannon and Zane Torelli, invited a group of women friends to be part of their "birthing team" when Kao delivered their daughter, Jessa Rose. One of those women remained steadily involved in the family's life, spending time with Jessa Rose twice a week.

And Beverly Stein has nurtured a decade-long relationship with the daughter of one of her closest friends, a woman to whom she has pledged lifelong commitment. "I have made her daughter, Ann, my friend. I do things with her. When she comes home from college, we go out to lunch. We write to each other a little bit. I feel a connection to her almost like a biological connection."

THERE is another choice, denied to so many women for so long—the choice not to bear or raise children, their "own" or anyone else's. Despite her relationship with Ann and with her niece and nephew, Beverly envisions her purpose in the world as something other than mothering. "Some people contribute by raising good children, who will grow up and help the world," she said. "I do it through my political work by helping to make things change, by making things better."

Why, then, is "mothering" the measure by which all other care is judged? Why, still, do people question the intentions, even the sanity, of a woman with no children? Why is the freedom not to bear children a constant political and personal struggle? Why have we no word for adult women without children that is not pejorative (such as "barren") or phrased in the negative ("childless")?

In struggling with these questions, with my mixed feelings about parenthood, I join millions of others striving for a world in which women voluntarily opt to mother or not—without coercion, with joy, with full knowledge of all the possibilities. A world in which each woman's freedom to choose her own life also frees her sisters. Knowing this, I feel less burdened, more confident that time and circumstance and careful thought will lead me into a decision that fits.

I have a clear picture of myself sometimes as the parent of a nine-year-old. I imagine my child going out, coming home, asking questions that make me pause—why people die and what happens afterward, why Jews are different from Buddhists, where dreams come from. She would bring me messages; he would show me a different world than the one I knew as a child.

Other times I see a different life, my days spun around writing, teaching, travel. I work until 2 A.M., spend all day Sunday with coffee and magazines. I live simply, at the spur of my conscience and inclinations. My family will be myself and Elissa, our friends, relatives, neighborhood. We will grow old together. We will be outstanding aunts.

At thirty, I am young enough to spend a few more ambivalent years. In the meantime, I watch for signs—the ravaged trees by the coast road, my nephew burrowing his head into my neck, the ways other women navigate this huge terrain. In the car, I squeeze Elissa's hand, then knuckle around the steering wheel and drive.

One Mom and One "Tia" Raising a Child

ON AN April evening in 1990, Cherry Hartman peered for the first time into the tiny face of Abra Helena Isabela Rosenthall. She'd expected the infant to look squashed, or at least weary from the transcontinental plane ride, the strange smells and unfamiliar voices. Cherry watched from the front steps while Susan Rosenthall eased her car into the driveway, then walked up to the porch, a blanketed bundle in her arms. The baby was beautiful. And Cherry's promise to spend one morning a week with Abra suddenly didn't seem like enough.

Cherry, a therapist and writer, had always wanted a child. She grew up in a large family—six brothers and sisters, twenty-eight nieces and nephews. But she was infertile, and her partners had been women who already had grown children or weren't interested in parenting.

Susan Rosenthall, also a therapist, was a graduate school classmate of Cherry's; their friendship had endured for more than twenty years. When Susan began to talk about adopting, several friends promised to baby-sit. But Cherry was more specific. "I want one morning a week," she told her friend.

Susan remembered an aunt who, along with her best friend, came to all her childhood birthday parties, took her on regular outings. She began to imagine Cherry in that role, doing the things that Susan didn't have interest or time for—taking Abra biking and canoeing, visiting the zoo, reading a favorite book twenty times in a row. They wouldn't be co-parents; Susan would make the decisions and pay the bills for Abra's care. But Cherry's role would be far greater than that of a baby-sitter or friend.

"One of the biggest voids about being single was—when she walked or talked, who would I tell?" Susan said. "I knew if Cherry were that involved, she would care. I could call her." More and more, she imagined Cherry having a lifelong, intimate role in raising Abra.

When Susan finally brought the baby home, after spending a month in Brazil waiting for court documents to be copied in longhand, Cherry waited at the house, leaning eagerly off the front steps. Susan extricated Abra from the car seat and carried her up the path.

"I remember," she said, "that Cherry looked at her and started to cry."

At first, Cherry watched Abra at Susan's house, just three blocks from her own. The baby was so small and seemed so fragile; taking care of her felt like an overwhelming responsibility. Finally Cherry took Abra to her house for just a few hours, then for longer stretches. Soon Abra was spending a few mornings a week with Cherry there. Later, their schedule became more regular—and a bit harder to engineer after Cherry and her partner, Helen, moved out of the neighborhood. They settled into a new routine, with Abra spending every Wednesday and some Saturdays with Cherry.

Their arrangement points to a new possibility for parenting: a single woman need not undertake motherhood entirely alone. And other women need not choose between a full-time commitment to children and none at all. Between those extremes lie a multitude of lives—many of them not yet named.

No English word works to describe Abra and Cherry's relationship. Cherry wanted a title other than "aunt," which her nieces and nephews used and which seemed too ordinary. A Portuguese friend of Susan's suggested "tua tia," which Abra shortened to "Titi." She calls Helen "Humma."

As one of the primary adults in Abra's life, Cherry complements Susan's strengths. The two women have learned to accept each other's quirks. They agree on basic principles: that children thrive on a lot of stimulation, that Abra will not play with guns or Ninja Turtles. But child rearing also revealed the differences between them.

Those inconsistencies didn't alarm Susan, partly because of her history. She and her ex-husband have raised their adolescent son, Simon, together for more than a decade. Although Susan retained custody, Simon spends time regularly at his father's house. What she has learned from that experience, Susan said, is that love and attention are the most critical constants; if small rituals and habits differ between households, kids can adjust.

Cherry used to put Abra to sleep by singing to her and rocking her for hours. Susan advised putting her down and letting her cry for a little while. Susan thought Abra's first solid food should be something chosen by her brother; he picked kiwi fruit, and Abra hated it. Meanwhile, Cherry was feeding her plain rice cereal.

Cherry is fastidiously clean and hates mud and dirt; Susan thinks it's wonderful for Abra to pick up bugs and play in puddles. Cherry takes Abra to the arboretum, a place Susan wouldn't ordinarily go. And to McDonald's, a place that makes Susan cringe.

"I try to let go of that," she told Cherry one afternoon, laughing. "For a while, I was teaching her to say 'yuck' about McDonald's. But *you* teach her to say 'yuck' when she sees dirt."

A more important difference between them stems from their unequal responsibilities. Susan's time with Abra, like any full-time parent's, is complicated by other demands—Simon, the telephone, errands, work, shopping. When Cherry spends time with Abra, she doesn't plan to do anything else, so the child gets undivided attention.

Their relationship to each other, and to Abra, requires flexibility and honesty in equal measure. "In an emergency, I can always call Cherry," Susan said. "I can call and say, 'Do you want her?' And Cherry can say yes or no. We have good boundaries.'" Both women know that a prolonged disagreement between them could disrupt the entire arrangement.

"My commitment is that I won't let that happen," Susan said. "I want it to work. But I've been scared at times. I've thought, Will this episode be the one we can't work through?"

"It's occurred to me that Susan might get mad and break the connection," Cherry said. "This relationship is very dependent on what Susan wants and doesn't want. But it's worth the risk."

Susan and Cherry crouched by the coffee table in Susan's living room, turning pages of a large and carefully assembled photo album. Together, they narrated the story of how Abra came from Cabedelo, Brazil, to her new home. There were pictures of Susan and Simon holding Abra for the first time, on April Fools' Day. Copies of adoption and immigration papers. And photographs of Abra's birth mother.

Susan pointed to one of them, a picture of a young woman in a two-piece bathing suit, her body still soft from pregnancy. There are other photos of her in Abra's album of people who are important in her life. That book holds pictures of Cherry, too, and of her partner, Helen.

"There's nothing more wonderful than having people love you. Abra has these other people who deeply love her, and not just because they've adopted her," Susan said. "I think about Abra, and I look at her, and I see this map that extends out from our home and goes down to Brazil.

"I have a sacred trust to fulfill—one that Abra's birth mother gave to me. I wanted to meet her and tell her I'd do what she trusted me to do. I think because Abra's adopted she's more a child of the world. There's no way to have traveled to where she lived and met her mom and not feel that. You can't be egocentric."

Choosing Not To

AT FIRST, Phyllis Oster kept finding reasons to wait. "I got married when I was very young. We were twenty," she recalled. "Warren had to go into the military almost immediately. We were stationed in Hawaii for two years, and we were broke. Then he was in law school and wanted to finish.

"We were in Washington, D.C., and hated it, and wanted to save money to move. It seemed like there was always a reason not to have children yet."

Looking back, she said, it was clear that logistical delays were not the only issues. For one thing, she'd never felt particularly drawn to babies. And while the two lived in Hawaii they had made friends with people who were involved in the movement for zero population growth.

When they returned to Washington, D.C., they watched their college friends buy suburban houses and wake up for 4 A.M. feedings. A new political lens shaped their vision. They began to save money to move beyond the Capitol Beltway and away from the automatic path most people they knew seemed to be traveling.

"I think we talked about children early on, joked about what our kids would look like, that they'd probably have freckles and red hair. But we didn't spend a lot of time on it," Phyllis remembered. "Growing up, I wasn't your perfect traditional young lady. I wouldn't wear gloves. I got sent home for wearing culottes to high school. I didn't conform to the notion of a nice Jewish girl. I went to college originally to find a husband, but once I fell in love, the idea of having a house in Potomac, Maryland, and baking cookies wasn't very attractive to me."

By the late 1970s, when the couple had resettled on the West Coast and Phyllis had gone back to school and earned a degree in communications, she had been taking birth control pills for ten years. A doctor advised that, for health reasons, she stop taking the pill.

"All of a sudden, we had to make the decision." She and Warren talked about their relationship, their ambitions, how a child might change their lives. They considered the world's overcrowded state and their reluctance to add another person to it.

"We'd had a long period of seeing how children changed other people's lives. We're very spontaneous people. We like to be able to get up and go. I'm not the kind of person who likes to have a lot of restrictions on what I do. Warren and I had a wonderful relationship. We really liked the way we lived together and had grown very accustomed to and comfortable with that. The thought of changing it wasn't appealing.

"I also don't think I ever felt the need to parent. You know how some women say they want to have children to feel fulfilled as women? It's not that I don't like children. But I never felt the need to be a mother."

After much talk, Phyllis and Warren reached a decision. Phyllis got rid of her birth control pills. Warren scheduled an appointment for a vasectomy. "We were ready to make the decision," she said. "I don't think there was any sense of loss. We felt we were doing something positive."

PHYLLIS curled on the end of a pale mauve couch in a living room filled with books and records. A vase of brightly colored blown glass stood on the mantel, near a photograph of herself and Warren in evening dress. At forty-five, Phyllis wears her red hair cut short; freckles are the only decoration on her expressive face. In her kitchen, a row of pro-choice and other political buttons stands on the windowsill.

Fifteen years after deciding not to have children, Phyllis's attention has shifted to other matters. Her job working for a congressional representative. Her sixteen-month anniversary of quitting smoking. Her relationship with Warren. Her work on the board of Planned Parenthood and the community relations committee of the Jewish Federation.

Recently she started a support and health care group for women friends. "Most of us are between forty and forty-five," she said. "Some have had hysterectomies. We talk about menopause. Children are in the past."

Sometimes, though, she remembers that her decision not to raise children remains anomalous in a culture that still points to motherhood as less of a choice than an inevitability. "If people ask if I have children and I say no, I often wonder what they're thinking. I know that some people will jump to the conclusion that something was wrong. They can't believe you'd *choose* not to."

When she and Warren were first married, she said, "Warren had one family friend who would ask me at parties, loudly, if I was still taking birth control pills. People would ask us all the time when we were going to have children and why we hadn't had any yet. My mother was very worried that she was going to die without grandchildren. Each set of parents thought the other spouse was crazy and was influencing the other not to have kids."

But when Phyllis and Warren actually made their decision, such admonishments took second place to their own inclinations. "The voices saying, 'Do it,' were the voices of tradition saying, 'You're *supposed* to do this.' Evidently, they weren't very strong."

What about her influence on the future, on the next generation? Phyllis's voice rises and her speech quickens. "I feel strongly about overpopulation. The resources are being used up. I feel like I've impacted the future a lot by *not* having children."

Three Moms and a Baby Open the Door to Adoption

For seven years, Sara searched, waited, and hoped for a child. First she tried to adopt through the state Children's Services Division, but it was clear the agency frowned on lesbian parents. Even if she could pass as heterosexual, single women faced poor odds; caseworkers told her she'd be unlikely to get a child younger than eight.

Then she considered an international adoption. But, as an early childhood educator who worked in a preschool, Sara couldn't afford thousands of dollars in attorneys' fees, airfares, and agency costs.

With her partner, Rita, she kept looking. She tried Open Adoption and Family Services, paid $2,000 for a home study, then languished on a waiting list for two years. One potential adoption foundered when Sara and Rita went to meet the pregnant young woman and her mother, who balked at the sight of a lesbian couple. Other clients, teenagers in church-run homes for unwed mothers, were uneasy because Sara is Jewish.

Undaunted, Sara combed through the Yellow Pages and wrote to every obstetrician listed; doctors, she thought, might know of pregnant women who were planning to give up their babies. Every time she and Rita went to a party or met a new friend, they talked about wanting to adopt. They imagined their message moving through the community like a persistent tentacle; eventually, it would touch the right place, the perfect person.

"One day I came home from work and the phone rang," Rita recalled. "It was my chiropractor. She said, 'Are you still interested in adopting? I know of a woman who knows a woman who's five months pregnant, lives on the street, and wants to give her baby to lesbians.'"

SHAENA was seventeen when she got pregnant as the result of a rape. When she was *still* pregnant, despite the trauma following the attack and the police department's routine D and C, she decided it must be a sign that she was meant to have the baby.

She'd been living on the streets, on and off, since the first time she ran away at age seven and ended up in a New York City department store. Later she slept in subway tunnels, befriended a hot dog vendor who fed her from his cart, and hitchhiked her way across the country.

For a while she was a pimp. Then she sold drugs. She carried a gun. Her nickname was Crazy. But the callous shell protected an idealistic soul; Shaena wrote long, impassioned poems about love, being a young lesbian, and her dreams for a more peaceful life.

For ten years, luck and a street-smart nature—gregarious, clever, and resourceful—helped her survive. Still, she watched other kids die, ruined by drugs and violence. She figured she probably wouldn't make it to twenty-one.

"When I got pregnant I thought, You have a baby now. You can't be doing twenty-four hours with no sleep, you can't go without eating. You've got to be concerned about this little life you're carrying.

"For a while I was thinking of raising the child myself. Then I thought, what kind of world am I going to bring this child into? A world where fear is there every day, where you don't know where you're going to eat or sleep next. That was the turning point. I had to find a family that would love him and take care of him, raise him with at least some of the things I would like to have given him.

"I tried a bunch of families who told me that juvenile delinquency and drug abuse and being gay were all hereditary. I thought, Get out of my face. Then I was talking to my counselor and she said, 'How would you feel about giving your child up to somebody who's gay?' I said, Is there anybody who'd want him? She said, 'Yes, are you kidding?'

"I got called back within two hours."

BY PHONE, the three arranged to meet. Still reeling from the adoption prospect that had fallen through, Sara and Rita kept putting on and rejecting different outfits. They took Shaena out for hamburgers and ended up talking for three hours. Rita, the youngest of ten in her Mexican-

American family, had suffered abuse while growing up; she could empathize with Shaena's troubled childhood. When she'd gobbled the last French fry from her plate, Shaena told the women she wanted them to adopt her baby.

"She really liked us. We really liked her. From the very first, she was straightforward with us," Sara said. "She was very intelligent. And there was no way she would have given up her child in a closed adoption."

Shaena got a lawyer. Sara and Rita got a lawyer. They began to work out the details, agreeing that Shaena would sign papers relinquishing the baby three days after the birth. What followed "was the longest four months of our lives," Sara said. Rita shook her head, remembering. "It was as if our child was having a child."

Shaena had decided to quit using drugs and alcohol while she was pregnant. But she couldn't give up the cigarettes. She twisted them nervously in her fingers, blew quick spurts of smoke from the side of her mouth. Every two weeks, Rita took her shopping for groceries, stocking up on bread and soup and fruit. Sara or Rita went to most of her prenatal appointments; Shaena visited their house and saw the room where her baby would sleep. By this time, Shaena was back in touch with her parents and arranged for them to meet Sara and Rita.

"We were worried because of the last experience," Sara said. "But her mom took one look at us and said, 'Oh, thank God it's you. I'm so relieved.'"

At the time, Shaena was involved with a social service agency's transition program for homeless youth. Even though her housing was stable and her counseling appointments regular, her life still lurched from emergency to emergency. "We'd get phone calls in the middle of the night: 'I have the measles.' Or, 'Someone kicked me in the stomach,'" Sara recalled.

"Fourteen days before the due date," Rita said, "she called and said, 'I'm tired of being pregnant. I'm tired of being fat.' There was a concert she wanted to go to, and she was talking about losing weight by then so she could get into her leather pants. She said she was going to have her labor induced."

Sara and Rita packed their video camera and headed to the hospital. A cluster of Shaena's friends were camped out in her room. Shaena was groaning and swearing her way through each contraction. She was desperate for a cigarette.

Simon was born two weeks early. Before and after work, Sara and Rita showed up at the hospital and Shaena would hand over the baby, saying, "Here's your son." After three days, she signed the papers that made it official. "We were so worried that it wouldn't actually happen," Sara said. "When she said she wanted to be with him for three days in the hospital, we really flipped out. But somehow it all worked."

IN TRADITIONAL, closed adoptions, a child's new family supplanted all mention of the old. That secrecy seemed to rise from a sense of threat, both actual and imagined. A birth mother might want her child back. Or the past might exert some invisible, irresistible pull, dragging the child away from her adopted life.

Open adoption rewrites that scenario. When Sara and Rita adopted Simon, they attached their lives to another world—one that included Shaena and her parents, the rhythms of urban street life, a history completely unlike each of theirs.

In this family, the fact of adoption is impossible to mask. Sara is tall, voluble and open, with masses of graying, curly hair. Rita is equally direct, but more quiet and intense, with dark eyes under a fringe of hair that is almost black. Simon, at three, is fair, corn-silk blond, and blue-eyed.

Once, when Rita was picking Simon up from day care, she walked through the door side by side with a tall blond mother who was carrying her Guatemalan child. A third parent remarked, "Oh, are you two trading children for the day?"

"I've become acutely aware of how much family conversation revolves around who resembles each other. And he will never resemble anyone in my or Rita's family," Sara said. "We were reading a children's book the other day that said something like, 'Most people look like their parents.' I thought, what is this nonsense?"

Hiding is not her style; with Simon, as with anyone else, Sara prefers to tell the truth. "We really wanted an open adoption. Everything I had read talked about adopted adults at some point needing to go through a search to find their birth parents. I didn't want my child to go through that.

"We agreed that we would exchange pictures and letters with Shaena twice a year. After we met her parents, we included them in that. We send photos on his birthday and at Christmas. Her parents have called a few times and asked if it would be okay to give him a present. Shaena calls regularly, lets us know where she is."

Sometimes they still get nervous. Once, when Shaena showed up at their home unannounced, Rita instinctively pushed Simon's high chair out of view. But she believes Simon has a right to all of his complicated history.

"I truly believe people should know where they come from," Rita said. "We thought if we were comfortable about it, he would be, too."

So far, he is. Now that Simon is old enough to ask, he requests the details again and again. "Tell me the story of how you got me, Mamas," he says.

WHEN I visited Shaena three years after the adoption, she pointed proudly to the wall of her apartment, where she displays the certificates of valor she earned from serving in the U.S. Army during Desert Storm. Then she pulled a wallet from her rear pocket and showed me a picture of Simon, dressed in bright colors. He has her hair.

"Even though I miss him a great deal, I think I made the right decision by him. When I came back from the war last year, I made copies of all my citations and sent them to him. So when he grows up, he can say, 'These are the medals my Mommy won.'

"I want him to have a mother he can be proud of, just as I'm proud of him. That gives me extra incentive to achieve. After he was born, I reached a depression stage where I wanted to die. I almost drank myself to death. The only reason I didn't commit suicide was that I thought, What's he going to do when he wants to see his mommy? I couldn't do that to him. I couldn't drop out on him.

"In a way, it's my baby who's kept me alive for a long time. It's because of him that I keep going."

Adoption is almost always framed as a zero-sum equation—one mother's loss becomes another's boon. For this family, the terms are not so simple. Everyone celebrates; everyone's scared; everyone survives. When it is Simon's turn to assemble a life, all the complex pieces of his past will be there, waiting.

Conceiving a Family of Two

"I DON'T have anything profound or original to say about why I wanted a child. It was just always there for me. As far back as I can remember, I wanted to have children. Every time I passed a playground or somebody with a child, I just knew I had to have that." That desire propelled Sandy Diamond from Cleveland, Ohio, to California, where, she thought, people would be more tolerant of a single mother and her child.

Today, she would have plenty of company, even in Cleveland; by the 1990s, one-fourth of all babies born in the United States were born to unmarried mothers. But in 1972, Sandy's was an unusual—and widely misunderstood—choice.

"When people say, 'Oh, you were brave to do it alone,' that is not true," Sandy said. "I was selfish. I was doing what I wanted. Courage really didn't have anything to do with it. Courage came in later, when things were difficult and I had to keep going.

"I was doing large oil paintings then. I had a friend who was a painter and had a child and she just put away her oils for four years, at least until the child was in kindergarten. I was ready to do that, too. That didn't feel like a problem at all. I worked for years at dreadful clerical jobs at which I had no aptitude so I could save the money to stay home with the baby.

"I was thirty-six when I had Gabriel. I wanted the child to be conceived in love and for the father to know what was going on. I was despairing of finding a man who would agree and who was worthy. And then, I did.

"It was at a Halloween party. I'd worked for three years. I had enough money saved up. This person came along. He was part Native American. He had dressed as a medicine doctor. He had the feathers, a papier-mâché mask. He was talking this pseudo war-chant stuff. He was absolutely magnetic. And he was very agreeable to my plan. I felt like I was stealing the baby from the heavens.

"He wanted to get married. I wouldn't take money from him, nothing. I didn't want anybody else calling the shots. I did leave the place I'd been living alone and found a three-and-a-half-bedroom house, so that I could have friends, a woman and a man, living there, a joint household. They were Gabriel's godparents. I did see that as family. But they were younger, in their early twenties. We all stuck together for a few years, and then they moved on.

"At least I had planned not to be mother and baby alone and isolated. We had friends who were around a lot; Gabe had a lot of attention. I wrote to my family in Ohio about it when I was about five or six months pregnant and tried to break it to them gently. It wasn't like I was a kid, trying to rebel. I wanted them to know. I was presenting them with a fait accompli.

"I got back some warnings and a lot of concern and then, closer to the birth, more and more loving support. I know I had some sorrow that he didn't have biological family around. I felt sort of guilty; the selfishness of what I had done hit me.

"And yet, using the word 'selfish'—it just seems like it couldn't have been any other way. I think something in me would have died if I could not have had a child. I called it selfish only to deflect all the reactions of people trying to make me into a kind of hero about it."

In Sandy's house, photographs lined the wall between the living room and kitchen. In one, she lay on the grass in a long white dress, her dark hair pooled beneath her, an infant Gabriel curled on her chest. In the living room were more recent pictures, including a high school graduation shot of a handsome, intent young man with dark hair and green eyes.

Sometimes, Sandy said, she felt pulled between nurturing her son and feeding her art. "No matter how much you love your kid, if you're in the ecstasy of writing, you would like your child to vaporize for a while because you can't stop.

"Once I went to a support group for single mothers. I thought they would all be like me—deliberate single mothers. But they weren't. They were all women whose men had left them. I didn't feel related to them at all.

"There were times when I wished it could have been otherwise. Especially as Gabriel got old enough to notice that other kids had fathers. I couldn't bluff that away. It was hard. I felt I had cheated him. And yet, he wouldn't have been there at all if I hadn't done what I did.

"Gabriel is a great companion. We have the same sense of humor. We have a lot of fun together. I really like him. I like how his mind works. He's a good, good person. And he's his own person. He doesn't follow other people's ways. I think he's way ahead of me. It took me much longer to realize I didn't have to belong to anything other than the human race.

"Eventually he's going to fly the coop, one way or another. And that's fine. I'm really on guard against being too grabby of him, because in a sense I've had him to myself all this time."

Sandy had a dreamlike way of talking, as if on the delivery end of a constant stream of visions. As an artist and a person, she latched on to an idea and pursued it down winding paths. She could not always predict her project's course. It happened with her collages. It happened during the Gulf War, when she and Gabriel and two other women and their kids stood on a street corner with a sign, protesting, and soon there were more than four hundred people flocking to weekly demonstrations.

And it happened again when she sold her city house and moved to a farm in a small coastal town. Some friends cautioned that she'd never be able to afford California property again. Others wondered how she could leave her child. "My child," Sandy repeated, laughing, "who was turning eighteen at that point and who *needed* his mother to leave him."

Gabriel, an aspiring actor, moved into a Victorian house in San Francisco, found work ushering at a theater, and quickly established a reputation among his housemates as an excellent cook. Sandy discovered that he wrote rich and funny letters.

"That's how I've done my whole life. I didn't know who my child's family would be before I did it. I couldn't know he would be mad at me when he realized other people had fathers. And I couldn't know he would stop being mad because half those kids' fathers went away.

"I think it's not single-mindedness, what I've done. I think it's mindlessness—hopefully, in the holy sense. Calligraphers practice alphabets all the time. B comes after A, and C comes after that. You just keep going. Gabe and I taught each other our ABCs."

One Parent, One Child, Two Cultures

ELIZABETH Des Camp remembers the day adoption suddenly meant more than stacks of paperwork and endless phone calls. She was shopping with her best friend, Julia, in a large department store. Julia grabbed Elizabeth's arm and dragged her toward the children's section. Racks of tiny jumpsuits, toddler T-shirts, and miniature overalls surrounded her.

"I was doing a lot of swimming at the time, and I saw this teeny little red swimsuit with ruffles. I just started to cry: Oh, I'm going to have a baby. That was probably the moment of knowing, buying that little swimsuit."

Elizabeth was thirty-two when she felt the pull toward parenthood. She'd spent time with friends' children—hours that were simultaneously too much and not enough. Sometimes she felt relieved to hand the kids back to their parents. At the same time, she craved a primary role with a child of her own.

I visited Elizabeth and her daughter, Maya, on a clear spring weeknight, warm enough to linger outside in the long evening. We sat on the porch of their wide house. Elizabeth had shed her work uniform of stockings, red pumps, and a linen skirt for jeans and a sweatshirt that read, "Honoring Our Differences: Through Diversity Comes Unity." On a recent impulse, she'd had her long blond hair chopped to collar-length.

Within minutes of my arrival, Maya, then eight, had shown off a book she wrote and illustrated about going to summer camp and demonstrated her jump-rope prowess on the porch. Hot pink clothes set off toffee-toned skin; her East Indian ancestry showed in her delicate features, espresso eyes, and satin-black hair.

"You can ride your bike as far as that green car," Elizabeth said, pointing halfway up the block.

"But that's *boring*," Maya protested, rolling her eyes.

THERE were eight Des Camp children in Elizabeth's family. Elizabeth was the fifth, a "rebellious middle child." She and her brothers and sisters spent days building imaginary cities in the Georgia swamps, catching polliwogs and looking out for snakes. At the tail end of a hurricane, her mother would let all the kids go outside in their bathing suits to be soaked by the last surges of wind and rain.

"We thought we were the luckiest kids in the world," Elizabeth said. "I realize in retrospect that she was probably out of her mind with us.

"I never saw myself as someone who'd get married and do traditional things. I just couldn't imagine that I would ever get married. It wasn't about sex. It was a matter of wanting so much not to have that life, being sure that wasn't a life for me."

When Elizabeth decided to have a child, she felt uneasy about bringing another infant into a world already crowded with children. Yet an international adoption raised other concerns. "I was really aware that sometimes parents in Third World countries are forced into selling kids. I didn't want to be a part of that. I had a real commitment to making sure the child didn't have other options."

She plunged into the adoption process with characteristic Elizabeth Des Camp fervor. Working with PLAN International Adoption Service, she attended weekly preadoption classes, gathered letters of reference from friends and employers, had home visits from a social worker, endured financial checks and questions about her emotional stability.

And then she waited. Finally, PLAN called with good news: Elizabeth had been assigned a baby girl from India, born six weeks premature but healthy. She drove to her parents' house with a bottle of champagne.

Still, the adoption seemed unreal. There was no pregnancy, no changing body to make motherhood tangible. There was only a photograph of a round-faced infant with a fringe of dark hair. The day the picture arrived, Elizabeth took one look and cabled to Calcutta. "Yes, yes, send this baby as soon as possible." Then she came home and stuck the picture to her refrigerator door.

WHEN Maya arrived at the airport, friends and family were there waiting for the plane. As it glided into view, Elizabeth's brother nudged her. "It's not much different from my kids' births," he said, "except for the size of the placenta."

Maya stayed awake for forty-eight hours straight. Even after that, she never slept much. She suffered severe milk allergies and vomited formula across the kitchen. Elizabeth fed her soy milk and walked her endlessly, over the black-and-white kitchen linoleum, up and down the long hallway, around the block.

"There is no way to anticipate the constancy of need that little kids have," she said. "But also the surprise, the delight."

And the slow building of simple routines. On Saturdays, a friend usually comes over to play outside with Maya while Elizabeth gardens. Sunday is Quaker Meeting day. Most evenings, Elizabeth leaves work promptly at five; the two always eat together, first joining hands to thank the plants and animals and people who brought their food. At bedtime, they cuddle and read out loud.

ELIZABETH'S passions about diversity proved easier to stamp on a sweatshirt than to enact in real life, particularly in a city that is 85 percent white. When Maya was an infant, a stranger in the park near their home muttered, "Get that nigger baby out of here," as the two passed. When she enrolled Maya in a day care center, play group, or camp, Elizabeth always checked the ethnic balance. Would Maya be the only one with dark skin, the only one who was seen as different? It wasn't easy trying to raise her daughter amid stereotypes of both gender and race.

"It gets more difficult as she gets older. There's a constant attention to her looks. People notice that she's pretty, not that she's smart or wiry or any of the other things she is. I've become much more aware of the racism nonwhite people live with every day," she said.

Elizabeth smiled ruefully, remembering her early resolve that Maya would be raised biculturally. She played Indian music at home from the time Maya was a baby; she often filled the kitchen with the scents of curries and raitas. When Maya got older, they joined the Indian Cultural Association, spent Saturdays learning traditional dances and celebrated cultural festivals. For a while, Maya went to a cooperative day care center with an Indian teacher. And her best friend, Mira, was the Indian daughter of a single woman from Elizabeth's preadoption class.

"I can introduce her to some of her culture, but I can't raise her to be an Indian. At a certain point, Maya said, 'I don't want that Indian music. I want Raffi.' I thought I could actually have her be a little Indian American. But she's a Des Camp. I've come to see that. And it's fine. It's complicated. I hope that her life is much richer for being a bicultural kid.

"We're alike about some things," Elizabeth said of her daughter. "We're both really verbal. We're both pretty affectionate. We're both intuitive types. We both have tons of energy. We can keep going and going and going. I couldn't have a daughter who's more my daughter than Maya is. That's quite clear."

Opting for Motherhood at Forty-One

WITHIN hours after her daughter, Julia's, birth, Nan Narboe understood one of the implications of being a forty-one-year-old first-time mother. She showed me photographs that brought the realization back in vivid detail. There she was in a flower-sprigged cotton hospital gown, one long forearm cradling Julia.

"I remember seeing how striped and veiny my hands were compared to how soft and dewy this baby was. That was one of the ways it registered: I am an older mom."

After nearly six years of motherhood, Nan told her story with articulate hindsight. In so many ways, her experience of conception, pregnancy, and childbirth was shaped by the parallel growth and maturity of two entities—herself and the feminist movement.

When she was eleven, Nan recalled, she read in a women's magazine that the ideal wife would greet her husband at the end of a day's work, with the salad made and the barbecue coals smoking. "I remember very clearly thinking, If that's what it takes, I can't do it."

She didn't. Born on the leading edge of the postwar baby boom, Nan took inspiration first from her own mother and grandmother, then from the feminist consciousness-raising of her college years. At nineteen, a college friend showed off her engagement ring and Nan blurted, "Oh, that's too bad."

In her early twenties, she founded a prominent French restaurant; in her thirties, she began to build a private practice in psychotherapy. She married at thirty-four. And she became pregnant just a few weeks before her forty-first birthday.

"I am so much a beneficiary of other feminists," Nan told me, and her eyes crested with tears. "My grandmother had her own business. My mother worked. And she had married late—she was twenty-eight. I came to hold two ideas: one was that I had better be self-supporting and have a good life with or without a husband, and two, I'd better have generation and satisfaction with or without a child.

"The feminist analysis I had to date made it clear that I had better examine the 'givens.' I got the message that the life you lived was a result of the choices you made."

By the time she became pregnant, Nan had grasped and practiced another important feminist concept: that women need the support of other women to make decisions that are right for them.

"A woman I liked, who happened to be my next-door neighbor, was a midwife. Before I conceived, I asked her to help me find a gynecologist.

"You are testing a lot of things when you say to a doctor, I'm shopping, and one of the criteria for my business is that you treat this midwife as an equal. It took two or three tries. I remember once walking out of a doctor's office in a rage. Then I found a doctor who felt right and had no qualms about delivering with a midwife."

Nan's forty-something friends had either long since given birth to their children or decided not to have any; the pregnant women she knew were twenty years younger. But she gathered practical support, care, and advice from sources she'd learned to trust: a few books, practitioners of Rolfing and massage, and a colleague with two children, who helped Nan figure out how much time to plan away from her practice.

For nine months, Nan had little interest in books describing the physical and emotional changes of pregnancy: she wanted to experience being pregnant, not study it. But once Julia was born, she became fascinated—and frustrated—with the available material on child rearing.

"Much of the information is written for naive consumers. As a grown-up, I knew I was being given a mixture of research and myth and convenience and things that were taught when the pediatrician trained twenty years ago. I was forty-one, and it seemed to me I was as likely to be right as the next person. You can't be twenty and take that position."

Nan pored eagerly over the writing of Magda Gerber, a Hungarian-born parent-educator whose theories were based on complete respect for infants and children. "She walks you through what that would look like—for example, getting the baby's permission before you pick her up," Nan said.

"The child-rearing and schooling practices to which I've been attracted are radical positions about the respect due every baby and every human being. Part of being an older mother, for me, was knowing I'd be more likely to find theories that fit at the edge than in the middle.

"The question had become, Is this right for me? rather than, Is this right?"

That confidence allowed Nan to stick to her beliefs, even when friends or medical providers were skeptical. She refused to own or use a baby thermometer because "I don't want things stuck in orifices"; if Julia seemed alarmingly hot to the touch, Nan took her to the doctor. She combed through child-rearing literature, even when friends scoffed that she was "intellectualizing" motherhood. She hired Laurie Todd, then a graduate student in history, as a caregiver, and arranged her life so that she, her husband, Daniel, and Laurie traded shifts caring for Julia.

And she talked freely, frequently, about the sensations, the fears, and the challenges of motherhood—a dialogue with friends and family that Nan said would have been impossible fifteen or twenty years earlier. At a wedding, she recalled, she traded snickers with another nursing mother as they talked about their anticipation of going home to feed their babies; nursing was better than sex, they joked. "At twenty, I don't think it would have seemed appropriate to have said that out loud, much less to make ribald jokes about it," Nan said.

Friends raised eyebrows at some of the decisions Nan, Daniel, and Laurie made about Julia's care. As a feminist historian, Laurie helped Nan deflect that criticism by reminding her that notions of "appropriate" child rearing vary enormously from culture to culture and decade to decade. And as a lesbian, Laurie brought a history of questioning society's conventions. "When you're outside the culture in some way," Laurie said, "you're able to critique things in the culture that are taken for granted. So many people have such limited vision about possibilities."

Nan, Laurie, and Daniel agreed that even the most mundane decisions about child care were steeped in values. "Here's an example," Nan said. "Julia's a toddler. We're discussing what to teach her about finding food on the floor: Do you pick it up and eat it, or do you throw it away? We had the understanding that this was a discussion about poverty in America, about middle-class fastidiousness.

"Many things that are done automatically, we did not do automatically."

Nan leafed again through the pictures snapped during Julia's first days, then showed a more recent photo, her daughter dressed in bright red, holding a camera up to her eye. Her own parents worried about spoiling children, Nan recalled. But her experience as a therapist convinced her that being adored is good for people.

"I was done fighting with myself about who I was," she said. "I'm grateful to be a mother who is happy to luxuriate in my child's beauty, in her intelligence, in her smell. Being older is being unafraid of my own passion for this person, my fierceness on her behalf. I'm a more extreme mother than I would have had the guts to be when I was younger."

When Nan was unable to find a private or public school that matched her values, she sought other like-minded parents and started Cascade Valley School, based on the Sudbury Valley School in Massachusetts. The school stresses children's autonomy and ability to decide what and when they will learn.

Instead of resuming a full-time psychotherapy practice, Nan arranged to see clients only half-time and spend the rest of her working hours at the school. She shook her head, in tears again, talking about the unexpected passion she found in motherhood and the unplanned places that passion had led.

"I said, Okay, this is hard *and* I'm going to do it. When you become a mother that way, you are choosing a transforming experience. Someone said having a child was like living with your heart outside your body. It is very unsafe, very powerful, very joy-giving.

"One of the pieces older mothers are going to contribute is this: We've had enough experiences of going after and getting what we wanted that 'This is not how it's done' is not going to be an adequate response for us.

"Part of being a mother, for me, is constant distress when other people treat questions of motherhood thoughtlessly, treat children thoughtlessly. I didn't know that in having a baby I'd be setting out on a path that would take me this far from conventional parenting."

Adopting as a Single Parent

BY THE time Becky Birtha was in her early thirties, she knew she wanted three things—to live in community with other people, to love a woman, to raise a child. What she got was more like a set of jugglers' plates. One item would be firmly in hand, while the others flew overhead or plummeted to the ground. First she had community, but no lover and no child. Then, for ten years, she lived with a woman who didn't want children.

By the time I visited her, Becky had Tasha, her three-year-old adopted daughter. A row house in West Philadelphia. A cat. And a perpetual, sometimes exhausting struggle to blend the grit of single parenthood with her ideals of community.

"As a little girl, I used to borrow books from the library whenever I found a story about a child who was an orphan," she remembered. "There used to be articles in magazines where adoption agencies would advertise, and you'd send your name and address and they'd send you all these pictures of children.

"I used to write to them, fill out the coupon. They didn't realize it was from a ten-year-old kid. I would get a little packet in the mail with pictures of Korean children. I can remember laying them out on the kitchen table and trying to interest my mother in discussing which would make the best sister for me.

"I never imagined myself living a lifestyle without children, even though in actuality most of my life has been spent without being a parent. Coming out as a lesbian made me recognize the concept of a lesbian or a gay family, and also the concept of people without children constituting a family. But I still wanted to have children. By the time I came out I'd already decided I wanted to adopt as a single parent."

After several years away, Becky moved back to her home city of Philadelphia. A Quaker-based group had set up an intentional community in

West Philadelphia, a neighborhood of row houses with linked front porches and stamp-sized yards.

Becky liked the group's philosophy—most members worked at part-time "bread labor" jobs and devoted the rest of their hours to social activism. She moved into one of the community's houses, purposely choosing one that included two children. The adults rotated cooking, chores, and child care; they made their own bread, granola, and yogurt. Bulletin boards at each house advertised potlucks, workshops on nonviolence, and other activities. Most friends lived within walking distance.

"It was really wonderful. You automatically had a group of friends who shared your values. Sort of like college," Becky said. It was the mid-1970s, and a women's community was just beginning to gel. After a year, Becky moved out of the community house and into a collectively run women's household. Then she fell in love.

"I lived alone with my lover for ten years. But my partner wasn't really interested in having children. I put my desire for children on hold for a long time. One of the reasons that relationship didn't continue was that I reached a point where I wasn't willing to put that on hold anymore."

TASHA crouched at the top of the steep staircase leading from the living room to upstairs. Slowly, one or two steps at a time, she inched down, shy of the stranger in her living room. Our meeting had been scheduled for the day before, but Becky phoned in the morning to ask for a day's reprieve. A friend had offered to take Tasha to the zoo, and Becky was desperate for the afternoon to write.

I knew Becky only from her stories and poetry, strong-voiced and vibrant with images of her African American roots. In person she was unassuming, a slight woman dressed in jeans and a light blue shirt, with a soft and thoughtful way of speaking.

She told me how she had envisioned raising a child amid a network of people—neighbors, friends from the women's community and the Quaker meeting she attended regularly. That kind of support seemed possible during the adoption process, when she didn't have a car and friends took turns driving her to the foster home where Tasha was living. Then Tasha came home, and the promises of support seemed to dim.

"Everyone thinks it's wonderful, but people just aren't available on the same kind of schedule I'm on. I need people who can see me in the daytime or are comfortable having half a conversation with me while I'm being interrupted every five minutes.

"Some friends are really jealous; some are impatient. People invite me to things that start at nine o'clock at night. They're on a different cycle. People do let me know about parties and poetry readings. It's just that most of the time I'm not able to do those things. I can't get there, because I don't have a car. There's a lesbian and gay adoptive parents support group, but it meets in a place you can't get to by public transportation."

Mornings were some of the hardest times to be a solo parent. Becky tried to wake up fifteen minutes before her daughter, enough time to tip-toe to the shower, get dressed and start breakfast. When she taught at Bryn Mawr College in the Philadelphia suburbs, she spent half an hour walking Tasha to day care, then took a trolley to the train station and a commuter train to campus.

In the afternoon, she'd follow that journey in reverse. She would hurry to put dinner together—often a simple meal of pizza or scrambled eggs—and spend time with her daughter. Sometimes they feasted on leftovers with a man whose daughter attended Tasha's day care center. Tasha often didn't fall asleep until 10 P.M. Then Becky got to work, grading papers, reading and preparing for classes, sinking into bed at 2 or 3 A.M.

"Having been a woman without children for so much of my adult life, I really can see the contrast—what you give up when you have kids. I also can see how it could be different."

Becky described her ideal: a deliberate community of people she already knew and loved. Gay men and lesbians. Quaker families. People of color. Each household would have private living space but also would share a kitchen and dining area. Adults would take turns with chores, cooking, watching the children. Outside would be grass and trees, safe places for kids to play.

"I haven't given up the idea of community. It wouldn't have to be an intentional community with everybody putting their money together, but just two or three households on a block who maybe would eat together a couple nights a week. Or every Saturday one of us would take the kids to the park and the others would get a break.

"It's an old dream that's not ready to die yet," she told me six months after our first interview. "And I'd love to meet someone who also has a child and wants to have more children. I'd like to have another child, but I don't know if I could do it. It's really hard to have one, alone."

There are things Becky wants, for herself, for Tasha. Parenthood makes the juggling act more frenzied. She continues to grasp for each spinning saucer as it soars and drops.

"Mostly, I would like Tasha to grow up with a larger sense of alternatives and possibilities than I grew up with. I'd like for her to know that there are people who live alone as adults, that there are people who have roommates. I'd like her to know about lesbian families and gay families and adoptive families and racially mixed families. I'd like her not to assume that the nuclear, two-parent, white, heterosexual, middle-class family is the norm."

Extending the Picture:
When Former Partners Stay Family

WHEN Elissa first broke the news, I wanted to run away. Portland was too small, the lesbian community too snugly woven. Of all the houses available in this city of half a million people, Elissa's ex-lover had chosen to buy the one next door.

I tried to be a good sport, but inside, I simmered. I could accept that Elissa and Peg sustained their friendship after breaking up. I could understand the car-sharing arrangement, the convenience and safety of holding keys to each other's home. But I preferred to keep the boundaries sharp, my present life with Elissa tucked neatly out of range from her past.

Now, here they were, Peg and her lover, Kate, moving into the peeling sea green house not fifty feet away, nothing but a raggedy border of rosebushes between us. The first time the four of us had dinner together, I managed to push only a few mouthfuls of fettuccine down my anxious throat. The conversation moved in fits and starts, and I was relieved when we finally turned on the VCR and no longer had to talk.

At Passover, Elissa and I argued bitterly about how, where, and with whom we would celebrate. For years, she and Peg had planned women's seders together; they wanted to continue that tradition, even though they were no longer lovers. I wanted to continue my own custom of hosting seders with Rachel and John. Finally we decided to have two seders, one at Rachel and John's house and another with Peg and Kate. I wanted no part in the planning of that one. But as I sat at the seder table, lighting candles and chanting blessings with Peg, Elissa, and a half-dozen women friends, I felt flushes of jealousy and resentment. How had I ended up in this configuration, this unfamiliar, unchosen family?

I thought about my relatives, how my father had married my mother's family. That's not what the rabbi said, of course. But it was the expectation my mother made clear, the first time she and my father visited the New Jersey beach house. This is where I live, she said; these are the people I love, and you will learn to love them, too.

For their part, my mother's relatives readily embraced my father. Bubie sent donations to the Oxford Circle Jewish Community Center whenever he returned safely from covering the World Series or a Las Vegas boxing match. My mother's cousins cornered him at parties to ask about the Phillies' chances that spring. As far as I could see, my family's connections—mapped by blood and marriage—were predictable and unambiguous. When one cousin was divorced, her former husband simply vanished from our midst and his name rarely came up. The lines were clear: you were in or you were out.

No wonder, years later, I felt frustrated and confused when the lines began to bend, cross, and assume startling new directions.

POPULAR culture depicts estranged couples as opposing forces in a permanent war of vengeance. It's the flip side of the romantic myth: either live happily ever after or become lifelong foes.

Clearly there are other possibilities. It's long been a custom—practically a cliché—for lesbian couples to remain friends after a breakup. That phenomenon might stem partly from a sense of scarcity; people in small, oppressed communities often feel reluctant to make enemies with each other. It may also be an effort to counter the invisibility lesbians face; perhaps remaining close with ex-partners helps to affirm, in the face of a hostile, doubting world, that the relationship *did* exist.

I think there's more. A habit of keeping former lovers in the family stems from an important vision, with impact far beyond the lesbian community—a recognition that relationships rarely evolve or dissolve in clear-cut ways, that it is possible to love a person deeply yet no longer wish to make a life with her.

When I began to look, I also found heterosexual women who had remained close to their ex-husbands or partners, making new patterns of kinship as both of their lives continued to change. These relationships called for more than the polite cooperation required to maintain joint custody arrangements; I saw women with and without children maintaining ties to ex-lovers and spouses for their own sakes. They didn't want to abandon years of shared history or lose an important, intimate friend.

These efforts to make family with ex-partners challenge the myth of eternal love and replace it with something more complicated and more pragmatic. Today, one out of every two marriages does not last. For both heterosexual and lesbian women, the ideal of a single lifetime partner is ceding to the reality of serial commitments that last for two, or ten, or twenty years, but not necessarily forever.

Still, we have no words, let alone models, for healing and maintaining relationships as they shift course. Existing terms always use the past as a reference—"ex-lover," "former partner"—while failing to articulate what the relationship means now. Sustaining such bonds requires not only semantic ingenuity but emotional endurance, two partners willing to paddle through jealousy, possessiveness, grief, guilt, and anger in order to reach friendship on the other shore.

I HAD tried it myself and found the trip a challenging one. From the time I was in high school, the pattern of my friends' breakups made no sense to me. On Tuesday you could be sweethearts, leaving flirty notes in each other's locker, celebrating your seven-month anniversary with pepperoni pizza. Then—boom!—by Friday you were enemies, cold-shouldering each other in the hallway, divvying up your friends, returning the ID bracelet and the borrowed sweatshirt. Through high school and college I felt determined at least to make peace, if not family, with my former boyfriends. Anything else seemed both painful and absurd.

In college, I dated Barry for nine months and ended the relationship shortly before we both graduated. In that time, he'd become close to my family, spending Thanksgiving with us, holding vigil by my grandmother's hospital bed, dancing the hora at my cousin's bar mitzvah.

When we broke up, Barry and my family stayed in touch. He and my parents exchanged notes. He visited them if business brought him to Philadelphia. My mother occasionally met him for lunch in New York. At first, those continuing ties made me angry and edgy; they seemed to undermine my desire to put distance between us.

Now, nearly ten years later, postcards in Barry's deliberate, squarish printing arrive in my mailbox several times a year. On the phone, we catch up on each other's family, commiserate about jobs. I think of Barry not as my ex-anything, but a friend of the family, a man who was, for a time, important to all of us. We appear and retreat from each other's life like cousins who, no matter how their lives evolve, will always hold a piece of one another's pasts.

At one time, you could diagram the *mishpocha* (Yiddish for extended family) with clear lines of blood, marriage, and legal adoption. But changing life patterns have built a new family, with connections scribbled out and drawn in again, convoluted links.

This new family confounds us sometimes. Do we continue sending Christmas presents to the former-partner-now-good-friend, as we always have? Invite her to holiday celebrations? What is the relationship of children, say, to a single parent's former lover? How does it change if a new lover enters the picture? If we don't oust the "ex" from our midst, how do friends and family acknowledge the relationship's shift and respect the changes in both partners' lives?

Instead of a pattern that rips each time a couple ends their relationship, the new *mishpocha* demands a more expansive vision. It refuses to choose sides, to split loyalties. Instead, it insists that there is enough: enough love, enough time, enough space for kinship to evolve in unpredictable directions.

FOR a while, I was merely cordial to our new neighbors. I waved when I drove up and spotted Kate or Peg on the porch. We traded pleasantries about the weather or the garden. Then, one night while they were working on the house, Elissa and I invited them over for an impromptu pizza dinner. We ate on the living room floor, spreading the pizza on a red-and-black-plaid tablecloth. Peg and Kate's clothes and hair were freckled with paint. It was a Sunday, and we were all tired and giddy. I remember a lot of laughter and a conversation that somehow shook loose the old tensions and jealousies.

A few months later, when vandals smashed my car window, Kate dismantled the door and installed new glass, saving me a hundred dollars in mechanic's fees. When Peg needed help with a mailing list, I typed addresses for an hour in the afternoon. I borrowed their gardening gloves and left a bag of fresh lettuce on the doorstep. Kate called to borrow a can of tomatoes.

In the spring, Peg and Kate began scraping the sea green paint from their house, the beginning of a months-long project. Elissa and I planted tomatoes that would not be red until fall. Clearly, we were all staying put for a while.

I recalled an interview I had read that discussed the effects of transience on our sense of family. "If you can always withdraw from relationships, you never grow up, you're not stimulated to look into your own motives, to exert yourself to see another point of view," psychologist Dorothy Dinnerstein said.

"You'll only go into social exchanges that are comfortable, and those will have to be transitory because nothing is comfortable for very long.... To be able to live amicably, or in some sense cooperatively, with people you wouldn't choose—it seems to me that is an irreplaceable humanizing experience."

I think about the notion of "extended" family, what that word means. When I extend myself, I go beyond an old limit, stretch in unexpected ways. I leave behind my assumptions about who I can include, who I must shut out.

Perhaps the exact junctures of family extension were once easier to find. They were the second cousins twice removed, the aunts by marriage, the kin acquired each time a couple wed. The links are less obvious, more complicated, now. But they are there, these points of necessity and affection, entrances to one another's lives.

One summer evening, Elissa and I walked outside barefoot, carrying a cold salad and a hot fruit crisp over the lawn to the house next door. In the dining room, we joined half a dozen friends for a shish ke-bab party, laughing as we speared cherry tomatoes, onions, mushrooms, and chicken on wooden skewers.

Kate barbecued on the wooden deck that another friend had built.

We sprawled outside, eating and talking. Joe, who had dated Kate in college, had just moved to Portland. Anne, exhausted from leading a two-week civil rights walk, curled up on the living room couch and went to sleep. Kate's cousin, visiting from Texas, plucked a banjo.

Night rubbed the sky indigo. The air smelled faintly of barbecue smoke and raspberries. Our talk pushed at the edges of the day until the edges themselves dissolved, and it seemed there were no limits—to the evening, the food, the growing place in which we met.

Different Shapes of Love

CELESTINE Wilson knows her friendship with Laurence Jones has never fit a conventional mold. They dated, but never exclusively. They became lovers twice but did not live together. They both married other people, and still they sustained their connection through letters, phone calls, and visits. They commiserated when each got divorced.

Today, twenty-five years after they first met, Celestine counts Laurence among a select and permanent circle of friends. Her impending second marriage will not change that, she said. "I have told my partner I will always love Laurence, that he is part of my life.

"My mother used to say you can only love one man in your life. But I know it's not so. Once you have really loved a person, I don't believe you ever stop loving them. Your love has different shapes."

CELESTINE'S first encounter with Laurence, though, was far from infatuation at first sight. She was a naive nineteen then, working as a hospital receptionist in Philadelphia, and he was a Howard University student fired with the emerging sense of black consciousness on college campuses. She thought he was arrogant. But as their friendship grew—through letters, phone calls, and Laurence's visits home—she began to enjoy their discussions about ethnic identity and male-female relationships.

"He raised my consciousness about what it meant to be black," she recalled. "We would have so many discussions. This was at a time when people were just beginning to talk about being 'black' rather than 'Negro' or 'colored.' We'd have conversations, and he'd say, 'Who *are* you?' and I'd say, 'What are you talking about?'"

As her own self-awareness grew, Celestine discovered she also liked Laurence's unconventional ideas about dating. Unlike other men she had been with, who grew jealous if Celestine wanted to see other people, Laurence believed both of them should date nonexclusively. He spoke candidly with Celestine and encouraged her to do the same.

Laurence loved to drive, and the two would often climb into the car for day trips with no particular destination. Sometimes they discussed their personal lives, books, or the politics of race. Other times, they were silent, each absorbed in private thoughts. "It was a comfort to know we were both there and didn't have to talk."

In general, Laurence was the more staid of the two. "I was the one who acted crazy, who would start dancing in the street, who'd talk love-talk to him and have him giggle, see him loosen up."

They became lovers twice—once for two-and-a-half years, and later for nearly eight years. In between, both married other people. "It was hard for me when he got married," Celestine said. "I felt like a part of me was gone. I felt that I no longer had the same accessibility to him."

But she found that the two could, and did, sustain the ease and confidences they had become accustomed to. "We could be very direct with each other. With Laurence, I knew I could say anything to him and still have a friend."

Those emotional ties stretched to include other aspects of their lives. At one point, when the two were lovers, they also launched a business together; Laurence was an attorney in private practice, and Celestine became his administrative assistant. Their small firm practiced bankruptcy law, and they split the proceeds down the middle. Later, Laurence helped Celestine buy a house so she and her son, Abdul, would have a stable place to live. Abdul, now twenty-one, treats Laurence like a beloved uncle.

Such connections have been difficult for Celestine's partners to understand. "My mates know how intense I can become; they fear someone else might be getting some of that. When I say I love this person and always will, it makes them feel very vulnerable.

"When I told my fiancé about Laurence, I said, This man was my friend at a very young age. I bonded with him. Maybe you weren't fortunate enough to have that kind of relationship happen to you. But I do love him. I will love him for the rest of my life."

Celestine drew her belief in that kind of inclusion partly from the examples in her own home. Despite her mother's counsel about finding just one true love, Celestine saw how her brothers' former wives were always included in family holiday celebrations, how they were welcome in her mother's house. When Laurence is in town, he drops by, too.

"I believe in continuity when it comes to relationships, unless someone is violent or is going to cause harm to the family. With Laurence, I wanted to continue a friendship with a person I thought was positive in my life. He was a gift. I don't want to let go."

THE two don't see each other often now, since Celestine lives and works in Philadelphia and Laurence's home is on the island of St. Thomas. He mails her articles about women's issues. She calls him to share news about mutual friends. And when they do visit, they talk as if no time had elapsed—the conversation ranging through politics, movies, friends, Abdul, their current partners, their thoughts about parenting and growing older. The last time the two got together, they surveyed each other and noted the signs of middle age. "You're gettin' wide," Laurence joked.

"He's balding; I'm graying. There may be periods of a year that go by when I don't hear from Laurence. But we always pick up. I'm looking for the end of this story, myself."

Maintaining Bonds with a Former Spouse

WHAT Rhonda Ray and Sven Solvik knew was that they didn't want a judge to outline the rest of their lives. When they decided to divorce, after an eight-year relationship and five years of marriage, they agreed on two things. First, they both felt equally devoted to their two-and-a-half-year-old daughter, Freya. Second, they were repelled by the idea of a protracted courtroom battle determining their financial and emotional arrangements. Besides, both recognized the bond that still existed between them—not just Freya, but a sense of mutual trust, respect, and affection.

"Neither one of us could justifiably blame the other person. There was a dynamic between us that sometimes created monsters out of both of us. And there was a love between us that never really died.

"Our bottom line was our devotion to Freya and her devotion to both of us. Sven had been a really equal parent. I didn't feel I could rip Freya out of his life. I was ethically against trying to get custody by taking him to court. Still, it was painful trying to work out how we could parent her."

Rhonda sat on the carpet of a large, cluttered living room, sipping tea. A midwife, she wore a pager clipped to the waist of her wrinkled khaki pants. In her kitchen, a confetti of pictures covered the refrigerator, including some of what she called "the umbrella family"—herself, her husband, Robert, her daughters Freya and Hopi, her ex-husband Sven, his wife, Sally, and their son, Elan.

That umbrella didn't spring open immediately. In the decade since Rhonda and Sven divorced, they invented their relationship spoke by spoke, a tenuous and sometimes painful rendering.

First, there were logistical considerations. They were living in Northern California, part of a loose-knit group of families who owned parcels of rural land and built their own homes. Sven was a carpenter; Rhonda a midwife. When the two decided to split, "We didn't have any role models for it," Rhonda recalled. "We just did it step by step. We didn't agree with a way of doing it that made enemies out of us."

Rhonda moved out of the state and began dating Robert, a man she'd met on a trip to Guatemala. Sven sold their land, and they split the profits. They agreed that neither would pay the other child support or alimony, and that they would share the expenses of raising Freya.

"We really worked at every step being equal, at there not being resentment," she said. "Sven joined me one or two months after I moved. From the time Freya was little, she said, 'I want to see you both every day—to wake up at one house and go to sleep at the other.' So we'd split up the time during the week, and then alternate weekends.

"We did that for six months, then I moved again. Freya did two weeks at his house and two weeks with me. The adjustment of her coming back was really difficult; she was resentful of Robert. It was terrible being without her for two weeks. I felt crazy: I wanted her to come back so much, then she'd come back and there would be a lot of conflict between her and Robert." When Sven left the area to earn a degree in physical therapy, Freya's relationship with Robert changed. She began calling him "Bobby-Daddy."

"Sven said, 'You two settle wherever you want to be when I get out of school, and I'll come there.' When he got out of school, he moved three blocks away from us. That's when we began the arrangement of Freya being here Mondays and Wednesdays, there Tuesdays and Thursdays and alternating weekends. That schedule has basically not changed.

"She has two homes. She has her own room and toys and games at both houses; she doesn't ever have to pack a bag." That setup continued even after Sven moved a bit further away; Freya, now almost twelve, can ride her bicycle to his house.

"When I got pregnant with Hopi, Freya wanted to be around here more. We had a big meeting—Robert and me and Sven and his wife, Sally. We added one more night, so she was here Monday, Tuesday, and Wednesday. We did it that way until her little brother was born at her dad's house. Now she's torn all the time. She says, 'I want to be with both families.'

"Mostly, this has worked for us. I know most child psychologists would say a kid needs one home base, but none of us have wanted to be without each other."

ON HOLIDAYS, the families juggle a solution that changes from year to year. Usually, Freya will be at Rhonda's house on Christmas Eve, then Sven picks her up in the morning to open presents at his house. Both families gather together for a late brunch or an outing.

"Our group of friends overlaps somewhat, especially the friends we've met through Freya. If we do birthday parties for any of us, Sven and Sally are friends we definitely invite. With other holidays, we try to remember what we did the year before and make it fair.

"Sven and I know each other really well. We never had conflicts in terms of parenting. We'll still call each other to talk about a mood Freya came home in, for instance. We'll have an hour-long conversation every few weeks.

"We have that knowledge of each other and our daughter—a respect for each other about parenting that is really solid. There are two people I really want to confer with when something comes up about Freya. I'll talk to Robert first. Sven is the other one."

Rhonda and the other members of her "umbrella" family feel frustrated, at times, by the lack of language to describe their relationships. Freya never liked the terms "stepdad" or "stepmom," and calls her parents' spouses by their first names. Rhonda refers to Sven as "Freya's dad," a term that fails to address their relationship as adults.

There have been times, Rhonda confessed, when she wished for sole custody of Freya—for an end to the discontinuity, the namelessness, the constant hellos and good-byes. Yet she also believes in the benefits of the more complicated choice they made. Sven remains a thread in her life, rather than a part of the detached past. Together, she and Sven offer Freya—as well as their other children—one more important possibility.

"It feels like we've really accomplished something special to be able to continue to care for each other and make decisions about Freya together and have each other in our lives," she said. "It's good role modeling for her—about the ability to change the structure of a relationship and still be close and have love for each other."

Partners in an Ever-Changing Pattern

ANN Hinds and Linda Kliewer used to have a bookkeeping ritual at the end of every month. They dumped all their receipts in the center of the bed—every magazine, every cup of coffee, every box of cereal either one had bought. Then they took guesses about the discrepancy between their totals.

They were never off by more than a dollar.

This equity in expense-sharing, they said later, was a sign of a nearly perfect complementarity. From the beginning of their relationship fifteen years ago, they knew they would be life partners. Linda and Ann still used that word to describe the bond between them. But explaining exactly what they meant required a long story, full of changing expectations and new definitions.

It was easier to say what the phrase didn't mean. They weren't sexually involved. They no longer pooled their money. They didn't plan meals together. They did live next door to each other, in two tiny rental houses, sharing a single phone number and answering machine. They each had lovers. They remained committed to each other for life.

"We're life partners," Ann said. She sat at the drafting table in her studio, which looked like the scene of a collision between two Crayola vans. Cups of colored pencils, felt markers, and crayons, bunched chromatically, sat on shelves near the slanted desktop. Vivid pastel drawings covered the walls. Even her calendar was color-coded.

Ann has a lion's mane of light brown hair and a high-speed voice that delivered her story in rapid, detailed bits, chopping the language apart and reassembling it in odd, idiosyncratic ways.

"'Partners' doesn't imply that we have sex together. It doesn't imply that we have money together. It's ambiguous. It's inclusive. We have to invent the words and demand that people listen."

When they first met, Linda was stunned to find that Ann treated her as an equal. Ann was startled to find herself responding sexually to a woman. They spent the first three years figuring out what it meant to be together. They got a dog. And a cat. And a van. Then one day they walked nervously into a bank and told the teller they wanted a joint account.

"That was our first time going into a patriarchal institution and announcing ourselves as two women sharing a life together. That was a kind of commitment ceremony," Linda said. At thirty-eight, she is lean and wiry, with short hair and intent eyes. Her voice races to the end of each sentence, and her laugh erupts like something let out of captivity.

From the beginning, Linda and Ann said, they felt sure they would be in each other's life forever. They felt equally sure they wouldn't be the only ones present.

"We maintained the idea that we would have the freedom as individuals to relate to whomever we pleased in whatever manner we pleased," Ann said. It was easier contemplated than done. "We practiced nonmonogamy in our heads for seven years before we practiced it with our bodies."

By then, they were comfortable as a duo. Several years into their relationship they signed notarized papers indicating they would act as next of kin for each other in case of a medical emergency. They celebrated that formality with a dinner party, and a friend planted a tree for them.

Gradually, their roles in the partnership crystallized. Linda made a good salary working as a camerawoman for a television station; Ann took care of their social obligations. Linda paid the bills. Ann fed the animals. When they went on trips, Linda packed the car and Ann arranged the food.

"We had developed interdependency to such a fine art that it crossed the line," Ann said. "I used to call it the amalgamated lesbian: one brain, two bodies." To extricate themselves, they decided to cultivate some separate interests. Linda became involved with local theater. Then she became involved with some of the women she met there.

"I felt that her attachment to them excluded me," Ann said. "That made me pretty cranky. For me, the idea of nonmonogamy or open relationship was the idea of being inclusive, not exclusive."

Ann's ideal was that her relationship with Linda remain primary while each had secondary relationships with others. In her vision, these other lovers would join the open circle she and Linda had created; the family would grow rather than fracture. Any newcomers would need to understand that her bond with Linda was "as lifelong as a biological family" and severing it as impossible as "trying to unmix paint."

For a short time, Ann took their vow of openness to its extreme. "I was sleeping with three other people at the same time. It became my worst nightmare. I had a different night with each person: 'If it's Tuesday, it must be Susan.' It was so open that everybody wanted structure. There was no room to be spontaneous.

"Finally, we stabilized. What we stabilized with was the constellation. We called it The Four Hearts. Linda and I explained to the other two involved that our relationship was primary and they had to know that. It went along for about three years."

When Linda's lover left, their carefully negotiated balance shifted. It changed again, a year later, when Linda became involved with someone new. The new configuration was dubbed CALM, for the first initials of their four names. But the acronym lost a letter when Ann and her lover held a "disengagement party" to mark the end of their sexual and romantic relationship.

At the same time, Linda and Ann were examining every aspect of their own bond. Did they want to continue sharing money? Should they remain next-door neighbors, with both names on the leases to their homes? Maybe, on the next vacation, Ann should pack the car and Linda should make her own lunch.

Ann wondered whether they were merely prolonging an inevitable split. "I hounded Linda for a while. I'd say, Oh, we're just breaking up in slow motion. You're spending all your time with your lover; why don't you just go live with her?

"It was an identity crisis," she recalled. "We'd set up something that had worked so well. Then came a phase of delight that we could break through those roles. We had developed enough confidence and security to be more fully ourselves."

That meant remaining next-door neighbors, coming and going frequently from each other's house. An intercom connects them. Ann borrows food from Linda's refrigerator; Linda drops by Ann's place at dinnertime. Their bank accounts are separate, and they no longer share a car. They do share a bed several nights a week.

"We can go for a couple of days and not sleep together," Linda said.

"Then it's really important to have that physical contact. It's a necessary part of my life."

"Linda and I spend less time together now, do fewer things together, share less, *and* the points where we intersect are deeper," Ann added.

Other people didn't get it. Someone would spot Linda being affectionate with her lover in public and assume Ann was no longer in the picture. Or friends would fumble party invitations, not certain who was paired with whom.

And their families, who had known Ann and Linda as a couple for many years, were confused. Ann's mother couldn't fathom what "partner" meant if Ann had another lover. Linda's father kept saying, "I don't understand what you're doing."

When Linda's parents last visited her, she tried to explain. "At this time, Ann and I are not sexual. My lover and I are. It's about loving. It's about support. My mother finally said to my father, 'They're loving each other. That's what they're doing.'"

THE women faced each other in two chairs. Linda's legs were propped on the drafting table; Ann hunched forward. They were both red-eyed. Ann grabbed a tissue. Their relationship would be fifteen years old soon, and they planned to celebrate it. But a ceremony based on traditional prototypes and pledges didn't fit the nuances of their lives.

In the past, they noted anniversaries of the day they met, the time they first slept together, the day they signed power of attorney papers. Gay Pride qualified as a holiday. So did their birthdays. Ann kept meticulous calendars—pocket-size books in which she printed microscopically and highlighted items in colored marker. Sometimes, she took the rubber band off the stack of calendars and paged through them to recall where she had been. They helped to ground her in a life unfolding largely outside society's boundaries.

Lately, Ann and Linda and Linda's lover had talked about finding a house where they could live together. "It's pretty unusual in the context of this patriarchal social system we're living in," Ann said. "I feel like we're way, way out on the edge. I have aimed for this place for so long—where I am not approval-oriented, I am not basing my life or my art on what anybody else wants."

"For me," Linda said, "the first conscious feeling I remember about Ann—I was twenty-four at the time—was that I'd met someone who had the same depth of caring as I did.

"One of the hardest things for me still is seeing Ann being intimate with other people. I fear I won't be as important. But for her, what I want is growth and happiness. The majority of the time, I'm secure in who we are with each other. I feel an enormous amount of joy and happiness and love. There's nothing I would change."

One Million Milestones:
New Junctures in Women's Lives

"TWENTY-TWO people? Mom, that's ridiculous." I tightened my grip on the phone. "No one else in the entire graduating class is having twenty-two people. They're only giving us five tickets. Why do they all have to come?"

I tried to imagine twenty-two members of my family crowding into my fifth-floor dormitory suite, traipsing to a New Haven restaurant—laughing, noisy, unbearably proud. There was a certain anonymous relief to graduating in a class of 1,250; with my family in tow, I would never manage a low profile.

My mother, of course, said I was the one being ridiculous. I should feel lucky that so many people wanted to see me graduate. What we did not talk about was my grandmother's death, just two months earlier. The family had last gathered for her funeral and then, a few weeks later, for a distracted, subdued Passover seder. My graduation was a chance to acknowledge something joyful with the aching, wakeful edge that a death brings.

In the end, Mom won or I capitulated, too preoccupied with finals to argue, not entirely sure what I was arguing for. Twenty-two relatives ruined their shoes in the mud of Yale's Old Campus, transformed by daylong rain into a giant swamp.

In a photograph from that weekend, ten of us are gathered in the leafy courtyard of my residential college. We all have that rummy look that comes from excitement, too little sleep, and drinking champagne before lunch. Over the years, the picture has taken on a particular charge that none of us, including me, imagined at the time. It may be the last occasion the family gathers to raise a toast in my honor.

So MANY traditional rites of passage are closed to me—or fit badly, like a hand-me-down dress four seasons old. I can cross the occasions off a mental list: no engagement party or bridal shower, no wedding, no silver anniversary. No pictures of me wafting down an aisle into the next chapter of my life, Mom and Dad beaming on either side. If I skirt the usual milestones, my future streams out blankly. How do I chart the time from here forward?

Birthdays come around each year, but they seem less poignant as more of them accumulate. I often forget exactly how old I am. Twenty-eight, twenty-nine, thirty—what's the difference? After a certain age, it seems, birthdays are supposed to recede into the background while family occasions take center stage. Engagement. Marriage. Children's births, and then *their* birthdays, confirmations, graduations, and weddings. It's as if a woman, upon adulthood, ceases to be a self, deserving of her own personal rituals, her private relationship to time.

I always write in my journal on significant days—birthdays, the start of a new job, the anniversary of my solo cross-country auto trip. But I know there are moments I neglect to record. The cultural myopia about women's lives helps to blur their importance. A lack of recognition out there, in the world, makes it hard to value my own internal landmarks. My uncertainty then helps to keep those truths invisible. In the end, we all suffer, robbed of the chance to know and share the critical junctures in each other's lives.

It is no accident that we assemble for a wedding but not a separation or divorce, that we mourn communally the deaths of people but not of cats or cedar trees, that we celebrate the anniversaries of marriages, not friendships. A subtext lurks under all that observance, a pyramid of values: it's better to be married than single; human companions are more important than those of other species; spouses rate higher than friends.

Some women are turning that pyramid on its point. They reject the ceremonial framework of women's lives, with its emphasis on heterosexual romantic love, marriage, and children, and assert an architecture of their own. Instead of complying, they invent. The resulting rituals do not merely substitute for old ones—say, a coming-of-age ceremony instead of a bridal shower—but offer profound challenges to old beliefs about women, the shapes of their lives and their right to celebrate themselves.

The stories I've heard about women's rituals rollick in my head. I let my mind loose to imagine a lifetime of new occasions.

•Birth and naming. On her first birthday, a baby girl is officially named and welcomed to the world. Her parents talk about why they chose her name. Friends and family take turns holding her and blessing her.

•Menstruation. From the time I was ten, I waited impatiently for my period to start, convinced it had begun every time I sweat enough to dampen my underwear. I'd inspected every item in the pink flowered box under the bathroom sink, read the little booklet "Growing Up and Liking It" at least fifty times. When I finally did begin to bleed, four anticlimactic years later, I told my mother and stuck a Modess pad in my pants.

Instead, it could be like this: when she begins to menstruate, a young girl is the guest of honor at a party for her friends and family. Women of different generations are invited—her grandmothers or older women who are neighbors, teachers, friends. Some tell their own coming-of-age stories. They talk about all the forms women's fertility can take—dance, song, political work, poetry, gardens, food, children.

•The celebration of a woman's twenty-first birthday could add depth to an occasion now marked—at least in the United States—by the ability to order a drink legally. This occasion would be a sign of independence and the entrance into the community as a person apart from her family. I know one woman who gathered friends to wind her and her twenty-one-year-old daughter in a tangle of bright yarn; the two then had to extricate themselves as a symbol of the young woman's independence.

•Risk party. Anyone facing a difficult decision—where to go to school, which job to take, whether to have a child—could invite friends to talk about their own hard choices. They could give the guest of honor tools that helped them, such as poems they read at the time, excerpts from their journals, music they played, runes or tarot cards or other instruments that helped clarify their decisions.

•Coming and going. We take mobility for granted, I think, and don't recognize the emotional wrench involved when people change homes. Judith Arcana, her partner, and her son do lengthy house-cleansings each time they move, smudging the new rooms with sage smoke, claiming the space. When Ellen Bass, a writer who had seen clients in her den for years, finally built a separate office, a group of friends and family gathered in it, sang songs, lit candles, and offered wishes for her success and fulfillment there.

•Recommitment ceremonies. A one-time dedication doesn't match the reality of long-term relationships, in which both partners must decide continually to remain together. Suppose couples—married or not, straight or gay—invited friends periodically to witness a recommitment ceremony, at which they consider the relationship's past and declare their wishes for its future.

•Separation parties. This is the flip side—gatherings to mark a breakup or divorce. Two women I know held a "disengagement" to note the shift in their relationship from lovers to lifetime friends. They let people know they no longer wished to be viewed as a couple. A private ritual can also help pave such a transition. I once saw a photograph of a stunning "divorce quilt" handmade by a woman, with panels depicting key moments in her marriage, its breakup, and her resolve to go on with her life.

•Leaving or returning parties. I had a goodbye party when I left the East Coast for Portland in 1986. Several dozen friends, family members, and former neighbors crowded into my parents' house to ask me about my plans (they were vague) and wish me well on my solo drive cross-country. But I would have liked a more structured ritual, a chance to talk about why I was leaving, to hear others' stories about moving, and to collect mementos from the people and places I would miss most.

•Anniversaries—not just of relationships, but of significant decisions and changes. Five years in a job, a decade in your first house, seven years since you learned to swim or began playing the clarinet or became a practitioner of Zen.

Such occasions can mark group, as well as individual, milestones. Just as a couple celebrates the date they met or married, women can honor the formation of their households, friendships, or groups—reading circles, acting troupes, support networks. Beverly Stein, for instance, planned a party for her closest women friends to acknowledge her twentieth anniversary of becoming involved in the women's movement. Such events are one way to map a life; they remind us that we live in a context, belonging to our times as well as to ourselves.

And there are new ways to mark customary occasions—alone or with family and friends. In a private yearly ritual, Dolores Kueffler used to dance her birthday. She played instrumental tapes of soft jazz or classical music and did a spontaneous, interpretive dance, trying to recount her year through movement.

My friend Cynthia received a fortieth-birthday quilt from her closest friends—a tradition the group began when the first among them turned forty a few years ago. One panel holds an embroidered Scrabble board as a memento of annual Thanksgiving-weekend tournaments. Another includes miniature appliqués showing scenes in India, where Cynthia spent her childhood.

When Tina Tau and a close friend turned forty, they sought guidance and perspective from older friends and relatives. They mailed sheets of handmade paper to eighteen women, all of whom had already passed their fortieth birthdays. "We want to enter the decade well-advised and well aware of the wonders awaiting us," they explained, asking each woman to write or paint on the page "anything you would like us to know or carry with us—memories, stories, poems, symbols."

One page holds a piece of lace that belonged to Tina's great-grandmother. One woman wove a silk handkerchief and attached it to her page. Others wrote poems about their lives. At a party, Tina and her friend read each sheet aloud, then bound them into a book that they now share, swapping it periodically from house to house.

•Menopause. Like rituals for first menses, this one's dropped by the wayside of Western cultures. A woman might gather friends who've also stopped bleeding—or soon will—to talk about what that change means. They could read Ursula K. Le Guin's essay, "The Space Crone," research another culture's menopause rituals, eat wonderful food, laugh and dance.

•Grief and mourning ceremonies. Perhaps the traditions surrounding death are the hardest to dismantle; in the midst of grief, few people have the energy or inclination to invent. Besides, we live in a culture that does all it can to deny death. Few topics are so difficult to discuss.

Yet even here, in such fragile territory, I know women who are finding ways to talk about and mark death as part of life's inevitable flow and ebb. When Barb's lover, Kathi, committed suicide several years ago, Barb invited dozens of their friends to the house the couple had shared. The two-bedroom bungalow filled with women—colleagues and friends, people who'd sat at Barb and Kathi's dinner table, helped build their back fence, house-sat when they went on vacation.

People brought food and shared stories about Kathi. Barb had decided to let friends read Kathi's suicide note, and some cried. Then she told everyone to look at Kathi's belongings and ask her if they saw anything they'd like to keep. Almost every guest took something home—clothes, photographs, knicknacks, paintings, jewelry. Each object, Barb said, was an emblem of connection between herself, Kathi, and their community.

I'M NOT likely to graduate again. Birthdays aren't enough. I crave ways to mark the important shifts in my life—decisions about work and family and where to live, commitments to my friends and to Elissa, losses and achievements. I want rituals to reinforce the things that make my life unique and the junctures I share with others—birth and death and the body's inevitable buckling, leaving homes and returning to familiar places, triumphs and disappointments.

It's not enough for me, either, to observe those milestones in solitude. In Hebrew, the word for "witness" shares a root with the word for "duration." That makes sense to me, that my tradition would require the presence of others to mark important times. Shared celebrations and griefs enter the common memory and language, part of the binding past from which we go on. We are related partly because of what we have been through together.

I envision one more occasion to add to the calendar:

Diana and I met at recess on the Penn Wynne Elementary School playground in September 1968. We were six years old and had dark brown pigtails. Mine were straighter. We both went to Yale. Diana majored in French and became a doctor; I majored in English and became a writer. We both cut off our hair—mine now much curlier.

When we are thirty-one, when we will have been friends for twenty-five years, I want to throw a huge party. Serve noodles with Cheez Whiz, our standard Sunday afternoon snack for most of grade school. Have someone paint faces, as they did every year at our elementary school's outdoor carnival. Maybe even reprise the five-character play we wrote at age nine, in which Diana played Miss Chiles and I played everyone else.

I picture the invitation: "Diana and Anndee invite you to celebrate with them a quarter-century of friendship. Dinner. Music. Face-painting." We'd send this announcement to friends, to the *Main Line Times*, the suburban weekly of our childhood neighborhood, and perhaps to our elementary school, in case any of our former teachers are still there.

We could make scrapbooks—one for each of us—filled with photos of us through the years: Our double date to the neighborhood bowling alley at age eleven. Our summers at tennis camp. Our appearances in the casts of *You Can't Take It with You* and *A Thurber Carnival*. Each guest could bring a story of a great female friendship—fictional or real. We could make a time capsule to open in 2018, when we will have been friends for half a century.

It is a rare and fine thing to know a person for twenty-five years. If I let the occasion pass unremarked, then I am agreeing with what this culture tells me—that women's friendships are invisible and unimportant, that only links of blood or marriage can gird me against the slipping away of time.

To imagine such an event—to create any of these rituals—requires pluck and imagination. I have to think beyond the automatic, beyond what I think people expect of me, what I expect of myself. I have to walk willingly into the unknown, trusting that my feet will land on something solid.

I borrow courage from the women who have dared before me; their ceremonies invite me to create my own. Together, one following the next, we will develop and pass down new traditions, fresh ways to hallow the ground, call sacred the time and gather a changing, growing circle of people we can call family.

Naming a Daughter

ROBERTA Lampert, a dark-haired artist, roundly pregnant with her second child, sipped tea in my living room one fall evening and talked about the ritual that *didn't* accompany her own birth thirty-eight years ago.

When Roberta was born—her parents' third child and third daughter—her father refused to call anyone with the news. "It was always made extremely clear to my sisters and myself that we should have been boys. That being girls really didn't cut it, was not quite good enough."

Jewish boy babies undergo a ritual circumcision when they are eight days old. The ceremony, called a *bris*, is also an official welcoming into the world, a party attended by relatives and friends. There is no equivalent ritual mandated for girls.

Roberta and her husband, James, were determined to change that pattern. When their first child, Gavrila Haness, was born, they wanted to celebrate. This baby had not come easily; months of medical tests seemed to indicate they wouldn't be able to conceive. They had decided on adoption when Roberta discovered she was pregnant.

"It was really important for me to say publicly and in front of everybody that this was a daughter I was really proud to have, and that we were going to treasure her and help her be everything she could possibly be," Roberta said.

When Gavrila was one year old, they invited friends and relatives to a naming ceremony at their home. The gathering should be small, they thought at first. But once they began making lists—friends who had been supportive when they were struggling to conceive, family from around the country, good friends and colleagues, Roberta's Jewish women's group—they came up with more than fifty names.

In the Jewish tradition, children are named after a dead relative whose qualities their parents hope they will emulate. Gavrila was named after Roberta's mother's identical twin sister, Goldie.

In the ceremony, they described Goldie's life, her curiosity about current events and the world, her determination and inner strength. Goldie, they remembered, never missed Ted Koppel's *Nightline* and learned drawing and handwriting analysis in her sixties. They explained that "Gavrila" means "woman of strength" and Haness means "the miracle."

They talked, too, about how parenthood had changed their lives. "We find that we are more aware of small things and new things, that we spend less time in introspection, more time understanding the world that Gavrila shows us." They offered wishes for their daughter to remain adventuresome and curious, to love learning, to give and receive love and to pursue justice and mercy in the world.

They read from the Song of Songs and from the Talmud, sang "Sabbath Prayer" from *Fiddler on the Roof*. Then family and friends offered their own hopes and wishes for Gavrila. "There was this incredible warmth and focus on her. Everyone was wishing her the very best that life could offer. That was very powerful," Roberta said.

Their second child, born several months after our conversation, was a son; Roberta and James named him Severin Michael, in front of a gathering of family and friends.

"Just as Gavrila's birth changed our lives completely, so has Severin transformed our lives again. We are learning to be parents all over again, with a different child whose approach to life is not remotely related to his sister's, to say nothing of our own," they wrote in the ceremony. "Our second child reminds us that each person is an individual, bringing us new means of understanding our lives and others' lives."

"I was not someone who went to synagogue a lot, but I've always observed holidays at home in some manner with family or with friends," Roberta said. "I never thought that much about a baby-naming or making my own family. I had been to one baby-naming, but had to leave because it was when I was trying very unsuccessfully to get pregnant, and it was just too hard for me.

"My mother has this theory of celebrating every event, like it's a law. I think she's right. It's important to acknowledge these things. You never know if you're going to be around for the next one; you never know how many people are going to be around for the next one. You invite who's alive. You do what you can do."

A Feminist Mother Marks a Son's Coming of Age

JUDITH Arcana made peace with tradition when she realized she could be a Jewish witch. The chauvinism of mainstream Judaism and its rituals was at odds with her feminist ideals. But she wasn't sure how to fill the spiritual gap.

"As I read and studied more, I found that Jewish women come out of a tradition of old religions in the Middle East. I simply incorporated them. I mix and match. Some people think that's kind of low-class. It's perfect for me. I am a woman whose history goes back, back, back. I am a witch of the old religion.

"Over the years we've done a lot of rituals that we've invented. On holidays and special occasions, we've done big-time stuff of the kind that binds people, where you light candles and chant and say very important things about your fears and hopes and who you are in the world, sitting in a circle, holding hands, having a magic stone passed.

"But, yes, I went through a period of feeling very bereft. I missed those weddings and bar mitzvahs, even though I didn't want those rituals for myself.

"When my son, Daniel, was thirteen, he chose not to have a bar mitzvah. I had a ritual for him in my house. I chose thirteen because, of course, we are Jews. Also because it is a magic, mystic number, part of sacred rituals in many parts of the world.

"I invited the members of my women's group, and my partner, Jonathan. Everyone gave Daniel a magic gift. Everyone gave him words of wisdom. It was like these wise women blessing him—the 'aunts,' if we were talking about blood relations. I said to him, You must make a reply to everyone who blesses you and then you have to make a final statement.

"One person gave him a bird's nest she'd found in the woods. One gave a small rectangular mirror in a deerskin pouch with holes in it. You could look at it through the pouch and see yourself as if you were looking through a mask.

"Another friend, the daughter of Holocaust survivors, gave him a white silk aviator scarf she'd found at a vintage clothing store. He put it on and said, 'I knew you would give me something Jewish. This is my tallis.'

"I designed a pouch for him like the ones Jewish boys get when they are bar mitzvah," Judith said. A friend who was skilled at needlework made the pouch according to her design, sewing on emblems of theater masks and Daniel's birth sign, along with those of his father and Judith.

"The ritual was definitely about being a Jew and a witch, giving my son a spiritual initiation, making visible that these people were our family. I said to him, These are the people of our everyday life, who give us what we need, who take care of you when I can't.

"He put all the gifts in the pouch. After that, every now and then he would take it out. I always knew when someone really mattered in his life because he would show them his bag of treasures.

"Years later, when Daniel was a senior in high school, he gave the magic mirror to a guy who was his good friend. I said, You gave it away? Daniel said, 'Mom, he needs it more than I ever will in my whole life.' And I thought, It worked."

A Ritual for Tubal Ligation

SHE lives at the peak of a woodsy spiral, at the end of a gravelly road, past a terraced garden. Up the steep back stairs lies the apartment Janet Riganti refers to as her "womb in the woods." At thirty-five, Janet still looks like the student who rushes to the front-row seat in English class. She wore a lavender jumper and round glasses; her long brown hair was caught with an Alice in Wonderland-style headband.

A year earlier, Janet had decided to have a tubal ligation. Her decision was prompted partly by health concerns (she was diabetic, and pregnancy could be risky), partly by emotional factors (she was single and did not want to raise a child alone).

But the surgery signified much more than ending the possibility of pregnancy. It meant a decisive step away from her family's values and the expectations of women in this culture. Having her tubes tied, it turned out, was one way to set herself free.

"I have six siblings. I come from a Catholic Italian family. A high value was placed on having a large family. I always lived with an assumption that everything I was doing was preparation for the next generation, for being a mother. Letting go of that was a real struggle."

Janet talked over the decision with a few close women friends and with the man she was dating at the time. She told her siblings—but not her parents—about the plan and made an appointment for a few weeks after a vacation she'd planned with a friend. At the last minute, her friend canceled, and Janet decided to go camping alone.

It was early September, a crisp night, when Janet sat by a snapping fire, writing in her journal. She could tell that she'd recently ovulated. This would be her last fertile period. She cried a little. The night felt like a rich, dark cloth around her, defining a safe refuge.

Janet remembered thinking about the purifying role of fire, how flames destroy so that something else can grow. There were some traits she wanted to shed—her naivete and tendency to doubt herself, her readiness to let others' values supplant her own. Symbolically, she tossed those characteristics into the fire and watched them vanish in licks of orange flame.

Two days before her surgery, Janet and six women friends sat in a circle in her small living room. She told them about her decision to have the tubal ligation and her time in the woods. Then each woman placed her hands on the bellies of the two women beside her, over their wombs. Janet looked around. These women were her confidantes and supporters, the family who accepted and encouraged her.

She'd asked them each to bring something that came from the earth. One friend gave a smooth, womb-shaped rock that felt just right in Janet's hand. She carried it with her into surgery, and when she woke out of anesthesia, her boyfriend slipped it back into her palm. "I felt so relaxed. I was so supported by my women friends and this guy I was seeing. I wasn't in any pain."

As her body healed, she felt stronger internally, too, more firmly rooted in her own life.

"So many of us are groomed to bear children," she said. "I always saw that as something that would be a part of my life. Once I was able to enter into the grieving, and make a conscious decision, it was a really freeing thing for me. I opened myself up to so many more possibilities."

At the same time, the choice brought Janet a new perspective on the continuity of her family. Perhaps her role wasn't to mimic the lives of her grandmothers and aunts but to carry their legacy across new boundaries.

She remembered a dream she'd had while alone in the woods. In the dream, Janet was hugely, awkwardly pregnant. But the womb wasn't inside her; it was outside, attached by a cord Janet carried in her hand. When the baby it held was born, she was surprised to see that he was healthy and intact.

"I think the message was that I don't have to have a child inside of me in order to give birth," Janet said. "I work with women as a nurse practitioner. That's a really tangible thing, providing health care. A lot of what I do has to do with empowering women."

Janet walked with me down the stairs. The hilltop garden was a knob pressed up against a dark blue evening sky. She stood at the crest of the driveway and waved as I backed out. "Something clicked for me after my surgery," she'd said before I left. "Something about connection to all the beings, to everything on earth. I feel sure now that what I'm doing is not in vain, even though it's not going to be passed on biologically."

Burying a Dog with Prayer and Song

BARNEY died on a Monday afternoon, and we put him in the ground by sundown. It wasn't a surprise. He was old—thirteen by the human calendar, a nonagenarian in dog years. In the time I'd known Susan Bryer, Barney's muzzle had gone from gray-laced to ash white. On walks, he lay down every few blocks. Finally he wouldn't eat, couldn't go outside or manage the steep stairs to Susan's bedroom.

In the last few weeks of his life, I'd wondered about Susan's decision to let him die on his own, without a vet's injection. Was he suffering needlessly? Was she?

Susan wasn't sure, either, until a veterinarian made a house call and told her Barney would die comfortably without intervention, if Susan could stand to let him. She moved her blanket downstairs and began sleeping on the couch in restless, anxious vigil. The afternoon Barney died, Susan was reading in the living room, listening while he breathed long wheezy breaths full of the liquid in his lungs, and then finally stopped.

"I want to do a *tahara*," Susan said when Elissa and I came over after work. Both Susan and Elissa had performed this ritual cleansing and praying for residents who died at the Jewish home for the aged where they worked. I'd never touched anything dead before.

Barney was on his side, on a blanket in the middle of the living room. I felt a spasm of recoil when I first saw him. I had to force myself to get close and touch his fur. It felt the same as his fur always had, just quieter.

Susan brought a bowl of warm water, two sponges, a brush, and three scarves for us to tie around our heads. Elissa's face was round under the scarf, her hair bristling out at the temples. "You look like your *bubbe* must have looked," I told her.

Elissa lifted Barney's head and sponged brown gummy liquid from his mouth, wiped his tongue, caught stiff and askew between his teeth. I brushed him gently, in long strokes, across the back, down the flank to the fluffy tail, over the stiff legs, until his coat was soft and glossy. Susan started to sing: "Draw water in joy…from the living well." Sudden tears welled in my throat and stung my eyes. I gulped and joined her: "*Mayim hayim…Shalom.*"

There is a special way to wrap a Jewish body for burial, in a white shroud secured with string tied in three-looped knots. We eased Barney onto a big white paper tablecloth and folded it over, leaving his head uncovered. "Are you ready?" Elissa asked Susan, who nodded after a moment. Elissa pulled the last corner of white paper over Barney's eyes and nose, a neat hood, and knotted the string.

We carried him outside, a bulky white-wrapped package. I was surprised at his weight. I'd been thinking of shells, I guess, with their inhabitants long gone, or the papery carcasses of moths on my windowsill.

Outside, we lowered Barney into the hole Susan had dug. And then we crouched in the long dusk, pushing in dirt by the handful, until our fingers were brown and the earth almost even with the rest of the garden, just a slight dip, like an intake of breath, to show something was there.

I helped Susan put together a death announcement that she could send to her friends and family, based on notes I took while she told Barney stories one night in the kitchen. Several months later, Susan went to dinner at the café where she'd once waited tables. A waiter said he'd hung the flier about Barney's death in the kitchen so all the staff could see it, and that it had made him cry.

"He told me how, when he lived two blocks away from me, Barney would just show up, knock on the door with his tail, come in, visit, and leave. I had no idea he was doing that.

"Barney was family. I never thought an animal would become family to me the way he did. Barney was a foundation in my life—probably more than most of my friends. I think in our culture we don't respect how much pets become family. They become an integral part of our lives."

Susan copied the text I wrote onto soft gray paper with a photograph of Barney. Every now and then, I take it out and read it again, the stories I now know by heart. How Barney lost his right front leg. How Barney sniffed out new tennis balls from behind a friend's closet door.

"He died quietly at home and was buried in the yard, at the site of an azalea bush and wisteria tree," the announcement ends. "Many people will miss him. Susan most of all."

Dancing to a New Biological Beat

Mɪᴍɪ Maduro rented a dance studio and filled it with the songs and costumes, voices and movements of women in flux. The occasion was her final menstrual period before undergoing a hysterectomy. For Mimi, that meant the cessation of a cycle that had patterned her life, regular as a metronome, for twenty-five years.

Ever since her first period, at age thirteen, Mimi had looked forward to bleeding every twenty-nine days. Even when severe endometriosis made her periods painful, her menstrual cycle remained regular. A hysterectomy meant an end to seven years of monthly pain—but also to the steady, predictable tides of blood.

"I realized that I was actually going to have a last period," she said. "That felt really important. Since I use my period so much as a life-cycle marker, I wondered what markers I was going to use in the future."

Mimi knew friends who had thrown parties when they turned fifty, or got divorced, or when their grown children left home. Mimi herself had gathered a group of women friends for a party before she and her husband, Michael, were married. She also hosted friends for a dinner dubbed "Seven Women on the Seventh Day of the Seventh Moon" when she decided to go to graduate school.

But this occasion was different. It marked an event most women did not celebrate, a turning point still surrounded by veils of taboo. For Mimi, who had decided not to have children, her period was not a reminder of fertility but a connection she shared with every other woman. Her party, she decided, would celebrate that link.

"I thought about having a barbecue. I thought about going on a hike with a group of friends. Or having a dinner party. Then I realized I didn't want the event to focus on food or talking. I wanted to dance with my women friends.

"It wasn't just about me acknowledging my last period, but all of the changes we all were going through. That's why I called it the Change Dance. This was the change my life was hinged around. When I hit upon that, it felt so right."

Seventeen women gathered for the Change Dance on a Sunday evening. Some had brought tapes of Motown, African drumming, Cuban salsa, marimba music. For Mimi, the party affirmed her connection not only with friends, but with the women in her own family, the biology that bound grandmother to mother to daughter. She set up photographs of her maternal relatives and labeled the display "The Uteruses from Which I Have Come."

"I wanted to serve some type of ceremonial treat. My grandmother, who was Slovak, used to make something she called a nut roll. I hadn't had it since she died twenty years ago. I couldn't find a recipe for it, so I wrote it down from memory and reconstructed it with my mother over the telephone. It came out wonderfully, and we fed pieces of it to each other."

Then everyone gathered in a circle. Each woman, one friend explained, would have fifteen minutes to create a performance piece about an important change in her life. They could use costumes, hats and props that belonged to the studio.

"That was the most outrageous part," Mimi said. "People were really taking a leap. The costumes helped. Once people got into hats and heels and wild outfits, they could take on a different persona." Everyone, it turned out, was in the midst of an important transition. One woman was going through a divorce. Another suffered chronic health problems. One was pregnant, another was entering menopause. One woman's mother had recently died.

On Mimi's turn, she pulled on a red silk skirt she'd found in the costume box. One friend had brought her a bunch of lavender, a variety Mimi had never seen before. "I put the lavender in my skirt so it looked like it was growing out of me. Then I said, I know I can grow something new, and I'm ready to do that."

Afterward, all the women gathered for a Period Dance. Holding lengths of red satin ribbon, they danced freestyle, interweaving the ribbon until they'd wound themselves together in a crimson web.

After the Change Dance, Mimi said, she discovered new ways of talking and thinking about her upcoming surgery. Not just about the details—which hospital, what kind of anesthesia, where the scar would be located—but about the deeper, emotional underpinnings. "It helped me to open up layers of discussion: What does it mean to go through menopause? What is it to be a woman?"

The Change Dance reminded Mimi and her friends of the fierce bonds created when women share the critical junctures in their lives. Such events literally make a space to recognize changes that have been overlooked or silenced; Mimi rented a room, and women flooded it with their stories. Her final period took its place amid the surge—not an isolating event but a magnet for support and community.

"There are so many women who have hysterectomies. I'm becoming more and more aware of how important this is. Whether you go through menopause naturally or surgically, it's a rite of passage. For me, it was about making a choice toward a fuller life. The ritual grounded me and prepared me more deeply for the many layers of change unfolding in my life.

"Bringing people together has always been my way of creating family. Part of me had wanted to celebrate, and part didn't want to just call attention to myself. I tried to make it focused on everybody's changes. Everybody had something they were going through. Our lives are so wild."

Celebrating Growing Older

NEXT to the tree, Smokey was just a youngster. The four-hundred-year-old sycamore was one reason she'd bought the house. It ruled the back yard with its knobbed trunk and huge umbrella of branches, focal point of the half-acre lot. Smokey called it the "grandmother tree." When she imagined her fiftieth-birthday ritual, she wasn't sure exactly what she would wear or do or say. But she had no question about the place.

"At 3:30 P.M., Grandmother Tree will host a croning," Smokey typed on the invitation. She scoured address books for names of all the people who'd mattered in her life, 150 invitations in all.

At work, where she was the environmentalist for a grocery and convenience store chain, people's fiftieth birthdays were marked with cynical jokes, black crepe paper, buttons proclaiming "You're over the Hill." In her biological family, older women were coy about their ages. "It was okay for the men to be older and wiser," she said. "But for the older women, age was a funny, tittery secret."

After graduating from college, Smokey became close with a friend's stepmother, and her perspective about age began to shift. "She was my model. I was struck with the vitality that came from the older women in her family through her storytelling."

Later, there were other mentors. Smokey resisted her mother for years until realizing recently that they shared an important bond, a love of plants and the earth. And just before her fiftieth birthday, Smokey spent a week with seven female cousins, all older than she, some of whom she hadn't seen in years.

"Part of my birthday passage was to meet these women who are part of my biological family and hear their stories," Smokey said. "They're all very strong, powerful women, proud of who they are in the world. They were kind of initiating me into my fifties. I thought, Hey, this is a beginning, not a downhill run."

She also remembered the women she'd met at a party when she was in her thirties. They were lesbians in their fifties, sixties, and seventies. During the party, one of them took Smokey aside. "You don't know what we've been through for you," she said.

As she neared fifty, Smokey could feel herself voicing similar thoughts. Young lesbians she met had never heard of once-thriving community institutions—the Mountain Moving Café, where local folk singers and actors had first performed, the monthly Lesbian Forum discussion groups. They couldn't imagine a time when more women were closeted than out. Somehow, time had nudged her into the older generation. Smokey thought about the party sixteen years earlier; the woman's words still echoed.

"It wasn't said in a martyr kind of way," she recalled. "It was like this: We've laid a lot of stepping stones with our lives that you're walking on, and you don't even know it. So be aware."

THE morning of her party, Smokey still didn't know what the "croning ritual" would entail. She put on a lavender blouse, a gift from her brother and sister-in-law, the first silk garment she'd ever owned. It felt lush next to her skin. She sat down at the computer and began to type.

"I wrote a little bit about my life, how I'd gotten to this point and how interlaced all these people were. I wanted to take time to celebrate those connections and make my passage into another level of my life." Gradually, the words began to flow. "Croning is a time of harvest when all that's learned is coming to fruition and ready to share. A time to consider life's gains and how to share them with all our relations." Soon she had an entire page of text.

At noon, people started to arrive. Colleagues from various jobs. Friends who'd driven hundreds of miles to be there. Old pals, buddies from her recycling projects. Ex-lovers. A woman she'd met once through the Lesbian Gardening Club on a brief tour of someone else's back yard. Men, women, young, old, reunited friends and people who had never met each other—about sixty-five of them in all.

Just before 3:30 Smokey put on a long Guatemalan dress. Everyone gathered outside. Light splashed to the ground in patches through the limbs of the sycamore tree. A cluster of bright balloons bobbed from the edge of her hot tub. She read aloud what she'd written that morning, then threw leaves of tobacco and handfuls of cornmeal—symbolizing earth and sun—to the four directions. A group of women drummers kept up a steady beat on hand drums. Then Smokey asked her friends to tell stories and memories.

One woman, a friend for about fourteen years, remembered running into Smokey a year earlier, when she was getting ready to move. She happened to mention her moving date, then raced off to do more errands. On that morning, without an explicit invitation, Smokey showed up at the door to help.

A former lover recalled the summer she and Smokey met, when they both worked on commercial fishing boats. Once, their two boats stayed out overnight. "We had this conversation back and forth over the CB radio. We were just starting to get together then, and you can't be too intimate on the CB, because everyone is listening for a thousand miles," Smokey said. "But we shared some personal thoughts about the incredible life of the sea. That was a magical night. She remembered that, and so did I. It never ceases to amaze me how much we impact each other's lives."

The ceremony lasted more than two hours, but to Smokey, it felt like minutes flying by. In the early evening, some guests started to drift out the door; at 9 P.M. Smokey realized she hadn't eaten all day. "I felt like I was definitely in another plane. I'm not sure I ever have felt quite as high as I did that day. I felt kind of filleted, unzipped, in a really positive way."

On the other 364 days, Smokey was simply a fifty-year-old woman, entering menopause, comfortable with the body, experience, and life that half a century had brought her. She wore her long gray hair loose, often with a bandanna tied around her forehead. When tears came, easily and often, she bit her bottom lip and let them flow.

"I think there is a subtle shift, a sense that I have gathered a lot of experience and energy and that it's my job to share that with other people. I've lived fifty years. I have half a century of experience, information, and understanding to my credit. I take those with me wherever I go.

"I have a number of friends in their thirties. They're interested in personal history, lesbian history, what I've seen. Women who are twenty years my senior have done that for me. It's important to pass that experience on so we don't forget."

When Smokey first planned the croning ceremony, she felt uneasy about making herself the focus of attention. But once her friends were gathered under the Grandmother Tree, a flood of support and warmth dissolved her fears of exposure. "We keep ourselves down by not risking that," she said. "We really need to celebrate ourselves more."

By Any Other Name:
Retitling Ourselves

I SPEND a lot of time spelling my name. I scribble out "A-N-D-Y" and "A-N-D-I" on magazine labels and send them back to the subscription office. "A-N-N-D-E-E," I say slowly to the secretary on the phone. I spell the last name, too, for good measure.

Our names are our first gifts, and they bring a mixed legacy of burdens and hopes. Names attach us to our families and tell us who we are supposed to be. Often whole sets of characteristics trail them: "She's got those Ochman thighs." The names are like envelopes, carrying the stories of our pasts, the expectations for our futures.

Some names bear witness to assimilation—names changed upon immigration because American tongues couldn't wrap around them, or altered en route because they were too "different," and difference meant danger. Or they may recall the hideous oppressions of slavery, the arbitrary names given to slaves by their white masters.

Women's names carry particular problems. For one thing, they have never been our own names, not entirely. We carry our fathers' names, which are *their* fathers' names. Traditionally, a woman's surname was merely a place-holder; upon marriage, her last name, and sometimes even her first, disappeared. Our female names have not always been strong enough to take us where we want to travel. Women have had to masquerade under male pseudonyms or hide beneath genderless initials to earn legitimacy and audience for their work.

Men's names clog the landscape and the marketplace—men's names on mountains and viruses, on buildings and shop windows, on cities and fountains. Names everywhere—arrogant and immortal, marking territory, declaring ownership. The results of that naming are buried so deep in our language we don't even think anymore: This is titled for some man. Pasteurization. Douglas fir. Nobel prize. Webster's dictionary.

I think of the Philadelphia suburb where I grew up, a riot of William Penn's progeny. Penn Wynne. Penn Valley. Penn's Landing. All those big, old woods, that spacious unfamiliar landscape, bearing the name of one mortal man. Perhaps giving a forest his own name, as if it were an infant son, helped bring the frightening new territory down to size.

These are old, tenacious habits. "Ms.," coined in the hope of making women's marital status as publicly irrelevant as men's, slowly took hold—but usually as an alternative to "Mrs.," while "Mr." still serves for all men, married or single. The New York Times held out against the advent of "Ms." for years, referring stodgily and absurdly to "Miss [Gloria] Steinem," "Miss [Rita Mae] Brown"—Miss, lacy and lingering, like a rustle of wind through magnolia trees. Ms., in contrast, sounds like a buzzer, waking us to the twentieth century.

CATHOLIC children choose a saint's name at confirmation; novitiates take new names when they enter a convent. I once interviewed a woman who said she befuddled the nuns and her family when she chose Saint Philip Neri as her confirmation saint. His was the only story in the book she admired. Change it to Phyllis, the nuns insisted, and she did. "But in my heart," she confided years later, "it was still Philip."

In other cultures, where names have mystical and not just economic or legal power, people take new names, or add to their original ones, at critical junctures in their lives. In puberty or coming-of-age ceremonies. At marriage. For women, when they stop menstruating. At croning ceremonies, an increasingly popular ritual to mark menopause, women often take a new name to signify their entrance into the "elder" stage of life.

Women sometimes choose new names, or peel the layers off old ones, to reverse the tide of assimilation, take back the ethnic echoes. Rachael Murphey thought about reclaiming her African American heritage by choosing a different name from that of her adoptive family. "I didn't know how I was going to tell my parents about it," she said. "I was going to be Rachael Lalique Shabar Baban-ra. Rachael Murphey, to me, is very vacant. "

Arturo and Esperanza, who rented the apartment attached to our house, used to be called "Underwood." One day I came home and found a pink printed card under our door, announcing that they had both adopted, as their surname, "Aguillon-Peraza," Esperanza's original last name and that of Arturo's mother.

I remember reading how the writer Melanie Kaye wanted to take back the name "Kantrowitz," which her grandfather had Americanized. A historian friend reminded her that the name change itself was part of her history, the history of Jews who feared visibility. So she took both names, Kaye/Kantrowitz, written like that, with a slash, a name that does not erase the old story but shows the segue from generation to generation, and back again.

Other women have flip-flopped the custom of passing on father-names by reclaiming maternal ones ("Rosechild," for instance, replacing "Mendelson"). Or they pull words from the realm of epithets ("Dykewomon") and make proud surnames of them. Still others rename themselves ("Wisechild") with the qualities they wish to have.

Naming can be strut and arrogance, a way of scrawling yourself on the world. But it can also be intimate, deliberate, an attempt to know and understand. To name yourself is to feel fully the weight of your own voice.

FRODO Okulam took her names from books. "'Okulam' is Chinook and means the sound of the sea," Frodo explained. "I read it in a book when I was a kid, and I liked it. I hung onto it. When I started writing poetry, I used that name. Then when I started hanging around the gay community, I used that name.

"Finally after I became a pastor in the Metropolitan Community Church, I decided it was ridiculous for my clerical name to be different from my legal name, and I changed it legally.

"I told my original family, but they're the only ones I let call me by the name they gave me, the name they're used to. I thought it was going to be harder for them, especially when I changed the last name. Of course, if I were straight and got married, the same thing could happen.

"I did feel some sense of loss about the last name. I feel very proud of my heritage. My given last name is a typical French name, impossible to spell. I don't have anything against it. I do have things against my given first name because it's a really typical female name. I never liked that. It was the name they yelled when I did something wrong.

"'Frodo' is from *The Lord of the Rings*. Frodo finds himself in a position where something needs to be done, and he's the obvious person to do it. I always felt that sense of calling. The name is of Scandinavian origin, meaning peacemaker. The same origin as 'Frieda.'

"'Okulam' to me means that the sound of the sea can be heard in all things. It sounds like a wave turning over."

Gwenn Cody, a therapist, changed her name from "Gwenn Janice Pereira" eight years ago as part of a resolve to detach herself from the unhealthy choices and relationships of her past. "I had a friend in Boston who had changed her name; for her it was a choice to disassociate from her biological family. I saw how it had empowered her."

Gwenn wanted to incorporate the surname of her aunt and uncle, whom she had "adopted" as a second set of parents. She transformed her uncle's East Indian name, "Satyanarayan," into "Tiana" for a new middle name, and chose "Cody" for her last name. That was a derivative of "Coyote," the crafty and mysterious creature of Native American mythology.

Initially, Gwenn's father was angry at what seemed a rejection of his family name. And since her marriage several years ago, her grandparents insist on addressing letters with her husband's last name, "Shostek." But most people, she said, react with curiosity and interest.

"Most women who have changed their names have done it either to get out of the patriarchal inheritance or to capture something mythological, like 'Moondaughter.' For me, the name is about freedom. I wish we could change our names easily and fluidly. I wish there was a way to wear those changing parts of our identity comfortably."

OTHER names signify new attachments. The day Laura Kern and Tere Wyatt appeared in family court to have their surnames officially changed to "Blue," they were on the docket following a divorce case. The man and woman stood in the courtroom screaming at each other, bickering about which of them should get their boat. At the time, Laura's smooth, medium brown hair was dyed a bright indigo. The judge dispatched the divorce case, consulted her files, and looked up at Laura and Tere.

"Let me guess what you're here for," she said dryly.

"We wanted to have a family name that represented our family, not an extension of our parents' families," Tere explained later.

Laura's surname, like so many others, suffered in the Ellis Island portals. "Gerstenkaren" became "Kern." And Tere never felt much affinity with "Wyatt," the name of her Tennessee family. Using a common name in public, they said, challenges people's assumptions about their relationship.

"We do a lot of education," Laura said. "I'll go to get a video card. I say, Put 'Tere Blue' on it. The clerk says, 'Your sister?' I say, No. 'Your mother?' I say, No. I let them guess. Then I say, My girlfriend."

Only some members of their biological families have acknowledged the change. Laura's cousin sent them a Christmas present addressed to "Blue," but Tere's mother still mails letters to "Miss Tere Wyatt."

For these women, the name change was a symbolic advance toward the family they are creating together. "I've always felt I would birth a child," Tere said. "The whole process of choosing our name and how we've thought about having children has been a more significant affirmation of our relationship than any ceremony."

Do people in a family need the same name? More and more, the surnames in any given household vary, tracing our tangled roots. I know a family of four in which no two have the same name: a lesbian couple, a teenaged daughter with the hyphenated surnames of her mother and father, and a five-year-old son with both women's last names.

I wonder sometimes whether we'd all live more freely if our families were conglomerations of people called different things, people who sometimes are like each other but many times are not, people who belong foremost to themselves and bear proudly their own names.

Or perhaps we need a ceremony, at age twenty-one or twenty-five or forty, at which the guest of honor explains why she is keeping what she has always been called, adding to it or changing it. There could be candles, music, and a cake—with chocolate chips, of course, spelling out the name.

If it were my party, I might tell the story of how a first-grade substitute teacher made me cry, insisting that my name must be short for Andrea.

Another year, my teacher distinguished me from the male Andy in the class by calling him Andy and me, Ann-DEE, accent on the second syllable. Occasionally I have received mail addressed to Mr. Andy Hochman, and one receptionist took it down as Abbie Hoffman in the message.

But it's my name, my very own. After thirty years, I can't imagine bearing any other. I like everything about it—its odd spelling, its refusal to be shortened to a nickname, even its androgyny and implied departure from gender roles. I like to see it on the tops of published articles, and little chills whisper down my back when it's said in the night. If I had the chance, I would choose this name again—which is to say, I would choose my own skin, my own life, with all the stories it does and does not contain.

ONE late August, under a full moon, I attended a party on the broad, sloping lawn of a house thirty miles from the city's buzz. The hosts had built a sweat lodge in the yard, a dome-shaped enclosure with a pit in the center that held steaming-hot rocks. About fifteen of us sat naked in the sweat lodge, and one woman talked about taking a new name. She was going to call herself Raven.

Heat seared the back of my throat and the flesh between my breasts. Streams of sweat washed down my back, and my vision smeared from the waves of warmth. Despite my altered state, I felt skeptical at first. If this woman dropped her given name, was she just treating her history as a commodity, easily cast off in favor of a newer, brighter garment? But perhaps names are sometimes outgrown, like snakeskin or baby shoes. Maybe it's not the name that is sacred, but the *naming*—the intention and the fit.

The woman now called Raven had black straight hair and a smooth, athletic body, glossy with sweat. When she said her new name, she sat up very straight, as if it filled her to the edges.

In Sickness and in Health: Unconventional Caretaking

In my biological family, sickness was a *shanda*, a shame, an aberration from the real lives of good people. My aunts uttered "cancer" in whispers, waited until the children were asleep to talk of a miscarriage, an accident, a coma. People did not "die," they "passed away," disembodied, like breezes.

Poor health, I learned, was a secret to be hidden even from one's own kin, particularly older parents or children. When my great-grandmother Ethel and great-uncle Bernie were dying, at the same time, in the same hospital, the family shuttled back and forth from one room to the other, not telling either mother or son that the other one was ill. I grew up believing that if I were ever very sick, my relatives would flock to my bedside, badger my doctors, pace all night in hospital corridors. They would be there, yes. But we would hesitate to *talk* about it, to name the pain, anxiety, grief, and fear.

For women, these silences are deepened by the shame we have been taught about our bodies, the societal flinch away from female flesh and blood. Besides, we are supposed to be the caretakers of others, tending the weak, the old, the ill, the young, ourselves impervious to breakdown.

Several years ago, I began to suffer occasional anxiety attacks so severe that rooms swung and floors rolled under me, my hands tingled and my throat closed in on itself. I couldn't escape the frightening feelings or the commands of my childhood to keep quiet about it. Panic terrified and embarrassed me, and my shame made the attacks more intense. My body's reactions, I thought, were stains on my competence. Somehow, I should have prevented them, and now that it was too late, I ought to fix the problem as quickly and quietly as possible.

When instead the attacks grew worse, so frequent and wracking that I began to consider carefully every public place I ventured, I wondered who would care for me if my world contracted, if I became afraid to leave the house, paralyzed by fear of fear.

For months I did not talk, even to close friends or relatives, about my jags of thudding heartbeat, roiling stomach, buzzing head. I didn't mention the anxieties that lurched like drunken buses through my mind. *Don't tell. Don't tell because they'll worry too much. Don't tell because you'll upset them. Don't tell because it's ugly and no one really wants to hear.* They are women's instructions. I followed them well, and they left me, for a while, with no one at a time when I needed people most. My burden was mine, unique, private, and humiliating.

Feminism urges women to tell the truth about all of our experience, including our experience *as bodies.* In consciousness-raising groups of the 1970s, women began to talk of their miscarriages and abortions, of cancer and mental illness. As a result, I now see women who do not hide their imperfect bodies, who know that silence brings exile and honest speech the only healthy way home.

I take courage from women who rupture these taboos. Kate Millett tells her truth about mental illness in *The Loony Bin Trip.* Nancy Mairs writes clear-eyed essays about being a woman, a mother, a wife, a person with multiple sclerosis. "The presence of pain in a family doesn't have to mean that the family's in trouble, ready to fall apart at any moment," Mairs writes in *Carnal Acts.* Her husband, son, and daughter, she suggests, are perhaps "a little wiser, not merely sadder and tireder, for having lived this way. We've learned...that the bodies we inhabit and the lives those bodies carry on need not be perfect to have value."

Women have begun to let their bodies exhibit the truth. Some, in the name of honesty and health, in rejection of male definitions of beauty, refuse implants or prostheses after mastectomies. Their flattened chests are not signs of shame but proclamations of survival. The late poet Audre Lorde, who wrote movingly of her illness in *The Cancer Journals,* was one of these proudly one-breasted women.

Once I saw a photograph of the writer Deena Metzger, standing bare-chested, her arms spread like wings, a tattoo of roses and leaves tracing the scar where a surgeon had removed her right breast. On the flat side of her chest, I could see the warp and weft of muscles, a finely sculptured plain. It is a stunning picture—joltingly frank, outrageous, and lovely. "Yes, I lost a breast," I imagine Metzger's voice saying. "Here's what it looks like. I'm scarred, but not diminished. And still, I celebrate."

WHEN I talked with women and wanted to know what distinguished "family" from "friends," illness often came up in the responses, etching a line between even devoted acquaintances and true confidantes: *Family are the ones you can call to bring you chicken soup. The ones who come over when you're too sick to see anyone. The ones you call when there's an emergency at 3 A.M.*

Typically, women have been the ones to answer these calls. As daughters, sisters, mothers, wives, and friends, the job of caring for ill kin fell to us with an unforgiving calculus. A woman could either suspend her life to tend a sick or needy person or, by refusing to ignore her own needs, risk being called selfish. This harsh either/or standard dismissed the toll that caregiving takes on the caregiver, and it offered no alternative.

One winter afternoon, Susan Bryer sat on the couch in my office, where papers were strewn over my desk and my crowded appointment book lay open on a chair. She explained her fears of depending on her "declared" family. Susan has chronic fatigue syndrome, a viral disease with erratic effects. Sometimes she feels energetic enough for a four-mile walk; other days, she can barely climb off the couch to cook dinner.

"A number of people have said to me, 'Call me, I'll do it, whatever it is.' And I believe them, but I also think it's an innocent offer. You have a busy life. And if I were to call you at four o'clock one afternoon and say, I'm exhausted. I'm too sick to make dinner. Will you bring me some? And you've got appointments or whatever. What would you do?"

I wait a moment, thinking. I would want to help. Yet I know how, on some crowded, work-crazed afternoons, I resent even the cat yowling to be let outside. I want to be with Susan in this chronic illness, but not by myself, and not all the time. I fight the shame of my ambivalence, which contradicts the expectation that women should care willingly and self-lessly for others.

"If I knew someone, a friend, with chronic fatigue, I would do it differ-ently," Susan continued. "I would drop by with food. Because I know how hard it is to ask. I wouldn't say, Do you need anything? I would just start doing it. It's only since I've been sick that I've developed that sensitivity."

Hearing that makes me feel my own lack, remember all the times I haven't checked in, didn't think to bring over extra portions of dinner, felt annoyed when Susan didn't have energy to go out. When I do care for her, when I stop my work an hour early, carry soup and biscuit dough to her house, my feelings are a thorough, perplexing mix of satisfaction and resentment, tenderness and impatience.

It is a source of shame, the suggestion that our care for others is not always cheerful and wholehearted. I am terrible, I think. I ought to be bet-ter. But even as I berate myself I remember that this uneasy subject is, among feminists, safe ground for consideration and talk. Hours after Su-san has left, I can still see her sitting cross-legged on my couch, her eyes tired, her face awaiting answer. I'll say yes when I can, I think. But I might also say no, sometimes. Mostly, I will do something neither perfectly self-ish nor utterly selfless. I'll make a choice out of my mixed feelings, a flawed and human act of care.

I KNOW there are ways of caregiving that do not depend on secrets and selflessness—in which the caregiver is not alone, omniscient, and stoic; the sick person is not helpless, mute, and ashamed. These are feminist models, based on a belief in each woman's right to govern her own body and on faith in what we can accomplish together.

These new types of taking care require a different way of thinking about illness—as communal rather than private, a part of life rather than a departure from it. They also demand a new vision of caregiving—one that encourages women to know and state their own limits, to take care of themselves even while nursing others. On the surface, feminist caregiving may resemble the models that still thrive in some communi-ties, where relatives, church folk, neighbors, and friends rally around a sick person's bedside. But a closer look reveals important differences.

Today, the people who come together in crisis don't necessarily share a biological, geographic, historic, or religious base. They form eclectic groups, drawn together by the choices they have made as adults. Best friends may assume important roles along with or instead of spouses or intimate partners.

These configurations are gaining public notice in forums such as obituaries and funeral programs. Nancy Ryles, a prominent Oregon politician who died suddenly of a brain tumor, was remembered in a memorial service that drew more than a thousand people. The program listed as survivors her husband, children, siblings, nephews, then a "trusted friend" and a "long time special support group of seven women."

Such kin cannot simply rely on sameness to get them through; they bring differences of background, ethnicity, sexual orientation, age, skill, and commitment to the collective task of taking care. What results is a way of coping with illness that looks and sounds different—more open, more honest, less embarrassed. It is the creation of a generation of women who grew up with feminism and learned, through long struggle, to ask for what they needed, to risk disclosure, to share tasks, to rely on community.

When Andrea Carlisle, a writer, went into the hospital for a myomectomy to remove fibroid tumors, she sent a letter to her friends telling them when and where the surgery would take place, where she planned to stay after leaving the hospital, who would make medical decisions for her in case she couldn't make them herself, and what she wanted in the way of help and company as she recovered. She also told them how grateful she felt for the support they had lent already as she weighed the risks and benefits of surgery. "Thank you for being my friends and for listening to me through all of this indecision and thrashing around," she wrote.

Other women have launched deliberate, organized efforts to inform and rally their friends during a medical crisis. When Nancy Conklin was diagnosed with an aggressive form of breast cancer, she asked a close friend to write a periodic newsletter that would be mailed to about forty colleagues, family members, and friends around the country.

"It was Nancy's idea," said Mabsie Walters, who wrote the newsletters. "She said that clearly she was going to need to muster the support of her friends. This was a way to keep people updated." The newsletters gave detailed, factual information about Nancy's diagnosis and treatment and specific suggestions for how people could help. One issue asked friends to send jigsaw puzzles, tapes of mysteries, and posters for her hospital room and advised that she did not want telephone calls. Subsequent newsletters thanked people, on behalf of Nancy and her husband, Jim, for their support, cards, and gifts.

"We tried to think of things that people who were far away could do," Mabsie said. "We tried to keep the letters upbeat, to put some humor in them." And while Jim remained Nancy's main caregiver, writing the newsletters allowed Mabsie to help in a way that was concrete, intimate, and manageable.

Women's new ways of caregiving allow a range of contributions from a variety of people, easing the burden on those providing primary, daily attention. When Susan Bryer learned she would need a hysterectomy several years ago, Elissa offered to organize a dinner brigade to provide meals seven nights a week for a month after the surgery.

Susan made a list of more than thirty names and phone numbers. She also set the guidelines: Friends could bring dinner at any time of evening, but they needed to call first. They should cook enough for Susan's mother and sister, who were staying with her for the first two weeks. Also, she requested soft, comforting foods—"things their mothers would have made for them," Elissa recalled.

"Through all this, Susan was always the decision-maker," she said. "When I called her friends, there was such a great response that we ran out of nights. They were so glad to be asked—it makes me cry just to think about it. It gave everybody a chance to see Susan and feel that they were doing something useful."

In all of these ventures, I see women working to re-vision illness, departing from the rigid prescriptions and taboos we have inherited. We need not talk in whispers. We need not embody secrets. No woman is required to give herself up in the effort to care for another. Divisions between the well and the sick are not so much a matter of category as of degree; sooner or later, all our bodies break down.

I work to quiet the old messages about illness, voice new ones. I dare, now and then, to tell my closest friends that I am sometimes spun dizzy with anxiety, that my whole body percolates with fear I can't explain. I try to stand by another's distress with honest, open eyes. I try to remember that there is nothing unspeakable about our lives.

I listen, fascinated, to the stories of women who help each other navigate their bodies' unpredictable courses with resourcefulness, pluck, and candor. In enduring pain with each other, we face our own frailties, our own mess. We grope toward a vision of family that can welcome each of us whole, a place to be seen and to belong. Here, in sickness and in health, are acts that flood me with faith—expressions of need and sorrow, the hundred small ways to give and receive comfort, the slow venture of illness out of shameful closets and into the healing light of day.

Candor and Kinship

ELIZABETH Waters remembers scanning a table of colleagues, other board members of the McKenzie River Gathering Foundation, a nonprofit group that funnels grants to grass-roots activists. When Elizabeth spotted Amani Jabari, she felt a surge of immediate kinship; his was the only other African American face in the group.

It was the late 1970s. As Elizabeth and Amani got to know each other, they discovered they shared more than ethnicity. Both were moving slowly from alternative, nonprofit work settings toward more traditional venues. Amani had lived in Washington, D.C., where Elizabeth's paternal relatives grew up. They both wanted to work with people of color.

Slowly, they started meeting for dinner after meetings, inviting each other to parties, talking on the phone. The two friends were well matched—they worked hard, sometimes compulsively, and unwound in the same way, drinking until they quit counting the glasses.

"There was a sort of instant connection," Elizabeth remembered. "It was like we were brother and sister, like we'd known each other all our lives." Soon the two were practically inseparable. They talked on the phone four or five times a day, lent each other money, bought each other gifts. Elizabeth spent holidays with Amani's biological family.

Not that they always agreed. Elizabeth was adamantly pro-choice; Amani thought abortion was murder. She thought he was elitist. He said she hung out with the wrong kind of people. "We fought," Elizabeth said. "The way Amani and I would interact in meetings, people thought, Are you two married, or are you brother and sister? We were honest with each other: Okay, you're doing this, I don't like it, I don't agree with it, but if that's what you need to do, do it. There wasn't the badgering, the Oh, this is really awful, How can you do this to me?

"No matter what phase I was going through, I knew Amani would be there and he would be honest with me. He might say, 'I think what you're doing is sick. You need to look at it. Now are you ready to go out and eat?' And we'd go out and eat.

"That's what I think family, in the healthy sense, is."

That candor included confronting each other when alcohol started to interfere with their lives. Elizabeth used to chide Amani about how much he drank; he'd respond, "Who are you to talk?" Eventually, he stopped drinking on his own, and, inspired by his example, Elizabeth resolved to quit, too.

"I went through a phase of my addiction when I thought no one knew. I sort of withdrew from people and tried to run away. Amani was right there. He wasn't leaving. Other people left me alone. But he didn't go away.

"I assumed Amani and I would be in each other's life forever."

WHEN Amani went to a county clinic to get the results of an HIV test, both he and Elizabeth knew what the outcome was likely to be.

"It was really devastating for me," Elizabeth recalled. "I'd had a lot of loss. A few people in my family had died, and I'd hired a couple people to work with me who were HIV positive. My father died when I was very young, and no one ever talked about it.

"I'd always thought that if I cared about someone, they'd die. I thought somehow I had jinxed Amani."

For months, Elizabeth refused to believe Amani would really get sick. He would be the one miracle, the person who lived forever with HIV disease. She'd been trying to stay sober—"white-knuckling it," she said later—but Amani's diagnosis jolted her back to old habits. She drank, then started using drugs to blot her grief.

Finally she called her friends together, told them she had a problem with drugs and alcohol, and entered a hospital treatment program. She started attending twelve-step meetings. She talked with a chaplain, an alcohol and drug counselor. Amani was getting sicker, and she was determined to be there, clearheaded, for him. She was also determined not to take over.

"I had an employee I'd become friends with who died of AIDS. What I learned from his death was that the person who's dying has the right to make all the decisions. It's his life.

"Amani could talk to me. When he got very sick, he'd say, 'I'm not going to take my medication any more.' I didn't say, You're giving up. How can you do this? I could say to him, I don't want you to die. You're my best friend. This is very painful to me. But I want you to make these choices. I was able to listen and be there.

"I remember when he decided that he was ready to die. He called me at five o'clock in the morning and said, 'I need to talk to you.' I went over there and he said, 'I want to die in the next two months.' He said, 'I want you to promise me that you won't let them put me on life-support systems, that it's not a sad funeral, and that they say I died of AIDS and that I was a gay man.'

"He died on a Sunday. On that Friday he was at a nearby hospice. I stayed the night with him. About three or four in the morning, he woke up. He had pretty much been out of it. He sat up in bed. He said, 'I gotta go. I gotta get ready.' The nurses said, 'What?' He said, 'I gotta get ready for the ceremony.' He was so alert. His eyes were open. He looked at me, and he said, 'I'm goin'.'"

AT AMANI'S funeral, he was eulogized as a gay man, a black man, a Christian who had died of AIDS. Elizabeth made sure of that. She stood up before the crowded pews, looked out at Amani's mother and sister, his colleagues, pals, ex-lovers, and talked about her friend.

It wasn't always easy, Elizabeth said, to find her place as "best friend" amid the cluster of medical providers and biological family. Amani's sister was designated to make medical decisions, and Elizabeth was her backup.

"I'd always assumed I was going to be the one who would make all those decisions for Amani. I had to learn to back down and respect the rights of his biological family, who had been in his life all his life. But he had also worked it out with them that he wanted me included.

"At the end, he became very mean. He would yell at his sister and yell at his mother. I'd get in his room and close the door, and he'd start yelling at me. And I'd say, You ain't gonna die from AIDS 'cause I'll knock you out of that bed if you keep talking to me that way, and you need to stop talking to your mother and sister that way.

"The family acknowledged and respected my presence and position. But it was hard for me. It had been Amani and me for so long."

For months after Amani's death, Elizabeth couldn't drive by his house, go to the church where they'd attended Sunday services, or bring herself to call Amani's relatives. Board meetings of the Oregon Minority AIDS Coalition, which the two had helped found, were too painful.

"It took me about a year to really walk through the grief and accept that this person is dead, he's gone and he's not coming back," she said. Two years later, there were still painful times. She got teary when certain songs, such as Bette Midler's "Wind beneath My Wings," came on the radio. Anything by Aretha Franklin made her laugh, remembering Amani's impromptu kitchen drag shows, how he would lip-sync his way through dinner preparations.

Elizabeth thought of Amani when she had to write a proposal or a speech, remembering how he had edited her work and reassured her that she was articulate on paper. She was tempted to pick up the phone and call him when a revivalist preacher appeared on cable TV; the two used to make merciless fun of such shows.

And she wondered sometimes how their friendship would have evolved without the haze of alcohol, who they would each be now and what they might have done together. "I always felt that with Amani, I was totally comfortable being who I was. That's unique," she said. "I miss him. I miss my friend."

Surviving Cancer with the Help of Friends

CLAUDIA Johnson woke up from a double mastectomy to a trio of concerned faces. Her partner of seventeen years, Susan Walsh. Her naturopathic physician. And a nurse.

"Where are all the people?" Claudia asked, her voice still steeped with anesthesia and fatigue. Just outside the room, where they'd been instructed to wait, a group of women heard her question. There was Andrea Carlisle, a friend of Claudia's since college. Jane Shearer, a friend and massage therapist who had promised unlimited neck and foot rubs. Other friends who had driven in from out of town.

This circle of women had entered one another's lives nearly twenty years earlier—and stayed, even as they moved and married, divorced, returned to graduate school, changed jobs, found new partners. Some had moved together from the Midwest to the West Coast; others had shared group houses, launched political projects and community newspapers. When one woman in the group divorced and received a large settlement from her ex-husband, she split the money with five friends.

Their commitment to each other was primary, fierce, and largely unspoken. It was in the routine of their lives—supportive phone calls, candid questions, long conversations—that the bond was made plain. When Claudia first learned that she had breast cancer and would need a bilateral mastectomy, she came home, wept with Susan, and then phoned her friends.

"It is so much in the fabric of our lives that we would be there for each other in committed, daily ways," Claudia said. "At the heart of it for me was a shift from the question everyone with cancer asks—What did I do wrong?—to, What's this a metaphor for? If this was a metaphor, there was obviously something about women and breasts and hearts and nurturing.

"It was clear that this was not a private matter."

YEARS earlier, Claudia had had a breast biopsy and endured the entire procedure alone. "It was awful," she remembered. "I thought at the time, I can handle this. Why bother anybody? This time, I'd learned." From the moment she discovered a discharge from one of her breasts, she brought Susan or someone else along to each doctor's visit, kept her friends updated through phone calls, sought advice on finding a female surgeon.

At dawn on the day of her surgery, friends met Claudia and Susan at the hospital. In the room where patients waited, each in a small curtained cubicle, some women lay alone. In Claudia's section, half a dozen women crowded around the bed, talking, laughing, cracking nervous jokes.

"She was in a green room, with curtained-off areas," Andrea remembered. "Completely cold. Then a resident came in who hadn't had any sleep for about three hundred years. The first few words out of his mouth made no sense, and we burst into laughter. We said, Been a long time without sleep, hon?

"Claudia had brought headphones with her, and music she liked. The staff kept saying she wouldn't be able to wear them in surgery, but she went through the operating room doors with the headphones on. We held her hands until she disappeared." Then they wandered through the hospital, consoling each other—and especially Susan—through the anxious hours of waiting.

"They said, 'You girls stay out in the hallway when she comes back from post-op,'" Andrea remembered. "We stood obediently out in the hallway. The door to her room was open just a crack. We heard Claudia say in a groggy voice, 'Where is everybody?' We just pushed open the door and went in.

"The hospital thought that someone just out of post-op wouldn't want company. They had this idea it had to be only one way. For us, there weren't any rules. We just took over. We had no intention of leaving her alone."

While Claudia was in the hospital, Susan slept there each night, dozing on an extra bed. Friends arrived daily with special soaps and favorite tapes, books and magazines. After Claudia wept at the sight of her first hospital breakfast, friends began to bring home-cooked meals, caffe lattes and rolls from nearby bakeries.

Jane massaged Claudia's feet, her hands, her throbbing neck and shoulders. Friends held her hand while she slept, swabbed her forehead with damp washcloths, and cheered when she got out of bed and took her first tentative steps across the room.

"The most comforting thing was being able to sleep and hearing the voices around me, knowing they were there, talking to each other," Claudia said. "I didn't have to entertain or take care of anybody. It was like when you're a kid, and you hear voices in the next room and know you're safe."

The support continued once Claudia went home. A friend had gone to the house early in the morning and practiced lying on the bed to figure out how to arrange the pillows. She moved the night table so that water, medication, and a tape recorder would be within easy reach; she placed bouquets of flowers where Claudia could see them without having to turn her head.

Susan waited tables in a restaurant at night, so other friends came and stayed while Claudia slept. Two friends from San Francisco came up for a week and virtually took over running the house—cooking, cleaning, doing laundry, fielding phone calls. One woman offered to handle all the insurance paperwork, filling in endless forms and arguing with hospital staff over discrepancies in the bills. Another drove by in her truck, planted a plastic flamingo in the yard where Claudia could see it from the window, then drove off. A colleague's husband showed up to mow the lawn.

"With biological families, I think, there are a lot of checks and balances: Well, of course I would do that for you; you would do that for me. Here, there wasn't anything at stake in taking care of me. They weren't doing it because they were related to me. They were doing it because of who they were.

"I don't think I understood what it meant to have a lot of friends around when something is life-threatening," Claudia said. "It was the way family is supposed to be. This was the first time I was forced by circumstances to allow that contribution, to allow that many people to be there for me."

Some old relationships grew new facets in the process. Claudia and Andrea had known each other for more than twenty years, ever since Claudia was a campus minister and Andrea a student. "Our relationship had been me taking care of her," Claudia said. "It totally turned around. It was great to see another human being emerge. She's very nurturing. I just hadn't been the recipient of it before."

For Susan, the experience drew forth capacities she didn't know she had. As an adult, she had worked hard to break habits of allowing herself to be swallowed by someone else's needs. Claudia's cancer diagnosis scared her: Would she be able to nurture her partner without erasing herself? Their friends' commitment turned the situation into "a healing crisis," she said.

"It wasn't just me and Claudia and one or two other people," Susan said. "It was our community coming together so no one person was overburdened beyond reasonableness. People were there for me, too, saying, 'How are you doing? Do you need anything?' I had never nursed anyone. The caretaking I did was not anything I ever thought I would do."

For Andrea, the experience was equally powerful. "We all needed support," she said. "It was a scary and strange experience. We talked about everything that was going on. That's something I think is often missing from regular families. It made me feel hopeful that if I had to be in the hospital, I could call on my friends in a way I hadn't really called on them before. It made it seem possible to go through something traumatic with real support."

A YEAR after her own surgery, Claudia got a call from her friend Philip. Both he and his partner had AIDS. They didn't want to die in the hospital. Claudia immediately began to organize a care team to provide the support the two men would need to go home.

"I'm like Anne Frank," Claudia said. "I believe that at the heart of it, people are very good, very dear. People had been there for me. That's what I got—the richness of being able to give that back. No, not give it back. Give it away. Give it as well."

And two years after that, she found herself back in a hospital corridor, waiting anxiously while Andrea underwent a myomectomy. The experience churned up images of Claudia's own surgery. This time, she was the giver, not the recipient, of care. But the feelings were similar—a sense of vulnerability, commitment, and "grace" that came not from biological ties or ancient obligations but from shared, conscious beliefs about how women can live.

"I looked at Andrea last night," Claudia said. "She was sleeping fitfully, and I was watching her, and I thought, I'm still here. I wouldn't be anyplace else. This is what it looks like to have chosen the relationships we chose." And she remembered learning of her own cancer diagnosis, deciding whom she would call with the news.

"I thought, Given that my life will alter irrevocably, who am I inviting to participate in this particular, very intimate, event? I chose Susan and my friends in a way I never had before. I invented a family. But I didn't have to look very far because I'd already created one, from those years of walking around in the world with women who were learning to choose themselves and others.

"I hold it as a responsibility to talk about what's possible when we take care of each other."

Living with AIDS, Relying on Community

NANCY Lawson wanted to tell a funny story about living with HIV disease. The one about having lunch in the elegant dining room on the tenth floor of a downtown department store, sitting with her daughter, her son, and her sister, discussing who would get her clothes and what to do with her body when she died.

Everyone was hysterical, she said. Seriously.

In March of 1987, Nancy went in for an HIV antibody test she was certain would turn out negative. It didn't. Dogged, street-smart, and resourceful, she hunted for information, read dozens of books, talked to countless people. Four years of learning and reading and raging and grieving later, Nancy knew a lot about living with HIV disease. And she was determined to tell others what she'd found.

The first time I met Nancy was at a dinner with the editor of an anthology called AIDS: *The Women*. I didn't know she was HIV positive. When a friend told me, later, I pictured Nancy again, measuring her graying hair, youthful face, and strong body against my stereotypes. Nancy wasn't male. She wasn't gay. And she didn't look ill.

A few months later, I interviewed her for a profile in a local gay and lesbian newspaper. We talked at a sidewalk café table so she could smoke—the one vice she couldn't give up, she joked, telling me she was already doing without drugs, alcohol, sex, and money.

Nancy navigated a story the same way she walked through life—with equal doses of brash humor and reflection, irreverence and hope. I was charmed by her fizzy style, the open, disarming laugh. In a voice grainy from years of smoking, she talked to me about her drug addictions and her recovery, her sexuality, her family, her disease.

Some months later, I interviewed Nancy again, this time in my living room. She was thinner than before, her face paler and more tired. I fought impulses to ask if she was cold, wanted more tea, felt too weary to talk. I wanted to know about her family: her two children, twenty-one-year-old David and fourteen-year-old Annie, a large and diverse circle of friends. How had their roles changed since she got sick? What did she ask of them? What were they willing to give?

"I never really had deliberateness about family until after my AIDS diagnosis," Nancy said. "All my life, I've just sort of been a coper. I've dealt with what fate or life has given me."

She was the oldest of five children and never gave much thought to a family of her own. "I was going to be a famous artist when I grew up, and I was the only one who was in my scenario. I never planned to have children. I thought I would be single or would live with people."

At nineteen, she was pregnant. It was 1969; abortion was illegal. Her high school sweetheart offered to marry her, and she accepted. Suddenly her life seemed cribbed from a TV commercial for dish soap—a mother, father, baby, and house in the New Jersey suburbs.

"I felt very much, at nineteen, as if I had really, really failed life and was never going to have an opportunity to do the things I thought I would. But there was a level of comfort about it, about playing nuclear family. What was comforting was that it was the scenario my parents and society had said was legitimate." She stayed married for two years, lived alone with her son for four or five, then married again and had a daughter. That marriage lasted a decade.

"I've been single for seven years," Nancy said. "Only seven years! This last period of my life has been the most satisfying and the most wonderful and the most amazing. Since my AIDS diagnosis, I've been really deliberate and focused and have chosen my life very carefully.

"Now my family is me and my daughter. My son is pretty close to us, but he's also got his own life. I have an incredible amount of intimacy for someone not in a relationship. I have a lot of people—thirty or forty or fifty—that I can be really honest and intimate with.

"Some of our best friends are a lesbian couple with two adopted Indian foster children. I have a friend who's a gay man and has a child. We also have the extended family of NA, Narcotics Anonymous. I can go to an NA meeting and see all my sisters. Annie has semi-sibling relationships with all their kids.

"Being sick—with the idea that I had a terminal illness—I started feeling like I don't have time for a lot of crap. I don't have time for people who don't want to be genuine. I don't have time."

THERE were practical needs—picking up prescriptions or groceries, driving Annie to school, tossing a load of laundry into the dryer when she was too exhausted to move. And there were the less tangible cravings—for company, for hugs, for straightforward talks about fear and love and dying.

"I've learned who can go to the doctor with me, and who can listen on the phone, and who can come over and make me a cup of tea, and who will go to the grocery store for me. I used to not know and thought I couldn't ask. I've found out a lot of my friends want to help but don't know how. I tell them, If it's too much, let me know. I can call someone else. I've got a long list.

"One of the things that's been a really interesting part of the journey has been spending the last couple of years really looking at my sexuality. I'm still coming to terms with it. Either I'm a not-practicing lesbian or, probably, bisexual. I'm attracted to people of both sexes.

"I haven't had any experience for three-and-a-half years. At first I said, I'm not going to have sex with anybody until I learn more about this. And as I learned more, other people got more scared of me. I've had both women and men be attracted to me and then kind of back off because of all the ramifications. It's a scary thing to think about loving someone who you know is going to die."

Members of Nancy's biological family had their own reactions, no two alike. One sister grew more distant. One brother surprised her with support and willingness to talk. Her daughter struggled with isolation, sadness, and embarrassment about AIDS. Her son was pragmatic.

"When I was diagnosed he said, 'Tell me all you know about it.' And I did. Then he said, 'Well, do you have any life insurance?' Which is a really good question. He was probably thinking, 'Well, maybe I can get a car if she kicks it.'

"I've always been open, wanting to talk about it and make jokes. One of the nicest times I had with all of my family was when my sister, my son, my daughter, and I had lunch together. My son is a punk rocker who dyes his hair black, has a pierced nose, and wears these heavy boots with five buckles and steel toes. My sister is a social worker. My daughter's a little preppie, and I'm an old hippie. So we were quite a crew.

"My sister said, 'When you die, I want you to be sure and leave me your clothes.' Then Annie said, 'No, I get some of them.' Then we had a serious discussion about what to do with me when I'm gone. My son didn't care if I was cremated or not. But my daughter said she wanted a grave to go visit. I'm opposed to that environmentally; it takes up too much room. I told Annie I'd get an urn and she could hook it on the car.

"I just did my will a couple weeks ago. It was really hard to do it. I started thinking about getting sick and dying, and I wondered who would be there. What I think is that I'm going to be surprised. People who are close and supportive now won't be able to be involved in it. People who aren't very close will all of a sudden get much closer.

"Sort of like a merry-go-round. The horses that are up will go down, and the horses who are down will come up. Maybe some of the people who are close to me now will stay. But I know that some of them aren't going to be able to be close. I don't know if I could. I've had guys in my support group get really sick, and I'm not able to be supportive.

"Even though I'm in an HIV support group, I haven't been able to be around the dying. I'm not quite ready to see my own death. So I have a lot more patience for people who can't be around me when I'm sick, or who go away when I get really needy.

"I did make myself go to the HIV Day Center for Thanksgiving. I chose to spend Thanksgiving with other people who either have AIDS or work with AIDS. It was this long table with twenty-six people, some of whom I'd never seen before. It was wonderful, a magical Thanksgiving.

"I took my daughter and a man I know. The man has AIDS. There were lots of kids, some older people, it was multigenerational. I'd told my relatives I wasn't coming for Thanksgiving. My son didn't want to be with us. We all went to different places. It turned out to be one of the nicest Thanksgivings I've ever had."

A year later, I heard that Nancy was very, very ill. A friend went to visit her and reported that she pleaded for a banana popsicle. She was lucid enough to impress on my friend that this request was an issue of quality-of-life versus doctors' orders to limit her fluid intake. My friend brought the popsicle.

For three weeks I had a note scrawled on my calendar: Visit Nancy Lawson. For three weeks, I found reasons not to. Then I saw her picture in the paper one morning, with an article about an AIDS hospice. Her body looked brittle, her hair thinned, her bracelets enormous on a spindly wrist. Her smile, huge in a drawn, pale face, made me want to weep.

NANCY was right, though, about support from unexpected places. Peace House, a community of activists who had lived together for six years, offered her a room and full time care until she died.

"When we invited her in," recalled Pat Schwiebert, one of four adults who form the core of the Peace House community, "it looked like she was going to die in a month. She had a fourteen-year-old daughter who needed a place to live.

"And Nancy thrived at Peace House."

She lived there for nearly six months. So did Annie. Nancy was not an easy guest—she broke house rules about smoking, sneaking cigarettes in bed at 2 A.M. She also grew healthier, strong enough to administer her own IVs, to sit on the wide front porch, near the poster of a tanker with a slash of red roses through it, rocking and talking to whomever walked by.

Visiting there, a few months after her death, I remembered what Nancy had said about people's responses to sickness and frailty, how comfort with the dying was a learned and practiced behavior. I remembered her generosity toward friends who shied away from her illness, and I hoped that compassion extended to me.

When Pat left the room for a moment to answer the telephone, I examined some photographs propped on the sideboard. There was a large color picture of Nancy, with a round button pinned to the frame. I picked it up to look more closely. Her face was gaunt, her smile a suspension bridge between thin cheeks.

"Nancy K. Lawson 1949-1992," the button read. "AIDS is everyone's disease."

Coming Out about Mental Illness

CAROL Steinel's resolution for a bleak new year was to end her life. For months, the activist, singer, and comic had been locked in a chronic depression that seemed impermeable to all the usual measures—regular counseling, creative projects, the upbeat "it'll get better" advice of friends. Just after New Year's Eve, Carol packed and labeled her belongings for delivery to various acquaintances and friends. She had finished assignments connected with her jill-of-all-trades business, Renaissance Woman. She performed a solo show of comedy and music at a local theater. After the final curtain call, she remembered, "I was going to drive into the mountains and freeze to death."

Instead, a longtime friend spotted Carol's distress and spent the night with her in a motel room after the performance, holding her, talking with her, and finally calling several of Carol's primary confidantes to help. In the morning, a small group of women brought Carol to the psychiatric ward of a nearby hospital. Eight days later, those same people helped her come home.

For the next several months, Carol said, "I was totally taken care of by my friends." For Carol, a fiercely self-sufficient person, the experience meant allowing herself to accept that care. And for the members of her support team, it meant confronting fears and assumptions about mental illness. This was different, they all learned, from caring for someone with a tangible physical ailment: How could Carol, in her admittedly unstable state, maintain some sense of control about her care and her life? Who would be told about her illness, and what details should remain private? How could the members of her support team inform, relieve, and take care of each other and themselves?

WHILE Carol was still in the hospital, a core group of friends rallied a larger support system. They phoned men and women who had worked with Carol on theater and musical collaborations over the years, her pals in political activism, her colleagues from the social service community.

"I asked Carol, Who do you want to visit or speak with you?" said Cathryn Heron. "We called and gave them the hospital phone number and visiting hours." Some brought small items Carol had requested—a stuffed animal, a certain book or magazine, her drawing paper and pastels. She had planned to move in with a woman friend after being discharged from the hospital, but that prospect suddenly collapsed when the woman changed her mind.

"I had no place to live. I had no money. Insurance paid for $1,000 of a $7,000 hospital bill. By that time, I'd missed two months of work," Carol recalled. "That was when the amazing network emerged. People crawled out of the woodwork. One peripheral friend, Heidee, said, 'You can stay at my house as long as you want, and you don't have to pay me anything.'"

After leaving the hospital, Carol remained severely depressed, her moods rising and sinking unpredictably. "She kept saying, 'I can't manage my life,'" Cathryn recalled. "So I said, There are people willing to help you do that. She didn't want to go back to the hospital. I struck a deal with her. I said, Would you be willing to have twenty-four-hour care? She agreed to that, and I said I'd organize it."

At first, Carol needed constant company and practical assistance with the most basic tasks of living. Her short-term memory was so flimsy she couldn't keep track of appointments; medication fuzzed her ability to think clearly. She couldn't drive. She was afraid to be alone. Often she felt suicidal.

Friends brought groceries and made meals, ferried her to doctors' offices, accompanied her to apply for disability benefits and food stamps, sat with her each day when she opened her mail. They wrote down schedules of things Carol needed to do and checked to make sure she didn't forget. Some spent the night and held Carol while she slept; others watched videos with her for hours. Many of them sought out books and articles to educate themselves about their friend's diagnosis of multiple personality disorder. Three people even attended a therapy session with her.

On paper, the task of providing twenty-four-hour care seemed straightforward: divide the day into shifts and phone people to fill them. In reality, it was complicated by some friends' uneasiness about mental illness and by Carol's own fluctuating moods. Sometimes, in a burst of energy and optimism, she would call people who had signed up for shifts and tell them not to come; later, Cathryn and other organizers of the care team would be upset that Carol had been left alone.

The primary caregivers held regular meetings to share information and discuss their anxieties and concerns. "We needed to negotiate how we operated as a group," Cathryn said. "We were people drawn together, but not necessarily because we had chosen each other. We entered this with no idea of how long we might be doing it. We had hope and faith that Carol would get better. But from day to day, we didn't know."

When someone new arrived for a shift, she or he would be briefed by the person who had been there earlier. In addition, Carol's caregivers began to write down all the decisions that they, along with Carol, made about her care—both for clarity among themselves and to give her a sense of control. And they traded the most draining tasks; after a week of organizing the schedule, Cathryn passed that job to someone else.

"It was really trying, emotionally," she said. "It was hard not to be drawn into Carol's chaos. Sometimes I just wanted to cry. But generally, there was someone to pass the ball to. We were good about saying, I'm burnt out today."

For Carol, being on the receiving end of such constant attention prompted its own problems. She had long counted on her boundless energy, drive, and seemingly infinite ability to bear stress. Now she could barely summon the physical strength to heat a can of soup or the emotional stamina for a long conversation.

"I was always the person who could push and push and push. I'd been a very self-sufficient person all my life. That's how I was trained: that you don't lean on people, you don't expect things from people. So to take huge generosities—such as Heidee opening her home to me—was very hard.

"It was critical to me that people knew their limits and told me what they were. It was so hard to accept the help anyway; if I had inklings that resentment was hovering in the background, I'd freak out. I wanted so desperately to get away from myself that I could not conceive that people wanted to be with me."

SEVERAL months after Carol was hospitalized, a stream of people filled the seats of the theater where she had last performed. For nearly three hours, local musicians, writers, comics, and dancers took turns on stage as part of "We Love You, Carol," a benefit that several friends had organized to help pay her staggering hospital and therapy bills.

Carol didn't attend the show; it was more than she could handle at a time when she was just beginning to venture out in public. But she did write a letter that was read, at the end of the performance, by one of the women on her support team.

That letter, she said, was an effort "to demystify my absence a little bit and say, I'm still here." It also was an attempt to "come out" about mental illness.

While writing it, Carol remembered a phone call she'd received from a friend several weeks before she went into the hospital. "The woman said, 'Let me tell you about my experience with depression.' That was very validating. This was someone I love, admire, and respect. Later, people who had been through similar things would come to the hospital and laugh with me. One of them said, 'Do as many crafts as you can; get your money's worth.' There was a camaraderie and easiness with them.

"Now, my friends are probably more cautious about telling people my diagnosis than I am. If I have spent a day with someone, they probably know. At some point, having been in the hospital did lose its stigma for me—at the point I realized it had saved my life."

In the frank and straightforward letter Carol wrote, she urged people in the audience to seek help and act promptly if they ever had a friend who was talking of suicide. Some women die, she said, because neither they nor the people around them reach across the gap of misunderstanding, denial, and fear. She named the people who continued to provide her with meals, company, and support. Without them, she wrote, she would likely have followed through with her plan to kill herself.

"Perhaps because I had worked in social service and was around a lot of people with mental illness, I never guessed the amount of fear and prejudice there still is even in the women's community. I thought, I can be a public voice about this and maybe make a difference."

Collective Inventions:
Dinner Groups to Co-housing Communities

KATHARINE Babad made a list: Change washers in the faucets. Paint and seal asbestos tape on the furnace ducts. Fix the leak in the garage. Add more electrical outlets. Replace the front door.

For two years, Katharine had accumulated a list of major and minute repairs needed in her seventy-year-old house. And for two years, she found reasons to avoid the tasks. She didn't know enough about wiring or carpentry. The weather was too brilliant, or too soggy. More exciting plans took precedence. Often, simple inertia halted her.

One day Katharine talked with three women friends who had similar lists, the same litanies of reasons to avoid the work. What if they shared the labor and took turns repairing each other's houses as a group? "We all had things we needed to fix. And we didn't want to do them alone," Katharine recalled. "We decided that every month we'd have a six-hour workday at one collective member's house."

On the inaugural day, the three showed up at Katharine's, clad in old clothes, tools in hand. She'd chosen some basic repairs from her list, tasks she thought the group could manage in one day. They patched and plastered a few holes in the living room wall, painted the basement floor, put the garden to bed for the winter, fixed the latch on a cupboard door, made a barricade in front of the basement crawl space so Katharine's cats couldn't use it as a litter box.

On her own, contemplating those tasks gave Katharine "an immediate sense of exhaustion," she said. "I'd rather spend a Sunday playing with my friends." The project was a way to combine company and work. "We took a break in the middle, had a snack, showed off our biceps. We had music going. It was also a social event.

"There's something about the isolation of women's work.... Your own task seems really daunting, but if you have someone else there, it becomes possible."

A push for privacy: that is one way of examining middle-class living patterns of the last century. Multigenerational households fractured into nuclear families, leaving people isolated from each other and bound to the repetitive, endless routines of managing a single household. Safe in our "little boxes on the hillside," with automatic dishwashers, clothes washers, trash compactors, and garbage disposals, American families managed on their own the jobs that once had been shared with extended kin or neighbors. Dishes, shopping, laundry, garden, child care, all the burdensome and necessary tasks of daily life, usually fell on the shoulders of one weary person—a woman.

A hundred years ago, Charlotte Perkins Gilman identified this problem in her book *Women and Economics*. Women thirsted to interact with people beyond their immediate families, she wrote. At the same time, they were chained to private kitchens, laundry rooms and nurseries, prisoners of a household economy that depended on women's unpaid labor. Only by changing that setup, she said, could women be free to venture into the world as whole people.

Gilman's solution: create cooperative cooking, cleaning, and child-care arrangements; design multifamily housing with central kitchens and nurseries; share the tasks of household maintenance. She imagined an entire society organized on this collective basis, the biological nuclear family dissolving into planned obsolescence.

Women and Economics, reprinted in the 1970s, took its place among feminist classics. Today, some women are putting Gilman's notions into action, collectivizing as a way to combat isolation, save resources, and manage daily tasks.

The word "collective" conjures up an idealistic era, when young city-bred adults headed "back" to land they'd never seen and set up communal dwellings where they shared money, land, food, and ideological passion for a new way of life. Some of those collectives lasted and still operate as permanently settled groups that require total commitment from members. Most ultimately dissolved.

But their principles stayed alive in a variety of smaller-scale collective arrangements. Women like Katharine are finding ways to bring collective models into urban neighborhoods and busy city lives. They might combine resources on just one aspect of life—for instance, meals or housing—while keeping other responsibilities separate.

"Aside from this collective," Katharine said, "I do spontaneous energy-exchanges with my sister-in-law. I go over to her house and we do some cleaning; she comes over here and helps put up shelves that need four hands."

These experiments span a huge range, from the simplest once a week child-care trade to highly structured co-housing plans involving a dozen or more families. They may even be one-time, rather than ongoing, events, such as a "naked lady" party at which friends swap their old or ill-fitting clothes for "new" ones from one another's closets.

These arrangements mean more than convenience. They offer a profound challenge to an economy in which money buys privacy and leisure and the poorest people (women, particularly women of color) clean up after the richest. Collectives, accessible to people of any income level, are one way to shrug off the grip of consumer culture with its plethora of empty choices.

A woman who belonged to a dinner collective told me that her participation in the group enabled her to say no to a limited, unsatisfying array of dinner "options"—either spending time every night to cook for herself, eating unhealthy junk foods, or spending money to eat out.

Collectives offer one solution to a resource-poor world, an antidote to the waste of materials and time in isolated households. Must every family on the block own a lawn mower, a washing machine, a snow shovel? Can't they share other things—cookbooks, power tools, magazines, canning equipment, community garden plots? Collectives subvert capitalism in important ways; they value what is shared, traded, and recycled over what is private, purchased, and new.

SEVERAL years ago, when Elissa and I wanted to attend a writer's workshop but couldn't afford the tuition, we decided to get a little help from our friends. But uneasiness set in as we began to plan a benefit dinner: Were we asking too much for a purpose too frivolous? Would people be willing to give?

We rented the multipurpose room in a local school building, cooked for two days, served a ten-course Indian feast to seventy people, read selections from our short stories and essays and charged each person seven to ten dollars to attend. Together, our guests raised about half the money we needed. Even some who couldn't make it to the dinner sent checks, saying they were happy to share in the project. I stood at the microphone that night, near tears as I watched friends and acquaintances spoon up vegetable curry and applaud our reading. The warmth and support were almost too much to absorb.

My father's mother, Rose, prides herself on never asking favors; she makes cookies with a single egg rather than borrow one from a neighbor. I've inherited some of her stubborn self-sufficiency, along with a rigid sense of reward. If I can't manage something on my own, I reason, maybe I don't deserve to have it. Collective approaches challenge such beliefs about what people will do for each other, what it is possible to ask.

In fact, collectives question the whole notion of individuality, the "freedom" supposedly attained by reducing attachments to others. When I visited a dinner collective, the women in it said prospective members often balked at the plan—an agreement to cook for fifteen people once every three weeks and attend as many dinners as they liked on the other fourteen weeknights. These women were used to the liberty of fending for themselves, even if that meant zapping frozen spinach in the microwave or gulping popcorn in the car on the way to a meeting. Once new members joined, though, they discovered the equation of self-sufficiency with freedom was skewed; their participation in the dinner collective, rather than clogging their schedules, actually gave them *more* time for other pursuits.

Susan Feldman launched a neighborhood dinner co-op when her first child was born eight years ago as a relief from the time crunch she and her husband felt as they tried to manage two careers and enjoy weeknight dinners together as a family. Susan recruited three families who lived within walking distance and who also had young children. Monday through Thursday nights each family took a turn cooking enough food for all four households; the others showed up at six-thirty, plates and containers in hand, to bring dinner back to their own homes. When the Feldmans moved to a new neighborhood, they started a similar co-op there; the original group found another family to join and is still going on more than eight years later.

"It's just as easy to cook for eight adults plus kids as for two adults plus kids," Susan said. "Cooking more food on one night gives you three meals for the rest of the week. Then you just have plates to wash, not pots and pans. The whole idea is that we can all come home and just spend time with our kids on those nights."

The night I visited Diana Cohen's dinner collective, I spooned up my own bowl of lentil stew, chewed on a steamy slice of bread, and felt a flicker of possibility. For days afterward, I examined my own life for wasted labor and materials, imagined all the ways I could share work or possessions. Buy one VCR for two households. Raise a dog together with the family next door. Rent space in a community deep-freezer. Invest, along with a few women friends of similar size, in one or two fancy outfits to share for dressy occasions.

Katharine suggested a mending collective, an occasional gathering to fix the broken zippers, lost buttons and ripped linings of all the clothes that end up heaped in the bottom of the laundry basket. Or, more ambitious, how about a work collective, in which members would take turns financially supporting each other's "sabbaticals" to study, travel, raise children, or simply reflect for six months or a year.

When I left the RAJ Mahal to move in with Elissa, all four of us agreed that subscriptions to the Sunday New York Times were too expensive for each couple to keep their own. Now we share a single subscription; we divide the Times each Sunday and swap sections on Thursday morning.

Splitting the Sunday paper hardly seems revolutionary. But even such small acts can break down the distance between households and families, revise our emotional and material relationships. The details matter: who wallpapers the bathroom, who buys the milk, who folds the clothes. In these smallest, most mundane aspects of existence lie the ingredients of change and the stuff of community, the possibility that we need not journey alone.

Feeding a Need for Community

IT WAS six o'clock on a Monday in the white house with the rainbow banner on the door, and dinner was ready. One by one, women arrived, shed their coats into a sloppy pile, and sniffed the food that was perfuming Diana Cohen's small kitchen: a stew of potatoes, carrots, and lentils, an oval of whole wheat bread on a cutting board, a bowl of salad. They filled plates from a mismatched stack, then settled in the living room, resting mugs of juice on chair arms or the floor.

The night I visited, the group included Carrie Bruck, Lisa Jonstrom, Leslie Abbott, Julia Peattie, and Gillian Leichtling—women ranging in age from twenty-four to thirty-five. On Tuesday night they would ladle soup in someone else's kitchen. And the next night, and the next, and the next. Every weekday evening, this dinner collective gathered to share food, conversation and one solution to women's struggle to feed both their appetites and their sense of community.

Carrie was one of the founding members, along with Diana. After ten months, the collective had reached a level of easy trust and comfort; Diana couldn't stay for dinner but offered her house and a meal as scheduled.

"Diana and a friend were brainstorming about how to make life easier," Carrie recalled. "They got really excited about the idea of having people feed each other. Economically, it was very appealing—only having to feed yourself once in fifteen weeknights. Not having to spend energy buying or cooking food. And it's about being with other people."

Lisa helped herself to a second bowl of soup. "In college," she said, "a group of us met at the same table each night at the same time. There was a familiarity about it. I really missed that when I left. Dinnertime was very stressful when I was a kid. There was a lot of fighting. It's not good for you; I developed lots of digestive problems. So, left to my own devices, I'd just skip dinner."

Gillian recalled subsisting on dinners of cheese puffs and popcorn before she joined the collective. Carrie ate makeshift meals, standing up in the kitchen or gobbling something in the car on the way to a meeting. Leslie might slice a banana into a cup of yogurt or toss frozen vegetables into boiling water.

"Diana kept calling me, saying 'You've got to come to the collective,'" she remembered. "But early evening was my down time. And I told her, Why would I want to see the same people every single day?"

Other potential members balked at the idea of a daily commitment. Or they felt intimidated about the prospect of cooking for fifteen, even if it was only once every three weeks. Some said transportation was an obstacle.

But others were eager to join. Over a period of weeks, the women met and agreed on guidelines. Dinner would be ready at six, but members could show up between six and seven. The meal had to be vegetarian. Members could bring guests if they cleared it with that evening's host. The person who cooked did all the dishes.

JULIA finished her dinner, stacked her plate in the sink, and stretched out on the carpet—a posture that soothed her backaches from a recently cracked vertebra.

"I didn't eat meals before. I don't like to cook. I'd either eat out or snack. When I joined, I went out to Goodwill and bought six plates for a couple bucks. I eat better now. I'm saving money. And it became an instant social life. Tonight I wasn't going to come because my day's been really long. But I decided it was a bigger hassle to cook for myself than to drive over here and have someone cook for me."

"I get off work at five," Carrie said. "And dinner is at six. So I have an hour of down time, when I can do errands or relax. In the spring, I go to the park and read for an hour before dinner."

The benefits of the dinner collective extend beyond the practical. In a fast-paced world where social engagements are set up by appointment, the dinner collective nurtures relationships that are at once casual and ongoing.

"You can have continuing conversations," Julia said.

"And there's no performance anxiety," Leslie added. "You don't have to be a scintillating conversationalist every night."

"In society, there's a lot of social etiquette," Carrie said. "People call before they come over. In college, I lived in big houses of twelve people, and we never locked the doors. I felt isolated when I left. Here, I have several people who know me well enough to say, 'You look really exhausted today. Are you okay?'"

Sometimes, conversation flares like wildfire, and collective members linger until 9:30 or 10 P.M., talking about politics or work or relationships, books or movies or their mothers. Other times, they eat quickly and head out to meetings or classes.

This night was one of the latter. Lisa and Leslie got up first, piled their dishes on the counter and pulled on their coats. Then Gillian left. Julia checked the schedule to see who was cooking the next night. Carrie, who wasn't hungry earlier, spooned up a bowl of soup.

The dinner collective, she said, reinforced her belief that women need not settle for unsatisfying options—about how to feed themselves, about any other aspect of life. Matters of emotion, as well as appetite, were at stake for her. As a child, Carrie was chubby and often endured relatives' chiding that she "ate too much." Through the dinner collective, she could spend mealtimes with other women who ate heartily and shamelessly, who enjoyed food and each other's honest company.

"One member's grandmother died recently. It was okay for the woman to be in tears, to be emotional, and just to be here. Other women would sit and talk with her, then return to the group. It was okay that she took an hour and a half to eat dinner because she had to stop and cry.

"Any experience that brings you out of the separateness that society has imposed has to be a good thing."

Turning a Home into a Hub for Women's Activity

AT SEVENTY, Silvia Dobson had no intention of launching a community. She'd moved to America from England in 1960 to live with a woman she'd met in Spain. The two built a house and lived together for twenty years.

"She died of lung cancer in 1980," Silvia said. "I was an old woman by that time and thought my life was over." Shortly afterward, Silvia met Betty Shoemaker, whose daughter had recently died. The two comforted each other; slowly, shared grief ceded to mutual attraction. But Betty was reluctant to move into Silvia's house. She thought they should begin anew, in a place they would buy together.

In the foothills of Santa Barbara, they found a house for sale by the bank; its owner, a concert pianist, had gone bankrupt. He had built an addition to the existing structure, a theater with a separate entrance, large enough for two grand pianos and an audience. A twenty-foot-high window peered over the canyon below. The wooden floor and stage gleamed.

"We thought, What fun to have that," Silvia recalled. They imagined inviting other women to live with them—not as part of a traditional landlord-tenant relationship, but as equal partners in the household. They named the place "Star Shadows" after Betty's daughter, Star. And for five years it functioned as their home, a locus of women's projects, and an experiment in semicollective living.

"There was one room with a bathroom that was $400; two rooms had to share a bathroom. One was $300 and the other was $250. Betty and I had our own bedroom, bathroom, and deck. Everyone shared the sitting room and the theater and the kitchen.

"We wanted to find older women to live with us there. But we found that much younger women would come. We had five or six people living there at one time, and we always had visitors. We did become like family to each other. But younger women tend to want older women as sort of grandmothers. It's very difficult for the old to find people to treat them as equals."

Star Shadows and its theater became the hub for women's dances, lectures, meetings, mailing parties, and discussions. "We had the first dance and thought twenty people might come. Eighty came. We had a DJ, really first-rate. People gave lectures there. Sonia Johnson spoke. We would have meetings there. Betty started a group for women who had left their husbands and become lesbians. Then we started a group for lesbians over fifty.

"We did experience a community there. It was a wonderful center, a most wonderful place."

After five years, Silvia and Betty decided the huge house was draining too much of their energy and time. They sold it, spent several years living alternately in a small house and a trailer in Mexico, then settled in downtown Santa Barbara, in one of the area's oldest two-story adobes. When they die, Silvia said, they plan to leave the house to a trust, set up so that low-income women can afford the rent; they imagine lesbians of varying ages living in there, supporting each other, making a family.

"There are separate entrances in this house, so people can come in and out with privacy. There are three bathrooms. We would visualize having a couple downstairs, in the two adjoining rooms. And two very happily upstairs.

"If I were ever going to start a new community place for old women, I would choose a motel that's up for sale, with each room having a kitchen and a bathroom. Lesbians who were born in the old days were so closeted that they have this sense of needing privacy.

"Nowadays young women can go to the gay and lesbian center and find other lesbians, or look up an organization in the phone book. In the old days you looked at a person and thought, I wonder if she's a lesbian. Maybe young women don't need that privacy."

Silvia and Betty's legacy will be the house, the study lined with books, the notion of women drawn together for financial savings and feminist kinship. "I'm now eighty-four years old. I'm at the end of my life. I have cancer," Silvia said, her voice a crepe de chine rustle on the phone. "In this town, there's a terrific need for lesbians to have alternative accommodations. The need is for women of any age, not just old people.

"I hope the women living here will be of different colors. There is room for unity. As the old women grow older and more feeble, they will need the support of younger women. It seems to me that women of different ages would make a better family."

Creating a New Kind of Neighborhood

JOANNE McClarty was certain it would never last. That's what she told the other five adults at the end of her first visit to the Shekinah community, an urban co-housing group. It was a Thursday night, the group's mandatory weekly meeting.

First, Joanne sat through the check-in, when each person offered a brief update on her or his week, then through a potluck dinner. Afterwards, they went upstairs to a wide, carpeted attic and sat down in a circle. "That was the center of the meeting—people sharing feelings, their own conflicts and struggles. I thought the level of the sharing was very deep. It was very warm and intimate. I was impressed.

"But I didn't believe that it would last. I had in mind that intentional communities were pretty grandiose ideas, mostly theoretical, and in reality they didn't work. I was steeling myself for the fact that I was going to be disappointed. At the end of the evening, I said, This is incredible. You people are incredible. And you won't survive."

By the second meeting, Joanne had changed her summation slightly. "I said, I don't know how long this will last, but I'm hanging in there with you."

Six years later, the Shekinah community, located in a modest pedestrian neighborhood, had not only survived but grown to include nine adults, five children under age eleven, and three adolescents. The youngest was an eight-month-old baby; the oldest was Joanne, fifty-six. For her, Shekinah represented the flourishing of a lifelong effort to live consciously as part of a group.

"About twenty years ago, I left a religious order," she told me, after turning off the phone in her office at a residential treatment center for children, where she directed a trauma recovery program for adults and children. "The powerful part of that experience for me was the communal living. I wanted to have some aloneness—or so I thought—so I bought a house and lived alone. But I kept exploring situations where the living was more communal."

She worked with a man who was a member of Shekinah and liked what he had to say about the group. Members lived according to the "rules of cooperation" described in the book *Scripts People Live*; those rules included equal rights, an assumption of "no scarcity," and a commitment by each adult to ask clearly for what he or she wanted. "No secrets" was another tenet.

Played out in daily life, those principles yielded a mandatory weekly meeting at which the adults aired any fears or resentments they might feel, resolved practical and emotional problems connected to the group, and talked about individual struggles in their work, home, or spiritual lives.

While each community member or couple owned a home privately— most of them on the same block—the group shared some financial and practical responsibilities. The adults split the costs of baby-sitters for members' children during the weekly meetings. The meals were potluck. They shared some lawn equipment and tools. If one person was going to buy a load of firewood, she or he checked to see if the other households needed any.

In addition to the weekly meetings, the group planned an annual three-day retreat and an annual vacation. They celebrated holidays to-gether—New Year's Eve, Easter, the sixteenth birthday of a member's daughter. And community residents frequently milled in and out of Paul and Joanne's house, the unofficial center of the cluster.

Although all the adults in the community were raised Catholic, their current spiritual practices spanned from Native American traditions to Zen Buddhism. The "prayer" that opened and closed the weekly meetings might be a physical exercise or a Bible reading, depending on whose turn it was to plan.

For her first four years in Shekinah, Joanne continued to live in the house she owned, about two miles from most community members. At weekly meetings, she would hear stories about what had happened since the last gathering; she craved that daily enjambment.

"I wanted to be part of that," she said. "I was also fifty years old, and I wanted to do whatever it was I hadn't done. At some point, someone said, 'What do you need in order to move over here?' I said, a doggy door for my poodle terrier and shitzu, and my own room. Then the house Paul was renting went up for sale, and he decided to buy it." When Joanne opted to move in with him, "It was probably the most spontaneous thing I've ever done in my life."

Still, she had numerous fears about the prospect. Would community living be too overwhelming after being alone for fifteen years? Would she be able to ask for—and get—enough time and space for solitude? Had she lost her ability to negotiate details of daily life with other people?

"I need to have some semblance of order and balance in my life. I had gotten so set in my ways. I feared it wouldn't work out. But I realized I'd lived out of community for too long."

Today, Joanne lives in the attic that was the site of her first lasting impression of Shekinah. She and Paul pattern their daily lives according to the same tenets of cooperation that guide the entire group. They meet weekly to talk over any resentments or problems. They share most food, taking turns buying groceries and halving the receipts at the end of the month. They split the utility bills. Because Paul owns the house and Joanne is renting, he pays for repairs that directly affect the house's value. But they share the costs of such additions as new curtains for the living room.

Paul maintains and fixes anything on the outside of the house and in the yard; Joanne cleans the inside. When Paul's eight-year-old daughter visits each Thursday and every other weekend, Joanne helps out with parenting tasks. They don't usually plan meals but eat together two or three times a week. They discuss everything.

"We were talking this morning about containers for sheets and pillowcases," Joanne recalled. "I said, Who's going to own those? We decided that since they would benefit both of us, we'd split the cost. It's in those small things—parenting, dividing work in the house—that our growth has occurred."

"THE major thing I like about Shekinah is this," Joanne said. "I think our community is a microcosm of how the world could be. There's a level of intimacy, care, and concern for each other and the world that isn't typical.

"It's wonderful to care about other people and have other people care about you and not live in a vacuum. It's a very supportive and loving environment—with all that that means, with all the struggles.

"The hard things are still to say what I want, to set boundaries on my private time. It's still somewhat tenuous to think about living on a daily basis in a situation that is so entwined with other people's lives."

Joanne sat back in her office, a room filled with masks and puppets, a heap of stuffed bears on the floor, children's artwork on the desks and tables.

"At fifty-five," she said, "I began to tap dance. At the birthday party recently, I was the entertainment. The community motivates me to do things I might not do without that support."

A Feminist Core in a Rural Collective

CAROLINE Estes was forty-two when she decided her lifestyle was not healthy for children and other living things. She had a husband, two adopted daughters, a job she liked with the American Friends Service Committee, eleven rooms of antiques in a vine-draped house in Philadelphia. It's not that those items weren't enough. They were too much. If everyone gobbled resources at that thoughtless rate, Caroline thought, the world might not last for the next generation.

She and her husband, Jim, sold nearly everything they owned, packed a pickup truck and, along with four other adults, drove west in pursuit of a life that matched their values. Community. Simplicity. Judicious use of resources. Peace.

That was more than twenty years ago. Today, Caroline and Jim are the only two founding members who remain at Alpha Farm, in the foothills of a Northwest mountain range. And a new generation of seekers has joined them—a total of twenty-seven people, including two infants.

Caroline looks like a hippie who has aged solidly and well, with steely-gray hair that tumbles down her back, ankle-length skirts, a ruddy face, utilitarian hands. In the early years, she recalled, the founding members were city people stumbling to learn about country life. The six adults sat down with a list of jobs and signed up—to shovel manure out of the chicken shed and convert it to a cottage, restore an attic into a children's bedroom, plant a small garden, launch the restaurant-bookstore-craft shop, Alpha-Bit, that would provide the farm with income.

As a matter of principle, they refused to split duties along traditional gender lines; everyone would cook, and everyone would help care for the house and the children. "Not always happily," Caroline said. "But that was our agreement." They began with two other rules—no guns and no hard drugs—which, since then, have been amended into a thick book of "agreements" governing everything from chores to clothing allowances.

The first members shared all income—a decision that prompted two of the original six to leave. After paying telephone and electricity bills, buying seeds and lumber and food, there was enough left for each person to have an allowance of one dollar a month.

Caroline remembered the mistakes of Alpha's early years. The tractor they left out in the rain—twice. The cow they overfed until it bloated and died. She also recalled the struggles to determine what it meant to make a working family out of a group of well-intentioned strangers.

"We had a lot of discussions about that: How to be close and love each other, to argue and have a hard time and still stay family." Every element of living prompted long conversations: How to celebrate holidays in December when one member wanted a traditional goose dinner and one thought Christmas was a crass extravagance. Whether they should slaughter chickens on the farm. What to do when the designated dishwasher let crusty plates pile up in the sink.

In mandatory once-a-month meetings that could last as long as sixteen hours, Alpha Farm's members talked about both philosophical and mundane issues until they reached consensus. Their insistence on that regular meeting, Caroline believed, was one reason Alpha had lasted when so many other intentional communities dissolved.

People did leave, of course; a mass exodus in the early 1980s left the farm with just five full members. But a decade later, times were hard again, more people saw that resources were running out, and ventures such as Alpha Farm held renewed appeal. Its brand of communal life was particularly attractive to single women with children and older women who were widowed or divorced. It also held promise for exuberant young feminists like Alitia Peterson.

ALITIA was a twenty-year-old college dropout when she found Alpha in the course of pursuing something else; she'd left Michigan and moved west to follow a boyfriend. After staying at the farm for three days as his guest, she was no longer sure about the relationship, but she was certain she wanted Alpha to be her new home.

People had been calling Alitia a feminist ever since eighth-grade science classes, when she challenged a male teacher who made sweeping put-downs about women. In college, she belonged to feminist discussion groups and Women Against Pornography.

At the time she joined Alpha, Alitia said, her outlook on life was unrealistically upbeat; often she masked her true feelings in a cloak of enthusiasm and cheerfulness. Residents of Alpha, and one woman in particular, challenged her immediately. "She'd say, 'Is that how you really feel? You don't have to impress people.' My relationship with her is probably what helped me to become more comfortable with conflict, with things not being nice or perfect or easy."

Alpha's practice of decisionmaking by consensus prompted Alitia to examine and express her views on everything from where the farm should place a new basketball hoop to how members could better function as one another's emotional supports. "I started to think about how I'd had little or no power in so many areas of my life. The more I thought about it, the more I felt challenged about the personal responsibility I'd be taking in living at Alpha."

There were practical skills to learn, as well. Alitia had never milked a cow or weeded a garden before coming to the farm. She learned to use an electric Skilsaw, drive a tractor, and hammer a sixteen-penny nail. She discovered a use for her organizational abilities through managing workshops at the farm and running Alpha's food booth at an annual region-wide fair.

"My mom was very much into traditional women's roles. When I came to the farm, I decided that if anyone asked me to do something, I would agree to do it, even if I had to ask how. I asked men or women, whomever happened to be handy. I felt intimidated by my own inabilities, but I decided I wasn't going to live inside my limits."

Within several months of arriving at Alpha, before she had become a long-term member, Alitia found herself looking to the farm community for practical and emotional sustenance. She found out she was pregnant and called a meeting of all the residents that night. People asked if she knew what she wanted to do, and Alitia said she needed more time to make up her mind.

"It definitely felt like a family, a strong sense of support," she said. "Caroline would check in with me every day. When I had decided that I wanted to have an abortion, I met with the residents' finance committee and said I didn't have the money. They decided that the farm would pay for it; if I became a long-term member, the abortion would be at farm expense. If I left, I'd pay it back."

After six years at Alpha, Alitia can see how her style and outlook have changed. She no longer feels compelled to gloss over feelings of unhappiness; in meetings, she is often the one to raise broad, provocative questions. When she visits her relatives in Michigan, the separateness and materialism of their lives feels odd, alienating. She envisions herself remaining at Alpha for "the foreseeable future," the expandable time period to which all long-term members pledge.

OTHER residents have come and gone, but for Caroline, the commitment to Alpha never dimmed. She treasures Alpha members' devotion to a simple life. They still have no automatic dishwasher, no television, just two washers and dryers for all the residents. Full members receive $25 each month, plus a $300 annual vacation stipend. The farm pays for necessities agreed on by the group—clothing for work and leisure, food, even movies if more than 80 percent of the group attends the show. When a long-term member leaves the farm, she or he receives back any initial investment, plus accumulated work-shares for each year spent at Alpha.

Part of Caroline's work entails visiting other intentional communities and lecturing at universities. She offers a grim message, telling people that the world cannot sustain our current level of growth, that everyone must change the way they think about land and possessions and families. Then she tells them about Alpha Farm. People related by their passions and principles, rather than by blood or legal ties, *can* take care of each other, she insists.

On a sticky summer day, she talked amid the clutter of dinner preparations. "Right now some people are digging up bales of hay and putting them in the barn. One's on the tractor still baling. Two are taking care of children. Two are making dinner. There are four out in the garden. There are two at the store."

When dinner is ready, everyone will gather around the table—adults, teenagers, children, infants—grasp hands, and sing, the ritual that has begun every meal at Alpha Farm for the past two decades.

"To live in the style we live, you have to feel it's okay to be cooperative, that you don't always have to get your own way, and that the good of the whole is more important than the good of the individual.

"You have to keep alive," Caroline said. "I'm aware that I don't think like most sixty-three-year-olds. I'm surrounded constantly with new ideas. That's not to say I don't think of leaving. We say, If you don't think of leaving at least once a week, you're not paying attention."

Living with a Cooperative Spirit

BEVERLY Stein and a handful of friends decided to wear their collective impulses on their sleeves. Literally. It was a dozen years ago, and the women belonged to the Wednesday Night Dinner Collective, gathering for a weekly meal that members took turns cooking.

"We saw each other often because we were eating dinner together once a week," said Nancy Becker, another member of the group. "Often someone would say, 'What a nice shirt,' and the owner would answer, 'Oh, God, I hate this thing.'"

Beverly had been in women's consciousness-raising groups and lived in communal houses in California. She thought combining resources made good economic and philosophic sense; such experiments turned her politics into something tangible. They had done it with dinner. Why not with clothing, too?

Each woman agreed to invite five friends to a clothing exchange party. "We all brought our leftover clothes—not the Goodwill pile, but the clothes we were sick of," Becker said. "We put them in a pile in the middle of the room. It was huge. We had champagne, little goodies to eat. Everyone wore leotards and tried on the clothes. It was a great success. The clothes that were left in the middle, we gave to a women's shelter."

For several years, the exchange became an annual occurrence. The idea spread to other friends; after a while, one woman remembered, a common response to a compliment about someone's outfit was, "Thanks. I got it at a clothing exchange."

"It was a kick to walk around town and see other women wearing your clothes," Nancy said. "Things that were a mistake for you were perfect for somebody else."

For Beverly, the clothing exchange was just one example in a life packed with experiments in sharing resources. She, along with many of her women friends, craved alternatives to the disturbing trends they saw in society—heedless consumption, wasteful privatizing, fractured community. Their approach to these problems "came out of the women's movement," Beverly said. They imagined a routine guided by values of cooperation, conservation and mutual respect, making feminist principles plain in their daily lives.

For several years, Beverly shared her 1976 beige Chevy Nova, then brand new, with two friends. None of them had much money, and they often were headed to the same political meetings. They kept records of gas and repair expenses and settled the bills equally, although Beverly retained ownership. Eventually, she recalled, "the car wore out, and our lives spread apart."

When computers first became available, Beverly bought one together with eight other people and worked out a system for each person to have access to it. Years later, she brought her communal approach to 1990s technology; she shares a fax machine with a friend in the neighborhood. "It's at her house. She runs over the faxes. Very high-tech," Beverly said, laughing.

OF ALL her collective arrangements, the Wednesday Night Dinner Collective lasted the longest, meeting every week for more than twelve years. The rules were simple and straightforward: The person who cooked would also clean up. People would arrive at 6 P.M. and leave by 7:30. The meal didn't have to be fancy, just nutritious.

The original four who formed the dinner collective—a politician, a lawyer, an artist, and a teacher—had hatched the idea during a twelve-hour car trip, talking about their work, their daily routines, their beliefs, and ways to bring continuity to their lives. What began as a way to share resources evolved into a deep, resilient bond. "At first, we thought we could pull it off because we all lived so close," Beverly recalled. "Then over the years, we added people, and people moved, and we found it still worked even though some lived in far reaches of town.

"It was not a revealing, intimate group in the sense of women's consciousness-raising. We'd talk about movies, politics, books, what was going on in the world, what was happening in our lives. The idea was to have some kind of regular thing. It's been a way for us—a group of friends—to touch base on a weekly basis. You get a sense of regular connection, which I find important."

Each year, the group went out to dinner as an anniversary celebration. They took weekend trips to the coast a few times and once constructed a group timeline, with pictures of all the women at different points in their lives and projections about where they might be in the future.

Occasionally, the collective would offer a dinner for eight as an auction item for a cause they all supported—the National Abortion Rights Action League, for instance—or stuff envelopes for a weavers' cooperative organized by a friend who lived in Guatemala. One woman's daughter grew up in the dinner collective, eating with the group from the time she was ten and joining the cooking rotation at fifteen.

Membership shifted a bit over the years. Some women got married; some were divorced. A few became parents. Beverly was elected to the Oregon legislature. People moved and changed jobs, acquired lovers and ended relationships. Wednesday night dinners were an anchor and a stopping-place.

Then, gradually, the collective began to dissolve. Members' lives seemed to accelerate; there were often empty seats at the table. Beverly's own commitments forced her to miss many of the meals. "It played out for me, too," she said. "We never really said it ended. It just petered out. We keep saying we should get together for a final dinner."

Beverly's accelerating political career now drains huge swallows of time. Her old friends from the dinner collective are equally intent about their own work, their partners, their growing children. Still, collective principles percolate through their lives. Nancy recently launched a reprise of the clothing exchange—this time, with a new group of friends who had never heard of such an idea. Beverly imagines her friends' lives as strands that will meet again as they age, the twin pulls of practicality and desire urging them into a new collective design.

At a recent dinner party, she and some friends played a game about aging. Each one wrote down three assets she thought she'd have in old age. The woman who brought the game took a card away from each player, then asked them to give up one more card.

"We were each left with one thing," Beverly recalled. "We talked about that: Okay, you've lost your sharpness; you've lost mobility; you've lost a loved one, you've lost money. What each one was left with was kind of depressing.

"Then we said, Well, if we put all our cards together, what would it look like? And it felt great. We said, Oh, *you* can do the shopping, and *you'll* be making phone calls for political causes. I guess we can carry it off.

"My vision for myself is still to live in a co-housing arrangement. It gives me a great deal of satisfaction to live that way and share resources and be efficient. One thing about the current generation of older women is that few have had the experience of collective living, so they don't know it's an option. But I have. I know how to do it, and I know it's viable."

Acquired Ancestors and Borrowed Kin: Hunting for Feminist Roots

AT THE shore, the big dining room table was draped with a cloth, an intricate, unlovely pattern of leaves, branches, and berries in Crayola reds and greens. Pressed into the vinyl was another pattern, a system of thin ridges, like railroad tracks. I traced them with my finger, making journeys through the plastic thicket as my relatives talked.

"So Bubie is your mom, and Aunt Charlotte's, just like you're mine?" I repeated to my mother. "Aunt Sadie is Bubie's sister, and Joni and Debbie are her daughters, right?"

On hot nights when no one could sleep, we played Password or Mastermind and told stories at the dining room table. I heard how great-Uncle Milt had startled my aunts when they were teenagers by sauntering through their room on his way to the bathroom, clad only in a cigar and a folded newspaper.

My relatives' names were as compelling as the stories they told. My grandmother, Sarah Ochman, had married Al Honickman. Their older daughter, my mother, then married Stan Hochman. This coincidence seemed magical to me, gave significance to the arbitrary meeting, and marriage, of two strangers. These names made my family seem more inevitability than fluke.

When I paged through albums of mercury-tinged photos or watched my grandmothers, my aunts, my mother, I grasped a sense of who I might become. I would develop sturdy legs, avocado hips, hair that frizzed on muggy days. I would keep lists and make do. They were my mirrors—casting not a direct reflection but an image bent through time. *Look closely. This is who you come from. This is where you may go.*

I learned to repeat my great-grandparents' favorite expressions, never quite as salty in English as in Yiddish. When someone sneezed, my great-grandfather Samuel, a baker, would say, "*Du zolst vaksn azoy vi a Purim coylech mit a rozhinke in der mit.*" You should grow like a Purim challah with a raisin in the middle. My great-grandmother, Ethel, told her granddaughters that if a man got fresh, they should "*Varf im in yam un pish im in oyer.*" Throw him in the ocean and pee in his ear.

The grown-ups talked about the Philadelphia neighborhood where my mother grew up, an enclave of Eastern European immigrants with the incongruous name of "Strawberry Mansion." To me, the name conjured images of sultry afternoons, sweet air, white verandas wrapped with shiny strawberry vines. Actually, it was row houses and brownstone stoops, a place where my aunt played with Gypsy children, fell into a bucket of lye in the basement, and once was bitten by an organ-grinder's monkey. I loved the stories of her mischief, a foil for my own more compliant nature. Maybe, I thought, such pluck was part of the family legacy, a trait I could grow to claim.

There were other traces of brave departure from the norm. Ethel, for instance, my great-grandmother, who hated to cook, managed the financial side of the bakery while Samuel made *babka* and was always described in family stories as "a feminist before her time." And Sarah, my grandmother, the only woman in her Temple University math class. My mother, too, ambitious and unconforming, delaying marriage until she'd found the work she wanted to do, continuing to do it after I was born.

On my father's side was my grandmother Rose. She was proud to be one of the first tenants of Rochdale Village, a high-rise complex in Queens. Her apartment there was a vast improvement over a four-flat house in Brooklyn where noise leaked through ceilings and showers ran cold. Thirty years later, she still lives in building 12A, apartment 12A. An elevator creaks its way up the cable, opens to speckled linoleum and identical black doors. I can never remember which way to turn.

Today, a live-in companion named Joyce cooks Bubie's meals, washes her clothes, helps her shower, and tries to make sure she doesn't fall, as she did a few summers ago, fracturing her wrist on the slick hall-way floor. Small rituals score her day: Lipton tea in a green melamine cup at 4 P.M.; visits to the library; late afternoons in the chair by her bed-room window, watching sunset bruise the sky while planes arc in and out of LaGuardia Airport.

On one visit, I sat with Bubie by the window for hours. She told me stories, sometimes the same ones half a dozen times. She is still fierce with anger at her father for insisting she take commercial rather than aca-demic courses, then pulling her out of school, which she adored, after the eighth grade.

She was proud of her handsome, American-born husband, Isidore. Some girls had to marry "foreigners," she told me, awkward men with ac-cents, fresh off the boat. But Isidore, a furrier, began to grow weak from multiple sclerosis soon after they married in 1924. She went back to work and supported the family for years with typing and shorthand.

"Let me tell you, when I was in my thirties, I never thought I'd still be here now," Bubie reported when I called on her eighty-eighth birthday. "There were days I wanted to put my head in the oven.

"You know who I'm grateful for?" she asked, and I thought, God? Her grandchildren? The neighbor who's lived in 12C as long as she has? What vision or courage or kinship kept her head out of the gas jet on those grim afternoons?

"I thank God," she said with tremendous conviction, as if invoking a spirit or an ancestor. "I thank God for Eleanor Roosevelt."

I, TOO, needed to venture beyond the family tree for images of courage; my female relatives, with all their spunk, could take me only so far. As my path veered away from the family's expectations, I became the odd daughter, the one geneology could not explain. As a lesbian, I was an interloper in my culture as well, missing from the history books, films, advertisements, all but a few novels. That absence delivered a clear message: You have no past. You came from nowhere. You do not fit.

I knew there always had been women who defied the times and their culture's expectations, who lived as they pleased, who found ingenious ways to gain love and support and companionship. Always, there were women who loved women, or who loved men but would not marry them, women who vowed everlasting commitment to best friends, who lived alone, who dreamed of communities, who gathered multiple families like strands of beads. If my own relatives couldn't provide sufficient feminist spark, then I would borrow some kin who could.

Julia was the first. I never met John's great-aunt; my picture of her comes from a few anecdotes, a single telephone call, and one long story, the one that made John's eyes glisten all the way back from Julia's funeral. At least, that was how I imagined it, later. I pictured him telling the story to himself, driving in the rain up Interstate 5, murmuring it on the ferry to Salt Spring Island, where Rachael and I had started our vacation.

He would not tell us, though, until after dinner. So we ate in silence. The scallops tasted sweet. I looked out the window. The sky closed down like a lid over St. Mary's Lake.

The cabin manager, a pale man with glasses, had squinted at us in his office, watched as Rachael and I greeted John with hugs, as we headed down the hill to our cabin, hand in hand in hand. Cousins? Sisters and brother? Three old college friends? Probably he would not guess right.

I knew John had come across Julia late in his life. And that she was the kind of relative you feel lucky to find in your late teens or early twenties, when it seems outrageous that the rest of your family is actually connected to you. She lived alone in a town near the Oregon coast and had never married. I had talked to Julia only once, on the phone. Her voice sounded like crepe being pulled over a washboard, with a slight drawl. "Just tell John his Ahhnt Julie called," she had said.

When she got sick, John was the only family member within reach. Every Sunday, he drove the three hours to the hospital. He sat in Julia's room and talked to her, fed her soup by slow teaspoons, listened while she groped for breath. Just after one of those visits, while he was back in Portland, she died.

Finally we finished dinner and John nudged his chair back from the table. "When I got back to Julia's house after the funeral, it was almost dark," he said. "Once, when we were talking about bank accounts and bills, she told me about a green carton that was full of old check stubs. She told me to burn it. I found the box, but there were no check stubs. Well, there were some—maybe a year's worth. The rest of the box was filled with photos.

"I started opening the envelopes, going through them one at a time. Finally I got to an envelope marked 'Germany' and one that said, 'Mostly

Mary and Willi.' I'd never heard of them. I was pretty sure they weren't relatives.

"In the 'Germany' envelope," he continued, "there were about twenty pictures of Julia, taped together and folded like an accordion. There were pictures of a cabin kind of place, maybe she'd rented it for the weekend, a cabin like this one. There was one picture of Julia leaning out of a second-story window. Her hair was shoulder-length and wavy. She was laughing. Then there were pictures of two other women. They all wore what looked like men's pleated wool pants.

"In the 'Mostly Mary and Willi' envelope there was another set. The same people. The pictures were different from all the others in the box. Careful. I mean, really *nice* pictures. And their expressions—kind of laughing, joking at the camera, glancing sideways, sort of mischievous.

"There was a picture of the taller woman dressed up like Charlie Chaplin, with a man's shirt and suspenders. Across her top lip, someone had drawn a pencil-thin moustache. And there was one of Julia and her sitting at a table on a balcony, leaning forward with their arms on the table, their arms really close together, almost touching.

"I think she might have been Julia's lover."

No one spoke for a few minutes after that. I could feel my cheeks flush, and my eyes got teary. I was thinking of family stories and the truths they withheld, and of links between our lives, glassy threads spun out across a dark place. For days afterward, I conjured images of Julia and her lover. I imagined conversations with them, the nods of understanding we'd exchange.

A few weeks later, John brought the carton of pictures back from Myrtle Point so Rachael and I could see them. We carried the box into the kitchen late one evening and pulled up three chairs.

Actually, they weren't very good pictures, just small, grayed snapshots hinged together with yellow tape. In the Charlie Chaplin photo, the woman's pencil-thin moustache was so faint I had to squint to see it, and I thought Julia's eyes seemed more distracted than mischievous. But we looked at those pictures for a long time, passing them carefully back and forth, leaning toward each other in the dim light over our own white kitchen table, almost touching.

I REALIZED that I'd been seeking feminist ancestors for years, trying to quench an inchoate hunger. My last semester of college, I became obsessed with stories of Elizabeth Cady Stanton. Three women in my class had been arrested for spray-painting antinuclear messages on government property near the Seneca Falls women's peace encampment. I interviewed them for an article, all the while imagining Stanton on a platform at the first women's rights convention at Seneca Falls in 1848.

I longed to visit the site, see Stanton's house, read her letters, examine her photographs. In her life I discerned seeds of my own, and that of my civilly disobedient peers. We were not adrift from history but linked to a defiant chain that stretched back beyond our sight.

Later, in women's music, art, poetry, and politics, I found other voices, encouraging, brash, and steady. They said: *You are not the first. There have been many of us. Take heart. Go on.*

To find these messages demands a careful reading between the lines. The pale photograph, the small brick house, the chipped gravestone—all are markers that say, *We were here. We lived. This happened.* But even those clues are not available to every woman hungry for female ancestry; concrete evidence of the lives of women of color, working-class and poor women, lesbians and immigrant women can be difficult, even impossible to find. Houses have been razed, manuscripts lost or destroyed, unmarked graves choked by weeds.

I remember walking through Bloodroot restaurant, where one long wall holds dozens of women's photographs—women old and young, in high collars and buttoned boots, in sepiatone and silvery print, framed and unframed.

"Mostly, we don't know who they are," said Selma Miriam, one of the four women who collectively own Bloodroot. "Some of them have obviously had very interesting lives. I feel that there have always been angry women, always been women who struggled, who have bonded with each other, who have had dreams together. It takes different forms in different times. And of course there will be others after us."

I trace my lineage now in paths that wander off the dining room tablecloth. My life descends not only from Ethel, Rose, Sarah, and Gloria, but from Ruth and Naomi, Charlotte Perkins Gilman and Harriet Tubman, Frida Kahlo and Emma Goldman, Zora Neale Hurston, Virginia Woolf and thousands of unknown others. As I listen to the stories of women's small subversions, everyday acts, I can hear these ancestors whispering encouragement. I take a breath and add my voice to the on-going collection.

Seeking Models to Mold an Identity

THE T-shirt was a gift from a boyfriend. "It's a black thing. . ." the slogan read. "You wouldn't understand." Rachael Murphey once wore the shirt home to the affluent, nearly all-white suburb where she grew up. It was a concrete symbol, she thought, of the gulf between her and her parents, the parts of their lives that lay beyond the others' comprehension.

Rachael, who is biracial and adopted, said she has never been tempted to seek her birth parents. But starting in high school, she began to hunger for cultural kin, the models her adoptive family couldn't provide.

The studio apartment where we talked showed part of what she found. Posters of Malcolm X, Toni Morrison, and Zora Neale Hurston decorated the walls; an advertisement from the film *Mississippi Masala* hung near her bed. A bulletin board was plastered with buttons, ribbons in the African National Congress colors of red, black, and green, and pictures of her parents, her sisters, her boyfriend, her friends.

Rachael's quest began on the small-town campus where she spent her first year of college. She'd graduated from her suburban high school, the only black person in her class. At college, she was determined, things would be different. Rachael vowed to date only black men—the darker-skinned, the better. She went to church with her dates' families, was baptized for the first time.

"I remember one time, when I was dating all these black men. I came home and my mom said, 'I don't know why you don't date somebody more like your father.' I laughed so hard I think I wet my pants. I said, Why in my wildest imagination would I ever want to date somebody like my father? My dad is from the South; he looks like Abraham Lincoln. I was trying to get so far away from that and be black."

That meant grappling—sometimes angrily—with her adoptive family. "I was trying to be this, you know, black power person, which is difficult when your parents are white and you grew up in a ritzy suburb," Rachael said dryly.

In high school, discovering for the first time the depth of American racism, Rachael wrote impulsively in her diary that she never wanted to clean her parents' house again. When her father, suspicious that Rachael might be using drugs, read the diary, he confronted her about what she'd written. "He said, 'I can't believe the things you said about your family. Do you really think we're racist?'

"At the beginning of my 'coming out' as a black militant, my Louis Farrakhan-Malcom X-black power-by any means necessary phase, my sisters in particular didn't understand it at all. They said, 'There's no difference between you and a white racist.' They couldn't distinguish between my struggling for self-identity and racism. They took it to be something personal. I regret that."

At home, Rachael often felt slightly foreign, looking around the table at faces utterly unlike hers. But attending Baptist church services with sisters and grandparents of the men she dated felt equally odd. Later, she moved to a mostly black section of the city "to be with 'my people,'" she remembered. "I've tried braiding my hair. I've tried making as many black friends as I could. I've tried a lot of things. Nothing really filled the void."

That is, until the day she met Avel Gordly, a state legislator and long-time black activist. "In the height of my militant resistant state I walked into her office and said, Can you give me some information on how I can get to South Africa and join the ANC? I was probably twenty years old. I was so serious. I called my dad and said, I'm going to Angola. He said, 'Great. Call me when you get there.'"

But Avel wasn't dismissive. "She took me under her wing. I think she thought I was a little wayward bird who had fallen out of the nest. I was so angry about the way things are in our society and the world. I wanted confirmation from the African American community that it was okay and appropriate and right to be angry."

Later, Avel invited Rachael to a black women's book group; Gloria Gostnell, a school principal, asked Rachael to be a counselor at a summer program to educate teenagers about racism and sexism. One contact led to others. One evening, Rachael found herself in a packed downtown lecture hall, seated between two black women she admired immensely, listening to Toni Morrison speak. It was the context she needed;

her African American "found kin" gave her a sharper sense of herself.

"I'm still overwhelmed every day when I read statistics, watch the news, take a bus through a poor black neighborhood, meet a Crip or a Blood. But I don't want to be miserable, either. Now it's different. My dad was telling me that I really need to focus on attainable goals and things I can change. I'd like to think it's a matter of maturity. I've never 'hated whitey.' That was never it. It was more about. . .time to be different, to be somebody different than my adoptive family."

Her perspective now, several years after marching into Avel's office, is as frank as ever, still passionate but less bitter. The truth about Rachael's identity is its complexity; with her adoptive family and her chosen kin, she continually faces the fact of her mixed heritage. To embrace her whole self is to accept the struggle of a life that does not conform to any categories.

"I don't feel any instantaneous bonding when I'm around black people, and I don't feel it when I'm around white people. You have a group of people on one hand who say I'm culturally white because of the way I was raised. Then there are people who say I've got one drop of black blood, so I'm black. I've decided there is a range of black experience, and my life is part of that range."

Rachael leaned back on the "Freud couch" in her apartment, a long shiny swoop of leather, and sipped a cup of whiskey-spiked tea, her mother's remedy for the cold that was clogging her voice. The infamous T-shirt lay bunched on a closet shelf.

"Three different black men I dated got me that same shirt," she said. "I used to wear that in front of my parents all the time just to get a reaction and drive my stake home. It was kind of like saying, There's no hope for you. There's no way you can ever possibly identify with me.

"If I had the shirt to do over again, I'd change it. I'd say, it's a black thing. If you try hard enough, you might be able to understand."

A Feminist Nun Vows to Question, Challenge, Continue

THE sister is wearing a sweatsuit. Powder blue, with a design in Santa Fe pastels. Her feet, in broken-down suede moccasins, are propped on the table. She is talking—rapidly and without much pause, the way she always talks—about the relationship between herself and the Sisters of the Holy Names of Jesus and Mary.

"It's basically an interracial marriage," Guadalupe Guajardo said without a laugh.

That "marriage," between the gregarious Latina activist and the cautious, mostly white institution of Catholic sisterhood, became permanent when Guadalupe took her final vows. That day came only after a decade-long courtship marked with friction, doggedness, and sincere questioning, from both sides, about whether this woman and that family could make a lifelong match.

As a teenager, Guadalupe would have been called "headstrong." She left home—a migrant family in constant financial struggle—at the age of thirteen and joined a convent.

"Being able to go into a community of young women made me feel like these were my sisters. And they were. That's the expression we used: sisters in community. For economic reasons, I didn't have family at home."

The convent closed with the advent of Vatican II; the young women were told to leave and "go out into the world," Guadalupe said. Later, she re-entered religious life as an adult.

"Now, my family is this religious community. Recently I made final vows. Why did I come? and Why have I stayed? were the questions I needed to ask myself. Part of my expectation was that I wanted to find God together with other people. I didn't know what that meant, but I didn't want to do it alone. I wanted to join with others who were committed to justice in an active way. And I wanted to be happier. It's simple. I wanted more love and companionship."

First, Guadalupe had to survive the novitiate, a three-year period whose first year she described as "a kind of endurance test, like boot camp." She lived in a house with two other novices and three professed sisters—those who had already taken final vows. She attended Scripture classes, studied and discussed the vows, ate dinner with the other women, prayed with them each evening and spent every afternoon from 1 to 3 P.M. in silence, writing in her journal, drawing, or taking walks.

Later Guadalupe was assigned to a different household in a semi-suburban area about 20 minutes by car from the city buzz she loved. The first time she drove there, she wept all the way.

The three women in the house were all reticent, shy personalities. "I was an off-the-scale extrovert," Guadalupe said. "It was a crash course. I asked what I thought were basic questions: What irritates you about living together? What do you like about community? Within the first month of living with me, they found out more about each other than they knew in a year of living together.

"One of them said one night at dinner, 'Guadalupe, when you talk, you have to let us know whether you want an answer or not. If you want an answer, you have to stop talking.'"

"Most of my life," Guadalupe said, "I've tended to walk away from difficult things. Because I had a car, because I was independent. And our society encourages that, walking away from situations."

In the years after completing her novitiate, Guadalupe weighed what a permanent commitment to the Marylhurst Order (the group's less formal name) would require, and what gifts it might bring. She thought of the three vows she would make: chastity, poverty, and obedience. And then she considered a fourth, a vow of stability taken by Trappist monks.

"That vow of stability is a very radical vow," she said. "It comes from the military, unfortunately, but it means to stay standing in the fight. Part of my commitment to religious life and family is a commitment to work things through and to see them through, particularly when they're the most difficult."

In the meantime, Guadalupe worked for an organization that advises nonprofit groups and for the Center for Third World Organizing in California. Together with a white woman and an African American man, she began to lead workshops on unlearning racism. Seeking her own ethnic identity and challenging the dominant white culture became more urgent. She wanted more women of color in her life as colleagues, friends, and housemates.

"It's not without tension and struggle that I made it through the ten years," she said. "There were questions about my bringing such a radical bent to the community. So I experienced exactly what members of families experience: Do we really want to claim this person as a member, because sometimes she is unpopular?"

And Guadalupe had her own questions. Could she pledge lifetime loyalty to a family founded on sexist and racist traditions? Would she be allowed to live with other sisters of color? Could the Sisters of the Holy Names of Jesus and Mary bend far enough, fast enough, to make room for her? "I had to ask myself, How can I be faithful in a way that doesn't do me violence? It's like any relationship."

I VISITED Guadalupe in her tidy house on the corner of a tree-lined street. Her housemates, both of them former officers in the order, are white. By consensus, one of the house's five bedrooms is always kept available for a sister of color. A women-of-color group meets at the house once a month. With Guadalupe's prodding, her housemates have begun to explore their own German and Croatian ancestries. At Christmas, they record their answering machine message in three languages.

The women designate at least three nights a week to eat together, with each taking a turn in the kitchen. Each meal begins with a grace. They plan a yearly budget that pools all their salaries and provides each with money for routine expenses. Guadalupe contributes about $25,000 to the household. About $3,000 a month goes to the order's headquarters, leaving each woman about $60 in monthly spending money. The household retains $2,000 for general expenses.

"It's really communist," Guadalupe said with a grin. "From each according to her ability, to each according to her need."

We'd covered poverty and obedience; I was hesitant to ask about the third vow. But when I managed to stammer out my question, Guadalupe responded with the same voluble attention that she applied to any other subject.

"Intimacy is a big deal in our society, as is sex. And so to be a celibate and not be married and have family in the traditional sense goes beyond most people's abilities to cope," she said. "I can't understand anymore when someone says, 'Are you in a relationship?' I'm in many relationships.

"I tell people, my love life is wonderful, and they say, 'Oh, I thought you were celibate.' I said my love life; I didn't say my sex life.

"I'm interested in being a life-giving celibate, a passionate celibate. That means being thoughtful and calculated—not leaving getting lonely to chance. Companionship doesn't happen accidentally."

Guadalupe looks first to her housemates, for daily check-in and support. Then there is her walking partner, whom she meets at 6:05 each morning. Members of the Portland Guitar Society. The man and woman who co-lead diversity workshops with her.

"I want my life more integrated rather than separated out," she said. "When I leave here, what I go out to do is to minister. That's connected to my faith and values, to empower people wherever I go. When I come back, I come back to share that and be renewed.

"It's a bit of a balancing act. But I love coming home. I love community. So they're choices I want to make."

And in making them, Guadalupe links herself to a world of other women—feminist peers and ancestors in her chosen family. Late in her period of discernment, when she met with the four sisters who run the Oregon province, they talked about what Guadalupe brought to the order and what it would lose if she left.

"The conclusion they finally came to was that all institutions need to have somebody challenging them and asking questions." The sisters named past members who were political activists and gadflies. That felt, Guadalupe recalled, like paging through a family photo album and having someone say, "Oh, you're just like Aunt Mabel." Suddenly there was a context for her activism, a tradition to uphold.

"It was wonderful when they said, 'You're carrying that on,'" Guadalupe remembered. "I just loved that."

Following Foremothers' Footsteps

JUDITH Barrington's search for female ancestors began by serendipity, amid the dusty contents of a postcard rack in a tiny café in rural France. Rifling through the faded cards, she found numerous pictures of George Sand. Intrigued, she examined the cards more closely until she found one that showed Sand's home in Gargillesse, where she sometimes lived when she wasn't in Paris. The village was about five miles away.

Judith and her partner hopped in the car and drove to the little village perched on the edge of an enormous gorge. Flowers bloomed in tubs outside the houses, and a little hotel sported blue awnings with "GS" in fancy script. Behind the houses on the edge of town, Judith could see silhouettes of rounded haystacks.

"We spent the better part of a day wandering around there, taking in the sounds and smells, the beautiful views. Sand's house had a little courtyard where we sat on the wall in the sun," Judith said. The house was open to the public, and when people began to gather outside the entrance for a guided tour, Judith and her partner got up and, without exchanging a word, walked away from the group.

"We wanted to hold onto the fragile sense of intimacy with George Sand's life that we had found, just by hanging out and absorbing the atmosphere. We thought a tour would ruin that."

Images of Gargillesse lingered with Judith throughout the rest of the trip, as she and her partner drove and camped through the French countryside. "I remember looking out," Judith said, "and having the sense that, hidden in the landscape, were all these women's lives, some of which were not as different from my own as I had once thought."

IT WAS that yearning for identification—with a place, with the past—that first propelled Judith on a hunt for feminist foremothers. As a child growing up in Brighton, England, she was bored by her family's trips to cathedrals and famous gardens. Later, she read biographies of male writers but found little that resonated. In her thirties, she discovered feminist biographies and history, books that made her fascinated, inspired, and angry to see how women's lives had been erased.

Still, the existence of those women seemed somewhat unreal. Judith craved something more than books or letters; she wanted to see the physical traces, the houses, graves, and gardens, of the women she admired. On a trip to England, she began to look.

"It was important to me to find feminist women who had unusual lives and lived them in the landscape I knew when I was growing up. It was important to me to find women's history in the culture in which I became who I am, to know that it had always been there, even though I hadn't come across it during my formative years.

"It made me feel less of an outsider there. Or at least that, as an outsider, I was part of a community of outsiders."

Judith began with a woman she'd read avidly, someone to whom she felt a strong sense of kinship. Virginia Woolf lived the last part of her life in Rodmell, not far from where Judith had ridden her horse on the Sussex downs as a young girl.

"I had read all her diaries and letters. I've always had the sense that if she'd been born later or I'd been born earlier, she's someone I might have come across. I've always had a sense of regret that I never got to meet her.

"Why was it important to me to go to Virginia Woolf's house and sit all day in the back garden? I felt I could get an insight into her daily life. Seeing the path Woolf walked from the house to her studio was different from reading about it, and somehow it made me feel I could create a life that accommodated what I wanted to do.

"I actually got very sad there. It was where she lived during the war; it was there that she committed suicide. That part of her history became very real. I felt like I had connected to her. Because I did, there was a loss, too."

ON ANOTHER trip to England, Judith set out to find Mary Wollstonecraft's grave. It was the early 1980s, just before the publication of Judith's first book of poetry. At the time, she was struggling to arrange a life in which her creative work could be central. As she made the transition from political work and journalism to poetry and teaching, she hungered for models: How did other women do that?

Both Judith and her partner had been reading Wollstonecraft and work of other women writers of the late eighteenth century. The relevance of Wollstonecraft's words to their own twentieth-century lives was both amazing and disheartening. Wollstonecraft had been brilliant and brave; and, in many ways, so little had changed.

"We must have read somewhere that she was buried in the St. Pancras churchyard, in the middle of London," Judith remembered. But there was a new St. Pancras and an old St. Pancras; their first stop was at the wrong one. A curate directed them to the older churchyard, practically hidden behind a large train station.

The grave—"a big square lump of stone"—stood among long grasses, under sweeping tree limbs. Buttercups bloomed among the headstones. "I remember lying in the grass by the grave and having the feeling of being in a meadow. It was quiet and hot. Birds were singing.

"Mary Wollstonecraft was so far back, such old history. I had the sense, sitting in that long grass, of her being a real person living her daily life and writing her books and being passionate about her ideas. It was a moment of communion with somebody from the past in the middle of a noisy, dirty city. It felt like one of those moments of illumination."

Judith's partner snapped a picture of her that day—a smiling portrait, with Judith's shoulder-length hair curling around her face. That was the picture she chose to appear on the back of her first book of poems. "I think of it as a very happy photograph."

JUDITH continued to hunt for traces of feminist ancestors. "Sometimes the process of looking for a particular woman's home was more interesting than the finding. We were looking for Elizabeth Robins's house—she was a suffragette, a playwright, and a lesbian. She wrote a novel called *The Convert* and a play, *Votes for Women*, which was where I first came across her.

"Her whole life really fascinated me. She was lovers with Octavia Wilberforce, who was Virginia Woolf's doctor. During the war, when there were ration coupons and it was hard to get cream, she and Elizabeth Robins took cream from their Jersey cows to the Woolfs' house.

"So it wasn't just about finding one woman, it was finding out how they were all connected. That aspect of their lives was very recognizable to me."

A biographical note in one of Robins's books said she lived in the village of Henfield in Sussex, near where Judith grew up. "In the course of looking for her house, we met some very old women in Henfield—one of whom had been a literary agent, with Eudora Welty and other prominent women writers among her clients—who invited us to tea and told us wonderful stories about interesting and independent women they had known who lived in and around Henfield in the early twentieth century. One of them had, as a teenager, heard Elizabeth Robins speak on women's suffrage at the local Women's Institute. One of them had known the painter, Gluck, who wore only men's clothes that she had made for her on Bond Street. There had been a women-only soapmaking business there in the 1920s. The women lived in Lavender Cottage and were referred to by locals as the Lavender Ladies. They supplied soap to the royal family. They didn't hire any men.

"I stayed in touch with those women, writing and visiting them for the next decade until the last one died."

Judith sat back in her light-drenched study, where a poster of the Barbara Hepworth Museum and Sculpture Garden hung above her desk. The opposite wall held bookshelves, crammed from floor to ceiling with journals, anthologies, poetry, and other work of women writers.

"On one trip, we discovered that the sculptor Barbara Hepworth's house and studio in Cornwall were open to the public. There was a walled garden with lush plants and sculptures in it. Being there, we had a real sense of who she was and what her life was like. We sat on a bench in the garden for a long time, talking about how difficult it is, if you're any kind of an artist, to make that central."

As the women she sought became more real to her, Judith also wondered about how their lives were preserved, how to balance her thirst for knowledge about them with respect for their privacy. "I was troubled at how Virginia Woolf would have felt about all these people tramping through her back garden. I wanted to be there in a way that did not offend her."

When we spoke, it had been more than ten years since Judith first hunted for Mary Wollstonecraft's grave. She had published a second book of poetry since then and had begun to work on a volume of memoirs. Although there were women whose homes or gravesites she still wanted to visit—such as Zora Neale Hurston's in Fort Pierce, Florida—she didn't crave those roots as she did a decade earlier.

Perhaps her searches yielded the best of a hunt for ancestors. We seek our roots not so we can remain with them, reliving our grandmothers' lives, but so we can choose our own existences more clearly, with full knowledge of their source.

"It seems important to know that women have lived lives like ours before. It feels too hard to think you're the first person who has ever created an existence that encompasses feminism and creativity.

"I was looking for the permission to create a space and a routine that made it possible to do the work I wanted to do. I don't think about it as much anymore. Maybe there are times when you really need those foremothers to say, 'Okay, you can take the leap.'"

What We Call Each Other

WE'D covered all the routine subjects—the weather in Portland, the weather on the Jersey shore (it was summer in both places). I'd thanked him for sending me a paperback copy of *The Joys of Yiddish*. Then my eighty-nine-year-old grandfather said, "So, how's your lady friend?"

I gulped. It was possible he meant Rachael, and "lady friend" was a quaint attempt to cover up the fact that he'd forgotten her name. But I'd never heard him use that phrase, with its tinge of old-fashioned, coy romance, to describe an acquaintance of mine.

Finally, I mumbled that she was just fine, thanks. "Rachael and John are fine, too," I said, testing. There was no response.

Later, I told my "lady friend" about the comment, and we both laughed. But I still don't know if my grandfather knew what he asked, if he grasped what he heard. Words are like that. They can swab the air clean of illusion, or they can fog the truth in a comfy, opaque veil.

So many of the words for romantic or sexual partners make women mere appendages of men, extend a long-standing power imbalance. What is the term to describe a relationship of equals, two adults trying to make a life together? I like "partner," with its hints of adventure and readiness, the idea of moving together through a love affair or a life. Most of my friends, gay or straight, use it to describe their romantic associates.

But even "partner" isn't perfect. For one thing, it conveys a sense of stability that doesn't apply to all relationships, especially brand new ones. Heterosexual couples have a whole vocabulary that hints at changing degrees of intimacy and intention. First "lovers" or "boyfriend/girlfriend"; then "fiancé/e"; finally "spouse." But unmarried or gay partners have no language to describe those shifts.

The words commonly used in such cases are designed to mask the truth rather than tell it. The euphemisms for gay and lesbian lovers—"constant companion" or "very special friend"—hide the true nature of the relationship under a cloak of decorum. But it's a cloak made to be seen through; everyone knows it's a cover for something else. It indicates that the real thing is too scandalous even for discourse; the word itself can't go out of doors unclad.

One lesbian couple I know dislikes "partner" for the same reasons I'm drawn to it—because it is democratic, gender-neutral. These women refer to each other as "girlfriends," refusing, even in casual conversation, to pass.

Slowly, slowly, names gather a new history; the weight of a word can shift. When lesbians and gay men appropriate the language of the mainstream, filling in their partners' names where government forms say "spouse," insisting that they deserve a "family" membership to the YMCA, they force others to reorder their mental maps. Those maps would change even faster if heterosexual couples boycotted marriage and its honorifics, if they, too combed the language for words that more precisely describe their bonds.

Girlfriend. Boyfriend. Mistress. Beau. Old man. Lady friend. Steady. Helpmate. Fiancé/e. Lover. Paramour. Spouse. Domestic partner. Soul mate. Significant other. Homeslice. Sweetie. Co-habitant. Ally. Longtime companion. Live-in. Partner. Collaborator. Consort. Intimate. Confidant/e. Familiar. Alter ego. Mainstay. Second self. Complement. Mate.

Even words that don't carry a gender bias can be suspect, quiet enforcers of the status quo. I used the word "single" to describe women without intimate partners until the irony of the term struck me. I was writing about these women precisely because they'd built networks of support through work, friends, housemates, yet my easy description of them conveyed someone alone and unconnected, with no important social ties.

"Are you in a relationship?" people inquire euphemistically, when what they mean is "Are you sexually involved with someone?" The notion of *a* relationship—primary, intimate, more weighty than the rest—doesn't fit the lives of people who choose celibacy, or who are in non-monogamous relationships involving two or more significant "others."

Then there's "friend," which doesn't begin to cover enough ground. It describes everyone from the colleague I chat with once a month at a writers' meeting to the woman I've known since infancy but haven't seen for a decade, to Rachael, whom I lived with for more than five years. The word, forced to stand for such a range of connections, erases distinction, implies all friendships are the same.

Names wake us to the particulars of a thing. If I call Diana my mainstay, Pattie my soul mate, and Rachael my sister, I remember that these women have different qualities, that my friendship with each is unique.

I say Rachael is my "sister," and then pause. Why is that the only term that seems to fit? I struggle to describe closeness and am left holding a simile, a stand-in phrase that only gropes at description. "He's like a brother to me," we say, revealing not only the assumed potency of sibling bonds but the dearth of words to describe intense, nonsexual attachments.

There's a level of intimacy that "friend" seems too small to contain. Then we make it even smaller, often denigrating it with the qualifier "just." They're "just friends," we concede, as if friendship were automatic and uninteresting, less full of potential than any romantic pairing. In fact, the vast majority of people in our lives fall into that maligned category; friendship deserves a vocabulary of its own.

Acquaintance. Colleague. Buddy. Bosom-buddy. Sidekick. Chum. Amiga. Compadre. Homegirl. Mate. Pal. Sister. Fellow. Right-hand man. Companion. Compañera. Associate. Cohort. Crony. Aficionado. Compeer. Confrere. Ally. Comrade. Familiar. Accomplice. Mainstay. Primary. Neighbor. Friend.

I'VE wrestled, too, with "childless." It's a gender-weighted word—we don't refer, with quite the same sense of anomaly and pity, to "childless" men. And it assumes childbearing is the norm and *not* childbearing a lesser version of life; it defines an existence by what it lacks. "Nonparent" makes the same mistake.

I've seen women use "child-free," which seems tipped in the other direction—as though children were a burden and only people without them have liberty. Besides, many women who choose not to be parents include children in their lives as nieces and nephews, neighbors, clients, friends. I thought about words like "adult-based" or "adult-centered" for women who don't have much to do with children. But I've yet to find a term that expresses, without judgment, the facets of this complicated choice.

And there are relationships, existences we scarcely have language to describe. The words for an unmarried woman—maiden aunt, spinster—are all pejorative. "Old maid," in particular, holds layers of judgment—a woman who contradicts her own nature, at once old and young, a perpetual servant. Thanks to Mary Daly and others, feminists are reclaiming "spinster" as a source of creative pride; one woman I know named her sewing business "Spinster Textiles."

Few terms exist to describe former lovers who now are good friends, or nonbiological parents, or relationships between the childhood families of a gay couple. I've heard a woman explain to her child, conceived through alternative (as opposed to "artificial") insemination, that there are "seed daddies" as well as the kind of daddies who live at home, and a lesbian friend coined "sister-outlaws" to describe her lover's siblings.

The contemporary women's movement and gay and lesbian liberation helped prompt people to create new honorifics, such as "Ms.," and reclaim old names, taking them back from the domain of those who hate. Queer. Dyke. Crone. Cripple. Faggot. Fat person. Fairy. When we use these words for ourselves, we become powerful, filled with the awesome responsibility that is naming. We print the words on buttons, shout them in parades. We repossess the names and, in the process, repossess ourselves.

Language changes from the edges; new terms ripple back to the center. Gradually, I have seen "partner" replace "longtime companion" in news stories about gay men and lesbians. Several papers even have begun listing gay commitment ceremonies. As such events become more popular and public, terms unimagined as yet may enter the lexicon.

Coupling. Espousals. Union. Match. Bond. Pairing. Knot. Joining. Dovetailing. Commitment ceremony. Intentional. Dedication. Webbing. Mingling. Intertwining. Weaving. Blending. Braiding. Concord. Alignment. Alchemy. Convergence. Handfasting. Tryst.

WHAT we call each other—how we refer to lovers and friends, partnerships and families—is more than a matter of etiquette. The words tell us who is owned and who is free, who really counts and who is merely secondary.

The language of the nuclear family continues to sway our speech, crowd out equally valid models of living. Homeless teenagers I worked with took the words of the families that failed them and applied them to each other. I heard them use "sister" and "brother" for their friends, but also "mother" and "kid," outlining large and intricate networks of street kin.

The actual people represented by those terms may have abused or abandoned these teenagers, but the words themselves seem to carry an infinitely renewable potency, a hope that someday someone will grow into the legend that is "mother," "sister," or "son."

"Blood family" itself carries that mythic power—"blood," with its symbolism of oath and source, a magical connection that cannot be undone. "Biological family" is less poetic but equally weighted. Married couples aren't related genetically, nor are adopted children. In families formed through remarriage, in foster families and extended families, "blood" connections have little to do with linkage.

I've toyed with "first family," "original family," and "childhood family" to describe the groups we grow up with, and "present family," "chosen family," or "adult family" for those we have now.

But the word "family" itself is loaded. The term can help justify secrecy ("let's keep it in the family") or serve as an argument for public hands-off ("that's a family matter"). And it is used disingenuously, as in "We're all one big happy family here" by businesses that want to promote childlike docility from employees and avuncular rule from bosses.

No mere noun, it's a way of categorizing society, even allocating resources, with "family" memberships and "family" fares on airlines and trains. "Family values" is political shorthand, evoking marriage, patriotism, and obedient children, a code aimed to halt a changing world.

Imagination is larger than language. The names claim who we already are and who we wish to become. We don't require them in order to live, but they make our living known, translatable, turn it into something we can talk about. There is room for more words, for the finest of distinctions, for as many possibilities as our minds can shape.

SOMEDAY, the white house in New Jersey will be mine. I cannot imagine selling it. I want it to remain in the family. Families. Meaning me, my cousins, our parents, our children, if we have them. And more than that. The partners and compatriots, lovers and allies, cronies and intimates, all those who share the everyday acts of our lives.

I can see it. Someone will tap on the glass between the front stairs and the kitchen. I will look up, out the window, through the house and the window beyond it, straight out to the ocean we all come from. I will recognize the face, and I will wave.

Welcome, I might say, to my tribe. My group. Cabal. Circle. Club. Nucleus. Team. Neighborhood. Community. Affinity group. Kin. Karass. People. Coalition. League. Assemblage. Confederation. Gang. Clique. Coterie. Set. Crew. Crowd. Cadre. We-group. Affiliates. Relations. Folk. Household. Brood. Collection. Cronies. Network.

Welcome to my company, my clan.

bibliography

Cronan, Sheila, "Marriage," in Radical Feminism, ed. Anne Koedt, Ellen Levine, Anita Rapone (New York: Quadrangle Books, 1973).

Falk, Marcia, "Notes on Composing New Blessings," in Weaving the Visions: New Patterns in Feminist Spirituality, ed. Carol P. Christ and Judith Plaskow (San Francisco: Harper & Row, 1989).

Firestone, Shulamith, The Dialectic of Sex: The Case for Feminist Revolution (New York: Bantam, 1970).

Gilman, Charlotte Perkins, Women and Economics (Boston: Small, Maynard & Company, 1898).

Kay, Herma Hill, Text, Cases and Materials on Sex-Based Discrimination (St. Paul, Minn.: West Publishing Company, 1981).

Kaye/Kantrowitz, Melanie, "Some Notes on Jewish Lesbian Identity," in Nice Jewish Girls: A Lesbian Anthology, ed. Evelyn Torton Beck (Trumansburg, N.Y.: The Crossing Press, 1982).

Le Guin, Ursula K., "The Space Crone," in Dancing at the Edge of the World: Thoughts on Words, Women, Places (New York: Grove Press, 1989).

Loewenstein, Andrea Freud, "Troubled Times: Andrea Freud Loewenstein Interviews Sarah Schulman," in The Women's Review of Books (Vol. VII, Nos. 10-11, July 1990).

Lorde, Audre, *The Cancer Journals* (San Francisco: Aunt Lute, 1980).

Mairs, Nancy, *Carnal Acts* (New York: Harper Perennial, 1990).

Millett, Kate, *The Loony Bin Trip* (New York: Simon and Schuster, 1990).

Morgan, Robin, "Changeless Need," in Ms. (August 1978).

Pogrebin, Letty Cottin, *Family Politics: Love and Power on an Intimate Frontier* (New York: McGraw-Hill, 1983).

Rich, Adrienne, *Women and Honor: Some Notes on Lying* (Pittsburgh, Pa.: Motheroot Publications, 1977).

Van Gelder, Lindsy, "Marriage as a Restricted Club," in Ms. (February 1984).

Weitzman, Lenore J., *The Marriage Contract: Spouses, Lovers, and the Law* (New York: The Free Press, 1981).

about the author

ANNDEE Hochman is a freelance writer of articles, reviews, profiles, essays, and short stories that have appeared in Ms., *The Washington Post, The Philadelphia Inquirer, The Oregonian, Glimmer Train Stories*, and other publications. She attended public schools in the Philadelphia suburbs, majored in English at Yale University, and graduated in 1984. Since then, she has worked as a metropolitan reporter for *The Washington Post*, a VISTA volunteer, a counselor for homeless teenagers, a creative writing teacher in Oregon's Arts in Education program, a theater critic, and a bartender. She currently lives and writes in Philadelphia. *Everyday Acts and Small Subversions* is her first book.

about the cover artist and book design

CLAUDIA Cave is a prominent Northwest artist. Her work is known for its feminist sensibility and its unique blend of the zany and the weighty. She lives in Salem, Oregon, and is represented by the Laura Russo Gallery in Portland, Oregon. The cover art is gouache on paper.

The text typography was composed in Novarese; the cover typography was composed in Matrix Tall. The book was printed and bound by Gilliland Printing on acid-free paper. Marcia Barrentine, a Portland freelance graphic designer and artist, designed the cover for *Everyday Acts and Small Subversions: Women Reinventing Family, Community, and Home*.

other books by The Eighth Mountain Press

LORI ANDERSON
Cultivating Excess

JUDITH BARRINGTON
An Intimate Wilderness: Lesbian Writers on Sexuality
History and Geography
Trying to Be an Honest Woman

ANDREA CARLISLE
The Riverhouse Stories

ALMITRA DAVID
Between the Sea and Home

IRENA KLEPFISZ
Dreams of an Insomniac: Jewish Feminist Essays, Speeches, and Diatribes
A Few Words in the Mother Tongue: Poems Selected and New (1971-1990)

ANNA LIVIA
Minimax
Incidents Involving Mirth

KAREN MITCHELL
The Eating Hill

MAUREEN SEATON
Fear of Subways

BARBARA WILSON
Cows and Horses

THALIA ZEPATOS
A Journey of One's Own: Uncommon Advice for the Independent Woman Traveler
Adventures in Good Company: The Complete Guide to Women's Tours and Outdoor Trips